THE GREATEST

THE GREATEST

WHO IS BRITAIN'S TOP SPORTS STAR?

Daley Thompson,
Stewart Binns and Tom Lewis

B▩XTREE
in association with Channel Four
Television Corporation

First published in Great Britain in 1996 by Boxtree Limited

Copyright © Daley Thompson, Stewart Binns and Tom Lewis
10 9 8 7 6 5 4 3 2 1

Cover design by Hammond and Hammond
Book Design by Martin Lovelock
Printed and bound in the United Kingdom by
Bath Press Colour Books for
Boxtree Limited · Broadwall House · 21 Broadwall · London SE1 9PL

A CIP catalogue entry for this book is available from the British Library

ISBN: 0 7522 1048 3

Cover photographs: All Sport

CONTENTS

PROLOGUE

This book, and the Channel 4 series to which it is an accompaniment, is the first thorough and methodical attempt to grasp the challenge of deciding who is Britain's greatest sporting hero. There are thousands of opinions and many previous attempts, none of which have been in any way systematic or reliable.

Our first task as authors, working with the producers at Trans World International (TWI) who are making the Channel 4 series, was to arrive at a definitive list of 100 superstars from British sporting history. This wasn't easy. Nearly 300 names came readily to mind. They were culled from other people's lists and from the lists of 'greats' contained in the various encyclopaedia and compendia covering Britain's sporting heritage. A short list of slightly more than 150 was then pared down to 120 in consultation with the TWI producers, who also sought the help of leading British sporting journalists, academics and statisticians.

The final list of 120 names were then 'scored' according to a set of five criteria designed to create a reliable method for comparison.

The five criteria eventually agreed upon took almost as much debate and discussion to determine as the choice of the athletes to be included. But, eventually, the following were thought to offer a comprehensive assessment of sporting 'greatness':

1. Achievement
2. Dominance
3. Style
4. Fortitude
5. Impact

These criteria were then applied to the 120 athletes in the list. The top 100 were then chosen as subjects for the book and the television series. But the demands of the medium of television are such that in eleven episodes, the series only had time to discuss the top 20 British athletes of all time. So, the twenty highest scorers in the list became the subjects for the television series.

HOW TO USE THIS BOOK

The book is divided into three main parts:

1. The Introduction.
2. 100 Biographies of Britain's Greatest Athletes.
3. The Scores for 'The Greatest' top 100.

1. The Introduction

The introduction offers some insight into the 'Art of Comparison' and the 'Science of Comparison' and an outline of the five criteria used in scoring the athletes.

2. The 100 Biographies

The biographies are the major bulk of the book and provide a detailed account of the careers of all the athletes considered to be in the category of the top 100. As much biographical information as space permits is included, as well as anecdotal background and statistical information. The material is intended to be the best possible guide to enable you to make your own judgements and decide on your own scores.

3. The Scoring for 'The Greatest'

The final section of the book lists the scores for Britain's greatest sports stars from 100 to 21. The scores for the top 20 are left blank in order for you to be able to make your decisions and fill in your own scores.

Each athlete is scored from 1 to 20 in the five criteria listed and their total score used to determine their ranking in an order of merit from 100 to 21.

The top 20 are the subjects for the Channel 4 series. 'The Greatest' series will use a combination of expert opinion, studio audience and public response to produce scores for the top 20 and, ultimately, to determine Britain's greatest ever athlete.

You can, of course, use this book to undertake exactly the same exercise, with or without the series. Give it a go, it's great fun. Read the biographies carefully and then do your own scoring. Good luck.

INTRODUCTION

Every athlete included in the pages that follow this introduction has reached the pinnacle of achievement in their chosen sport, many of them several times over. They are all 'legends'; they are all 'stars'; and they have all been described as 'great'.

All of sport's many cliches apply to each of them. They represent the best that Britain has had to offer for close to a hundred years; in effect, since the beginning of modern, organised sport. They are a tiny fraction of an elite corps of sportsmen and sportswomen who have played their sport professionally or at representative level over those years.

Beneath the 'Top 100' listed here are two or three hundred more who deserve consideration and about whose omission there will be severe criticism from many quarters. They, in turn, are an elite from the tens of thousands of gifted athletes who have played professionally or at the highest level, who are themselves, of course, but a tiny fraction of the millions who have played at least one sport reasonably well, or have dreamed of doing so.

As such a tiny rarefied group, 'The Greatest' in these pages are equals, in the same way as the members of a great orchestra, or an elite unit of soldiers. But it is the nature of sport, driven by its philosophy – the pursuit of excellence – that we still have to make gods out of idols and idols out of heroes; we must go on eliminating until we find the tallest tree in the forest, the mightiest of them all.

Not content with a near-perfect cover drive, we yearn to see a better one. Having witnessed the apparently faultless drop-

Left: Daley Thompson, savouring the moment of victory.
Below: The real moment of truth in sport. Lennox Lewis in full cry against Tony Tucker.

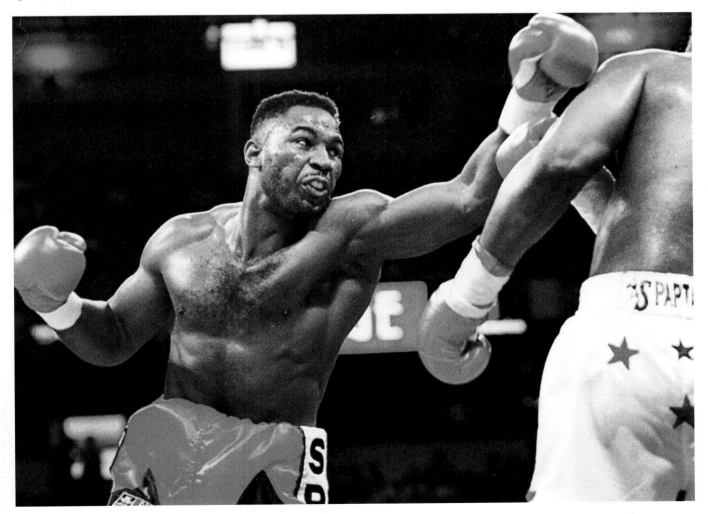

volley, we are reminded of someone who could play it crisper or firmer. There is a search for purity in sport and a striving for perfection. That is why it is surrounded by records, statistics and superlatives – to allow comparisons to be made.

This book is about comparisons. It is a guide to the art of comparison, with a little help from the science of comparison. It is a guide to be taken seriously, as all the great subjects in sport should be taken, but it is also a guide to be approached with enough lightness of touch to allow the thought that sport is what it is because it doesn't matter.

The late Bill Shankly, the founder of modern football's most famous dynasty at Liverpool, summed up the significance of sport better than any philosopher when he said, 'Football isn't a matter of life and death, it's far more important than that.'

What Shankly said about football is true of all sport. It is important because it's something we've invented to allow us to forget about the things that are really important. Sport is about joy and pleasure, fun and excitement. We invent games and competitions to create capsules of adrenalin that exist in an unreal world. The fields of play and the arenas of competition exist in their own time and space, suspended above the humdrum of everyday life.

Paradoxically, having created this unreal world of sporting fantasy, we have to allow in the things that really matter in order to heighten the thrill: money, the rule of law, bureaucracy and organised competition. The 'fields of dreams' have to be built and organised and the 'heroes' have to be trained and rewarded if the adrenalin we seek is to be stimulated as often as we would like.

So, sport has to be unimportant and trivial and earth-shattering and vital, all at the same time. You should approach this book with the same contradictory confusion: It's only a bit of trivia – but make sure you can defend your opinions, or your life-long friend may threaten to rip your head off!

Sporting passions run deep. Try telling a Scot that Jimmy Greaves was a better goalscorer than Denis Law, or a Yorkshireman that Compton was a better batsman than Hutton. For that matter, try telling Scottish football fans (as we authors must) that Alex James, Jim Baxter and Hughie Gallacher haven't made it to the top 100 in these pages, or squash fans, of all British regional shades, that Jonah Barrington didn't 'make the cut'. But don't let your passions run away with the sport – remind yourself that everyone who plays sport at the highest level is a hero and raise your glass in praise of their mighty deeds.

This book is dedicated to everyone who has played sport,

A beautiful blend of man and machine. Geoff Duke at the Monza Grand Prix in 1956.

watched sport and made the magic happen. The 100 special individuals listed in the following pages represent everyone in sport. Their success is but a reflection of the efforts of all the rest of us.

THE ART OF COMPARISON

The arguments are endless. You can hear them in factories and offices, on trains and buses and in pubs and clubs all over the country:

'They all go on about Matthews, but ask anyone who really knows his football – they'll all tell you Finney was a much better player.'

'You can say what you like about May and Cowdrey, when it came to scoring runs, there was no one like 'Sir' Geoffrey.'

'When push came to shove, Edwards was a winner. He made the great Welsh teams tick, John was just the gloss on the surface.'

'I never saw Cotton play, but Faldo's proved one thing – he went to America and won.'

'Clark and Stewart may have been better drivers, but Mansell has done it in a more competitive environment.'

'There's no comparison between the era of Jimmy Wilde, when boxing was a brutal game, and the kid gloves of today. Bruno and Lewis wouldn't have survived in boxing's heyday.'

Eulogising about sporting performances is a central part of the nostalgia and mythology of sport. It forms a major part of the art of story-telling in sport. Hero-worship is often the spark which ignites a life-time of devotion. In sixty years time, future grandfathers (and grandmothers) will talk of the great days of English rugby in the 1990s; of Will Carling and his mightly forwards, of the dashing Andrew, Underwood and Guscott. Men and women, who are youngsters now, will talk of Mike Atherton's famous match-saving innings in 1995 in South Africa, when they sit with their grandchildren fifty years into the next century. And it will be the exploits of Alec Ferguson's young pretenders who will create the next generation of fanatical Manchester United fans, just as Matt Busby's three great teams each produced a new legion of the Old Trafford faithful in the fifties and sixties.

Much of the mythology of sport involves comparisons and hierachies: 'Britian's greatest sprinter', 'Scotland's most prolific goalkicker', 'Wales' finest outside-half'; we pick 'Footballers of the Year', create 'Halls of Fame' and 'England's greatest forward line'; and we have 'Dream Teams' and 'Terry Venables' greatest eleven'. We love it. We argue about it, we think one another's choices are ridiculous, but we still love it.

The art of comparison is based on judgement; the judgement of the life-long devotee, the seasoned observer. Any realistic comparison of talent or athletic achievement must be based on experience. It is difficult to compare Sir Jack Hobbs with David Gower, because few people alive saw the former bat and there is very little film of him to form a judgement. In many instances you have to rely on the judgement of others to help form an opinion. Unless you are fortunate enough to have a lifetime of watching and viewing behind you, you should be cautious about the strength of your own convictions, they may be the most biased factor you could bring to bear on your thinking.

When indulging in the art of comparison, treat it like an art form: look, listen and learn; read the biographies and works of the great reflective journalists and sports-writers; listen to those who were there and can remember; and watch the videos to see for yourself the great talents from years gone by.

The biggest problem in comparing contemporary performances to those of the past is the obvious difference in standards. There is no doubt that yester-years' footballers looked amateurish compared to modern players, that athletic and swimming times were much slower and that tennis players seemed less mobile. But appearances can be misleading. An athlete can only be as good as the era in which he or she performs – a product of the training, diet and standards of the day. The key question is a relative one. For example, how much better a boxer was Jimmy Wilde amongst his peers in the era when he boxed? If he was regarded as significantly better than his peers, then you should assume that that would be his status today. Unless, of course, the circumstances pertaining to boxing have changed between the two eras. If you feel, for example, that boxing is less competitive (i.e. fewer young men or less talented athletes taking part) than it used to be, then you might consider that Wilde's exalted status may be worth even more today, relatively speaking. Alternatively, there are some sports where, it could be argued, competition has increased dramatically. Track and field was, for a long time, a traditional, amateur sport with a high standard only in relatively advanced countries. However, in the last thirty years the base of athletics has broadened dramatically, thus increasing the pool of talent within which the best athletes have to compete. For example, middle-distance and long-distance running now has Arab, African and South American stars who have deepened the reservoir of competitive athletic prowess.

Kenny Dalglish in his great days at Liverpool. A big fish in the very big pond of modern football, the world's most popular game.

Similarly, there is a good argument to suggest that the world of top quality football is far more competitive now than it was thirty years ago. Countries like France, Denmark, Holland, Romania, Portugal, Colombia, Cameroon, Nigeria and many more have added a new competitive edge to the traditional football powers, making it more difficult to shine brightly in the football firmament. Traditionalists might disagree, but theirs is surely a difficult argument to sustain.

In rugby, players are considerably bigger, stronger and quicker than even twenty years ago. They train more often and take the game far more seriously. Indeed, rugby is now on the threshold of a professional revolution which will change it even more dramatically. These changes provide several interesting questions. Would the great Welsh stars of the seventies have played much longer, and created even greater reputations, had the lure of professional reward been available to them? But, would they have survived and prospered as well now, amidst the giants of the modern game, as they did in their era? Would Edwards have made so many heroic dashes to the line, if he had contemporary forwards like Bayfield and Johnson hanging around his neck? And would JPR Williams have made so many of his famous last ditch tackles if the opposing backs had been on the Jonah Lomu scale?

Motor-sport faces a similar conundrum. Modern cars are quicker and thus demand keener judgement, but they are also safer and easier to handle. So, who are the better drivers, the aces of the past who struggled manfully with monstrous death-traps, or the modern drivers who have but a milli-second to make a decision at speeds which defy comprehension?

The answers to all these questions should be based on your judgement using the art of comparision.

THE SCIENCE OF COMPARISON

There are the hard facts that help bring solid statistics to the art of comparison. Sport is replete with records, tables, strike-rates, averages and orders of merit that offer hard evidence to reinforce or refute opinions.

'Yes, but look at his record!' must be the most frequently heard retort used in the midst of a heated debate about comparative sporting talent.

Many sports are festooned with statistical bunting, especially sports like baseball and cricket. But American encyclopaedia of baseball make Wisden look like the random scribblings of an amateur statistics freak.

The following is an extract from the American magazine *Inside Sports*, published in 1990. It is an assessment of Wade Boggs, one of baseball's greatest hitters:

> *'Hitting in the Clutch*
> *He does all right hitting leadoff, but has also hit third. He drove in 89 runs in 1987, but slipped to 58 and 54 the following two years. He's at .358 lifetime, with runners in scoring position.*
>
> *Last year Boggs hit .351 with runners on base and .341 when they were in scoring position. With bases loaded though, he hit only .091 and he was just a .268 hitter in 97 late-inning at-bats.'*

Cricket's first class averages seem relatively simple compared to all that!

But statistics are important. Scoring goals or tries for your country is impressive by any reckoning. However, a striker who scores twenty goals may take sixty appearances to achieve that total, whereas a fellow international may do it in forty-five. Similarly, fifteen tries in a rugby career may be considered much more impressive if achieved from centre or even scrum-half.

Other hard evidence is an important part of the science of comparison. Length of career is a stark fact. It is clearly impressive and highly laudable to have played over a hundred times for your country, or to have competed in three Olympic Games. Almost inevitably, such longevity is a sure sign of enduring greatness. However, there is an important caveat. In some sports, especially amateur ones, it is often difficult or unusual to have a long career. You should thus be careful in dismissing short careers in certain sports. Also, you might consider another factor in the two-edged sword of longevity. What should we make of the remarkably short careers of a Barry John or an Ann Packer for example? Should we be even more impressed that they had the impact they had, given that they were in the public eye for such a short period of time?

The most obvious statistical evidence for sporting comparisons is, of course, honours, championships, victories and records. These offer reliable hard evidence of sporting prowess. In most sports an Olympic gold medal is the ultimate accolade, but not in everything. In some sports, football being the obvious example, the World Championship (the World Cup) is the highest honour, while in rugby and especially cricket, the World Championship itself is not yet the most prized honour.

You should also remember that in the case of some sporting legends, their reputation was made without the prestige of an international career of any note. George Best is perhaps the best example of this. Although he played many times for Northern Ireland and in one famous European Cup Final, his reputation was based almost entirely on his performances for Manchester United in the English domestic league.

World records and first places in statistical lists are clearly the ultimate measure of achievement. Holding a world record, especially for a very long time, or repeatedly breaking it, is a sure sign that the athlete concerned is the best in the world. Similarly, to be a world record goal-scorer, run-maker, try-scorer or wicket-taker is an absolute measure of achievement. The only reservation to consider here is to be sure to compare like with like. It is not a fair comparison to equate being Scotland's highest goalscorer with the world's greatest wicket-taker. Neither is it justified to compare any domestic honour with an international honour – unless of course, the domestic honour is itself at the pinnacle of the international game, like the (British) Open Golf Championship or the All-England Tennis Championships!

THE FIVE CRITERIA

After much thought and great debate, and after taking into consideration the need to create a method that could be used on a mass scale by a national television audience, the following five criteria have been devised to answer British sport's most fiercely contested sporting question.

The criteria are designed to meld together the 'art of comparison' with the 'science of comparison', in order to produce as close to a definitive conclusion as it is possible to get.

It is a difficult task. But the biographies in this book, the five criteria, and the debate inspired by television and followed up in the press, should allow the British public to come to a conclusion in a way that's never been attempted before. Use the criteria carefully and try to be consistent with your scoring.

Fred Perry in Wimbledon in 1936. His achievements are easily forgotten after the passage of more than sixty years of sport.

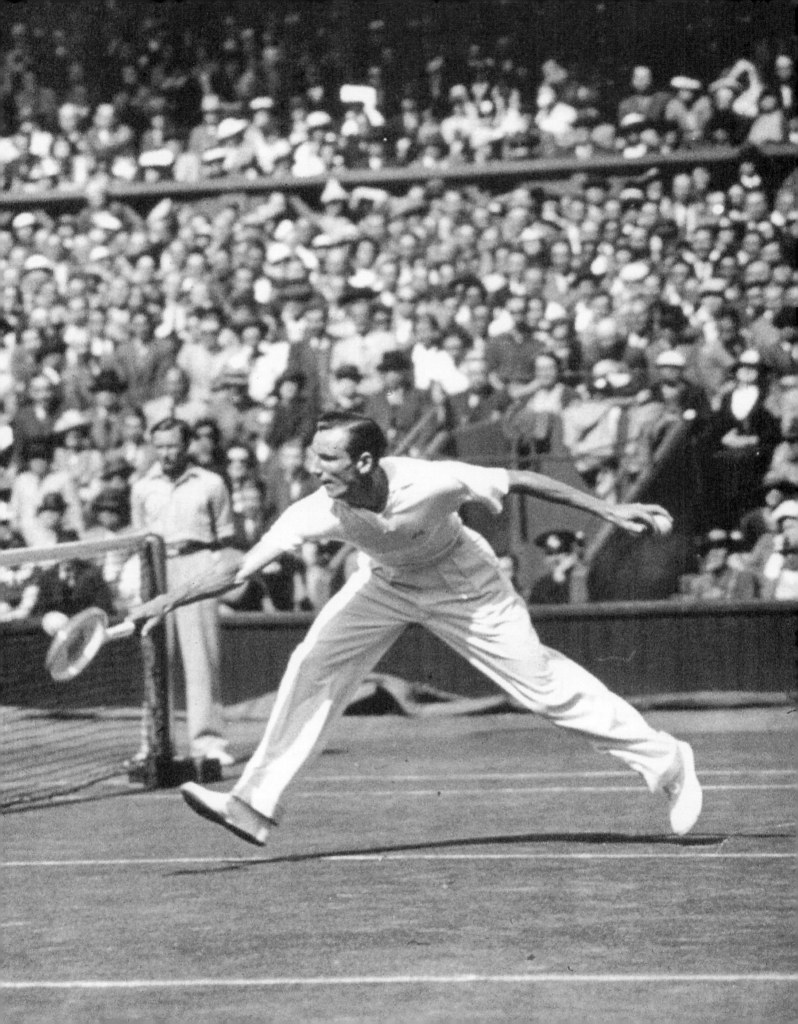

'Besty', still admired, loved and even revered, despite everything.

1. Achievement

This is a hard and fast statistical measure. It is the place for giving marks for quantifiable successes: olympic medals (especially the gold variety), world championships, world records etc. It is also the place for recording special honours, like being the top of a world ranking or being regarded as the best in the world. It is particularly important in this criteria to compare like with like and to remember that all the great athletes in this book have largely achieved their reputations on a world stage, not just on a British one.

2. Dominance

This is a more relative factor. It should allow comparisons between eras in one sport and between the relative pools of talent in different sports. You should pose yourself various questions: when did the athlete concerned compete and what was the status of their sport at that time? What was the quality of the opposition like when they competed? Were they dominant in their era? How were they regarded vis-à-vis their peers? For how long were they at their best within their sport?

3. Style

This is a more subjective factor, but covers lots of quite tangible elements. It is about technique and flair; it is about sportsmanship and image; and it's about the suitability of the athlete as a role-model.

Inevitably, one person's role model is another's villain and one observer's exaltation of supreme flair is another's condemnation of flawed technique. But it is possible to reach some common ground. This category presents the opportunity to reward those whose legacy is more in the mind's eye than in the cold evidence of statistics.

4. Fortitude

Fortitude covers a multitude of virtues. It is a reflection of the background and underpinning of sporting success. It is about mental toughness and the will to win; the essence of a champion. It is also about the building blocks of success: discipline, self-control and dedication to training and preparation.

This category also provides an opportunity to reward those whose sporting achievements are earned in less glamorous competitive environments, where commitment, dedication and motivation are so much harder to find.

5. Impact

The final criterion is the most subjective in the list. It is perhaps no more than something we all sense. It is the 'x' factor. It's been called 'charisma' and 'transcendance' and describes those athletes who become exceptional even among an elite group of their peers. It is perhaps best illustrated by examples.

They are drawn from experience outside the British confines of this book, in order not to colour your judgement of the people in these pages.

In America, people get goose-bumps at the mere mention of names like Gordie Howe in ice hockey or Babe Ruth in baseball. Michael Jordan is probably the only major sports personality who is reverentially referred to by the simple use of his christian name; there is literally only one 'Michael'.

Within Europe, the passionate world of cycling is currently aghast at the awesomeness of the presence of Spain's Miguel Indurain. Closer to home, in the thirties and forties, English hearts missed a beat at the news on the radio that, 'The Don,' Donald Bradman was on his way to the crease. Everyone in football knows instinctively that Pele had a quality that will probably never be equalled in the history of the game. While finally, the whole world knows the most famous, the most transcendant, the greatest athlete of them all – Muhamed Ali.

They all personify 'impact'!

SUMMARY

The 100 Greatest British Sportsmen and Sportswomen includes 91 men *, and 10 women *. There are 72 English **, 11 Scottish, 12 Welsh and 6 Northern Ireland athletes. Altogether, there are 18 sports represented with the following distribution:

Football	21	Swimming	3
Athletics	19	Horse Racing	2
Cricket	13	Tennis	2
Boxing	9	Table Tennis	2
Rugby Union	8	Skating	2 ***
Motor-racing	6	Equestrian	1
Rugby League	5	Rowing	1
Golf	4	Yachting	1
Motor-cycling	3		
Snooker	3	Total	105 ****

*   Includes Jayne Torvill and Christopher Dean as separate entries.

**   Includes Torvill and Dean as two individual entries.

*** Includes Torvill and Dean as a single entry.

**** Includes the following as double entries:

    Denis Compton – cricket and football

    Ann Jones – tennis and table tennis

    Fred Perry – tennis and table tennis

    Eric Liddell – athletics and rugby

    John Surtees – motor-cycling and motor-racing

Several legendary figures from the era before the First World War were excluded because of the difficulties of making genuine comparisons with modern athletes. Many of them have reputations and records which would put them close to the top of any all-time list, but our view was that the context of sport has changed so much in the last eighty to ninety years, so as to make it extremely hard to make national judgements about them, especially as there is almost no film evidence of their performances and few, if any, people alive who saw them in their heyday. The exclusions include famous names like C.B. Fry, W.G. Grace, Harry Vardon, Fred Archer, Sidney Barnes, Lottie Dodd and Bob Fitzsimmons.

There are also omissions involving several contemporary athletes who are rapidly developing a status which will demand their inclusion, should this book be revised a year or so from now. Mike Atherton, Paul Gascoigne, Damon Hill, Naseem Hamed, Will Carling, Chris Boardman and many others, look like they are amassing a body of evidence to stake their claim to a place among the very best of British sport. Indeed, during the final preparation for the book, we felt that Jonathan Edwards' achievements in 1995 warranted a late inclusion in the final 100. The events of the summer of 1996 may well demand more amendments to the top 100.

The final choice of 100 names was thought through, argued about and based as thoroughly as possible on hard evidence to try and make the decisions as objective as possible. Nevertheless, the decisions reflect the subjective views of everyone involved in the Greatest project, especially those of the three authors of this book.

There are many great British sportsmen and sportswomen not included in the list. We tried to think of all the obvious candidates and (hopefully) all of the not so obvious candidates. If we have missed anyone, or underrated their achievements, we can only apologise. We did consider several hundred. Below, in no particular order, are but sixty of the very special talents, who, in our view didn't quite make it.

In broad terms, their exclusion was based on a strict application of the criteria for scoring. Simply put, they got less than 45 marks (Ann Jones' score ranked 100th in the list), when compared to the people in the top 100. Their achievements were not as impressive, they didn't have the same impact, they didn't dominate their sport and they didn't exhibit the same style or fortitude as our illustrious 100 Greatest:

Beryl Burton	Sir Chris Bonnington	Bill Beaumont
Jonathan Davies	Johnny Leach	Danny Blanchflower
Sir Harry Llewellyn	Reg Harris	Joe Brown
Sandy Lyle	Jimmy McIlroy	John Barnes
Ted Dexter	Duncan Edwards	Chris Chataway
Lloyd Honeyghan	Ian Woosnam	Jonah Barrington
Brendan Foster	Tommy Simpson	Jim Baxter
Chris Brasher	Liz McColgan	Ivor Allchurch
Alex James	Jim Sullivan	Neil Fox
Hughie Gallacher	Wavell Wakefield	Dickie Jeeps
Jim Watt	Howard Winstone	Charlie Magri
Frank Tyson	Godfrey Evans	Chris Eubank
Alan Knott	Duncan Goodhew	Sharron Davies
Ray Reardon	Chester Barnes	Sarah Hardcastle
Barry Sheene	Virginia Wade	Brian Phelps
Gavin Hastings	Gillian Gilkes	David Broome
Andy Irvine	Danny McGrain	Karen Briggs
Sean Kerly	Derek Underwood	Peter Scudamore
Robin Cousins	Malcolm Cooper	Kitty Godfree
Joey Dunlop	Steve Hislop	Neil Adams

HAROLD ABRAHAMS

HAROLD MAURICE ABRAHAMS
ATHLETICS – SPRINTER
BORN: BEDFORD, 15 DECEMBER 1899
DIED: ENFIELD, 14 JANUARY 1978

Facts about Harold Abrahams

- Abrahams was selected for the long jump at the Paris Olympics, but was excused after an anonymous letter criticising the decision was published in a newspaper. Abrahams had sent the letter himself.

- There was no medal ceremony in Paris, and he was sent his medals through the post. The French authorities had not put enough stamps on the envelope, and he had to pay the excess postage himself.

- He was awarded the CBE in 1957 for his work as Secretary of the National Parks Commission.

- After the Olympics he became a barrister.

Harold Abrahams's Career

1920 Olympics (Antwerp)
100 metres (did not qualify)
200 metres (did not qualify)

1924 Olympics (Paris)
100 metres (1st)
200 metres (6th)
4 x 100 metres (2nd)

AAA Championships
100 yards (1st) 1924
Long jump (1st) 1923,1924

Records

100 metres (equalled Olympic record)	10.6 seconds 1924	
Long jump (British record)	7.38 metres 1924	

Abrahams's name, like that of Eric Liddell, will forever be associated with the Oscar-winning film *Chariots of Fire*. He did far more than just compete in the Paris Olympics, though. He was as good a long jumper as a sprinter and, after his competitive career was over, he became a noted athletics broadcaster and statistician.

Abrahams grew up in an athletic family. His two older brothers were both athletes, one representing Britain in the 1912 Olympic long jump, and young Harold set out to emulate them. He won the 100 yards and long jump at the 1918 Public Schools' championships while at Repton, but his career really took off when he went on to Caius College, Cambridge.

In 1920, he represented England in a triangular match against Ireland and Scotland, winning the 220 yards. He was then selected for the Antwerp Olympics in both sprints, the relay and the long jump, but failed to win a single medal. The next year, though, he showed considerable improvement. A combined Oxford and Cambridge team toured America very successfully, and over the next two years he did well on the domestic scene, twice setting an English long jump record in 1923.

That winter, he trained for the Paris Olympics, determined to succeed. Famously, he engaged a professional coach, Sam Mussabini, to oversee his progress. Abrahams had a very dedicated and scientific approach to training. His methods would not seem unusual now, in fact, they would seem lackadaisical, but such an approach was virtually unheard of at the time. However, Mussabini did pass on one vital piece of advice. Before the Paris final, he told Abrahams, 'Only think of two things, the report of the pistol and the tape. When you hear one, just run like hell until you break the other.'

It was clear his hard work had paid off when the 1924 season commenced. He ran a wind-assisted time of 9.6 seconds for the 100 yards, and then extended his own English long jump record to 7.38 metres, a mark that stood until 1956. He then took the 100 yards and long jump titles at the Amateur Athletics Association (AAA) Championships.

In Paris, he decided to concentrate on the sprints rather than the long jump, and it rapidly became apparent that he had reached the peak of his form. In the second round of the 100 metres, he equalled the Olympic record with a time of 10.6 seconds. In the semi-final, he was left behind by two yards at the start, and still recovered to win in the same time, beating the Olympic champion Charlie Paddock in the process. He ran the final magnificently, and at the tape was almost a yard in front of Jackson Scholz of America. His time, once again, was officially 10.6 seconds, although an electronic timer recorded 10.52 seconds. He was the first European to win an Olympic sprint gold medal. Abrahams also reached the final of the 200 metres, but this time he finished last. However, he did get a second medal, a silver, in the sprint relay.

The 100m, AAA Championships, Stamford Bridge, 1924 – finishing first as usual; something that seemed to preoccupy Abrahams throughout his life.

- His father came from Lithuania, and could never spell his adopted English name.

- He became obsessed with time in later life, always rising at six, going to bed at ten, and wearing three stopwatches.

- He married a light opera singer, Sybil Evers, who he met in 1935, not before the Paris Olympics as depicted in *Chariots of Fire* .

- Arthur Porritt, who finished third in the 1924 final, became a life-long friend, was surgeon to the royal family and, as Lord Porritt was governer-general of New Zealand. Abrahams and Porritt, and their wives, met every year for dinner at the precise time of the 1924 final.

Abrahams still had not reached his full potential, especially in the long jump. However, the next season, when he was still only twenty-five, his career was brought to a premature conclusion when he injured his leg while jumping. Once his active career was over, though, he devoted himself to journalism and broadcasting. He was the *Sunday Times* athletics correspondent for over forty years, and became a founding member of the Association of Track and Field Statisticians.

He joined the AAA General Committee in 1926 and, after fifty years of service, became President. He also served as honorary treasurer, and later chairman, of the British Amateur Athletics Board. While he was not universally popular, his disposition not allowing him to suffer fools gladly, he was a much-mourned loss to the sporting world when he passed away in 1978.

'*Chariots of Fire* is my favourite film, I've lost count of the number of times I've seen it, and I know I would watch it again. I met Abrahams when he was working for the British Amateur Athletics Board, still sprightly at 76. I understand that he was the first to use PR to his benefit, when he started writing reports for athletics meetings that he was involved in. Also he resisted the introduction of paid coaches which is odd as he employed one for the 1924 Olympics in Paris.'

ERIC ASHTON

**ERIC ASHTON
RUGBY LEAGUE – CENTRE
BORN: ST HELENS, 24 JANUARY 1935**

Eric Ashton was much more than merely the other half of that famous Wigan duo with Billy Boston. He was a tall, stylish centre and an inspirational leader. Most importantly, he provided the ammunition that allowed his colleagues, especially Boston, to bombard the opposition with a fusilade of tries.

His own tally of points was not insignificant – 231 tries and 448 goals for Wigan – but it is for his qualities of leadership and for his creative playmaking that he is best remembered.

At six feet two inches and with a long, raking stride, he had a deceptive turn of pace. His outrageous dummy was as potent as Boston's famous hand-off. Their collective ploy, the scissors, was a joint strategy they revelled in.

He captained Wigan in six Wembley Challenge Cup Finals between 1958 and 1966 and collected the trophy in the famous cherry hooped jersey on three occasions: 13–9 in 1958 against Workington Town; 30–13 in 1959 against Hull Kingston Rovers; and 20–16 in 1965 against Hunslet.

As an international, he led Great Britain to victory in the 1960 World Cup and on the triumphant Ashes tour in 1962. He had also toured in 1958 and played in the 1957 World Cup. In the Ashes tours of 1958 and 1962 he scored a prolific fifty-one tries, a measure of which is the fact that his famous wing partner, Billy Boston, scored only seven more. In all, his Test career spanned twenty-six Tests in six years.

Ashton's leadership and quiet dignity led him into management. He rarely had to raise his voice, preferring instead to lead by example. He was Wigan's player-coach at Wembley, in 1965, and took them back again in 1966. In 1970 he was at Wembley with Wigan again, this time solely in a coaching capacity.

He then moved on to Leeds and eventually to Wigan's rivals, St Helens, and guided them to Wembley, in 1976 and 1978, twenty years after his

Eric Ashton's Career

Challenge Cup winner

1958 v Workington Town	13–9
1959 v Hull KR	30–15
1965 v Hunslet	20–16

Challenge Cup runner-up

1961 v St Helens	6–12
1962 v Wakefield Trinity	10–25
1966 v St Helens	2–21

Championship
1958–59, 1961–62

Championship play-off
1960

231 Career tries

448 Career goals

26 Test appearances for Great Britain

'Eric is best remembered for his ability to get the best out of others. He really was a team player in the best sense of the word, in that, as long as it produced the right results, he was happy to play second fiddle to his team mates. So, for our style category Eric would score very highly because he had all the ingredients of technique, image and role model.'

first victory with Wigan.

In 1979 Ashton took charge of the Lions tour and added the final accolade to a full set of honours as player, captain and coach of both club and country.

In June 1966 Ashton's immense contribution to the game of rugby league, his demeanour and his qualities of leadership were rewarded with an MBE, the first to be given to a player from the thirteen-man code.

Facts about Eric Ashton

- Like his counterpart, Billy Boston, Ashton's talent first came to prominence when he played rugby union during his National Service.

- Much to their subsequent regret, he was turned down by his home town team of St Helens before joining Wigan.

- His signing fee for Wigan, in 1956, was £150 compared to the £3000 for his more flamboyant partner, Billy Boston, in 1953.

- His MBE, awarded in 1966, didn't quite get the recognition it deserved as England's Association footballers occupied the headlines as they began their assault on the World Cup.

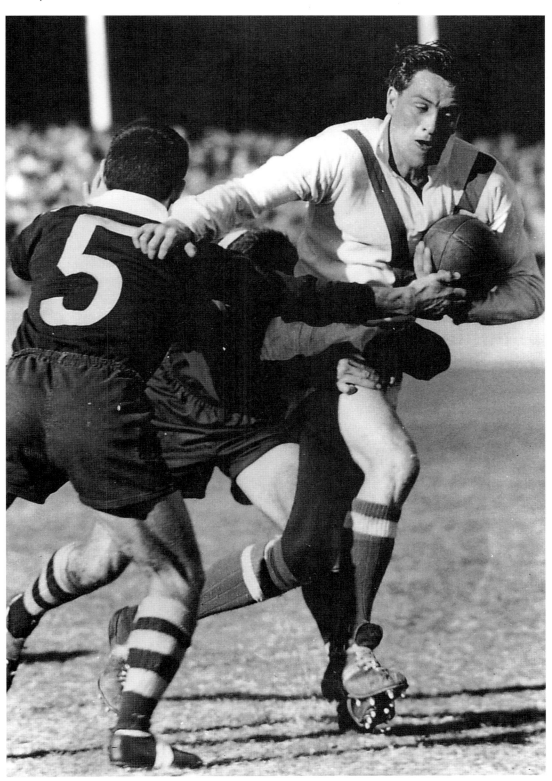

A leader of men, an inspiration to others. There can't be many better epitaphs for a team player. Ashton against Australia at the Sydney Cricket Ground 1962.

GORDON BANKS

GORDON BANKS
FOOTBALL – GOALKEEPER
BORN: SHEFFIELD, 30 DECEMBER 1937

Gordon Banks's Career	
Football League appearances	510
International appearances	73
World Cup winner	1966
League Cup winner	
(with Leicester City)	1964
(with Stoke City)	1972
Footballer of the Year	1972

'As safe as the Banks of England' was the cry and, as England ruled the football world, they had a custodian who made opposing forwards lose heart. Gordon Banks has a powerful claim to be the best goalkeeper of all time. He was over six feet tall, and quite powerfully built, and this was combined with incredible agility and reflexes allowing him to pull off some quite miraculous saves.

He was born in Sheffield, but the two local giants allowed him to escape to Chesterfield, where he made his debut in 1958. He only made twenty-three appearances for them before Leicester City snapped him up. Banks quickly became their first-choice goalkeeper in a team that, having only recently escaped the Second Division, never really challenged in the League. They were a good cup team though, reaching the final in 1961, where they succumbed 2–0 to Tottenham's double-winners. They were back in 1963, only to lose 3–1 to Manchester United. The next year, they won their first, and so far only, major trophy. The League Cup was still a fairly new competition, but Leicester reached the final where, over two legs, they beat Stoke 4–3 on aggregate.

He had done enough to impress Alf Ramsey, who selected him for England in April 1963 against Scotland. They lost 2–1, but a month later he was back in the team against Brazil. This was a 1–1 draw, with Banks beaten by a swerving free-kick from Pele, unfortunately the very shot against which Alf Ramsey had warned him. However, Ramsey had seen enough to regard Banks as his first-choice goalkeeper, especially after good European Championship displays against Czechoslovakia and East Germany.

In 1966, the World Cup came to England, and Banks had an inspired tournament. As England failed to spark fully into life in the early matches, Banks kept four consecutive clean sheets, and he played well against Portugal and in the final against West Germany, keeping his concentration even after the Germans equalised so dramatically in the last minute.

In 1967, Leicester, having discovered a young keeper called Peter Shilton in their ranks, felt free to cash Banks in and, for £52,500, he moved to Stoke. The move didn't affect his place in the England team, and he was a member of the team that took third place in the European Championship in 1968. Two years later, England travelled to the World Cup in Mexico knowing that they were one of the favourites. They met the other favourites, Brazil, in a group match in Guadalajara, and, although England lost 1–0, Banks made perhaps the most famous save of all time.

Midway through the first half, Jairzinho escaped his marker, Cooper, on the right flank, he reached the byline and sent over the perfect cross for Pele, who leapt high above Mullery and directed a lethal downward header towards the left corner of the net. Pele and the crowd thought it was a goal, but Banks had managed to fling himself right across the goal, thrust out a hand, and directed the ball over the bar. It was a save in a million, a masterpiece of physical agility, and is still talked about to this day. Pele said, 'At that moment, I hated Banks more than any man in soccer. But

A superb illustration of Banks' agility, one of his greatest assets, saving against France in 1963.

Facts about
Gordon Banks
• Banks's most embarassing moment was being tricked by George Best, who flicked the ball away from him as he was attempting a goal-kick for England against Northern Ireland. The goal was disallowed for a non-existent infringement.

• Banks was responsible for getting Stoke to their first Wembley final in 1972. He saved a Geoff Hurst penalty with three minutes left in extra time of the second leg. Stoke won the second replay 3–2.

• John Farmer, Banks's colleague at Stoke, penned this poem, entitled 'For Gordon Banks':
All down the days and thro the years
that now must be,
Your magic moments of inspiration
will serve me well:
For in the cheers and in the air
I now must breathe,
Your winding spell will never fade
or die.

when I cooled down, I had to applaud him with my heart. It was the greatest save I had ever seen.'

Unfortunately, a bottle of beer excluded Banks from the quarter-final against West Germany. He had a serious stomach upset, and his deputy, Bonetti, could not stop the Germans coming from two goals behind to win.

Banks remained England's first-choice when the team returned from Mexico, although Shilton, by now his understudy, was given the occasional cap. He was still playing well at club level and, in 1972, helped Stoke beat Chelsea in the League Cup final at Wembley, their only trophy. Later that year, though, he was involved in a car crash. He lost the sight of an eye, and his career was over. It was a sad way for such a great player to have to leave the game.

'Few goalkeepers are said to be the best keeper in the world, fewer still are called the greatest of all time. Add to that the fact that he made the greatest save Pele has ever seen. That says more about Gordon than I ever can.'

ROGER BANNISTER

SIR ROGER GILBERT BANNISTER
ATHLETICS – MIDDLE-DISTANCE RUNNER
BORN: HARROW, 23 MARCH 1929

Facts about Roger Bannister

- The PA announcement of the record at Iffley Road was made by Norris McWhirter who went on to compile the famous Guinness Book of Records.

- Another record was set at the Iffley Road meeting that evening. Malcolm Pharoah threw the discus 160 feet four inches for a British and Empire record. His achievement was largely ignored.

- The famous athletics trio also found fame in later life: Chataway as a leading Conservative politician, Brasher as a journalist and organiser of the London Marathon and Bannister as a neurologist, academic and Master of an Oxford College.

One moment in time. A great day in athletics history, six tenths of a second inside immortality for Bannister.

Most sportsmen and sportswomen gain their place in the sporting history books because of a succession of achievements throughout their careers. A few, like Sir Roger Bannister, write their page on one special day with one towering achievement. Bannister's ever-lasting contribution lasted just under four minutes. It will be remembered, like Bob Beamon's 'leap' in the Mexico Olympics and Sergey Bubka's six-metre pole-vault, as one of the great watersheds in athletics history.

Bannister's career was butterfly-like, not because of a lack of dedication, but because he was a product of his era and his sport. In the 1950s, athletics was an amateur affair, his career goal was to become a doctor and so he retired after the momentous events of 1954 at the age of twenty-five.

A mile in under four minutes had been a highly tempting goal for nine years following the exploits of the Coe and Ovett of Sweden, Gundar Haegg and Arne Anderson. Over eight years they had reduced the world record by five seconds in six record breaking runs, between them, until Haegg set the mark at 4:01.4 in 1945.

When Bannister went to Oxford a year later, in 1946, as a very long and stringy seventeen year-old, he had a considerable way to go. Although he won the Freshman's mile, he was over fifty seconds slower than the world record. However, the lightweight bean-pole soon developed into a long-striding thoroughbred. By the Amateur Athletic Association (AAA) championship in July 1948 his time had come down from 4:53.00 to 4:17.2.

His potential was already apparent, but he declined an invitation as an Olympic 'possible' for the London Olympics, in 1948, knowing that 1952 was a more realistic option. Always in command of his own destiny, he brought his own scientific discipline to the track. Fashionable training techniques abounded at the time but Bannister kept his own counsel, picking up ideas from the likes of Percy Cerutti and especially Franz Stampfl, but preferring to keep them at arm's length.

His equally thoughtful and dedicated training partners, Chris Brasher and Chris Chataway, were just as important to his plans, and subsequently, to his famous 239.4 seconds of glory.

Roger Bannister's Career

Commonwealth Games
Gold: 1 mile 1954

European Championships
Gold: 1500 metres 1954
Bronze: 800 metres 1950

World Records
4 x 1 mile relay 1953	16:41.0
1500 metres (indoors) 1954	3:43.0
1 mile 1954	3:59.4

The Helsinki Olympics, in 1952, were a great disappointment for Bannister. He missed a medal finishing in fourth place in the 1500 metres, behind the winner, Josy Barthel, of Luxembourg, who set an Olympic record of 3:45.1, McMillen of the USA and Lueg of Germany. It had been a great race, but Bannister's meticulous planning had been upset by the sudden introduction of a semi-final. He came close to retiring from athletics. He eventually came to the vital decision to run for two more years, 'To prove my attitude towards training had been the right one, and hence restore my faith in myself that had been shaken by my Olympic defeat.'

Immortality beckoned at Iffley Road, Oxford, on 6 May 1954. Bannister, Brasher and Chataway ran for the AAA against Hulatt, Dole and Gordon of Oxford University. Brasher set the pace to 800 yards, covering 400 in 57.4 and 800 in 1:58.0. Chataway took Bannister through to three-quarters of a mile in 3:00.5 before Bannister struck for home 230 yards out. The dramatic finish is etched in everyone's memory, with Bannister collapsing into the arms of his supporters before being engulfed by the delirious on-lookers. The time: 3:59.4.

Bannister's recollection of the last few moments of the four-minute mile in his autobiography, is one of the most revealing passages ever written about an athlete on the cusp of greatness: 'Those last few seconds seemed never-ending. The faint line of the finishing tape stood ahead as a haven of peace after the struggle. The arms of the world were waiting to receive me, if only I reached the tape without slackening my speed. If I faltered, there would be no arms to hold me and the world would be a cold, forbidding place, because I had been so close. I leapt at the tape like a man taking his last spring to save himself from the chasm that threatens to engulf him.'

The record lasted only six weeks. John Landy, the brilliant Australian miler had also been thirsting for the record. In Turku, Finland, on 21 June, Landy set an astonishing mark of 3:57.9, in many ways an even more remarkable time than Bannister's. However, it was the Englishman with the long, loping strides who had first crossed the great divide.

1954 had two more dramatic instalments. Landy and Bannister were due to meet in the Commonwealth Games Mile in Vancouver, on 7 August. It was called the 'mile of the century', the 'miracle mile' and almost anything else enthusiastic journalists could invent. Most importantly, it confirmed that Bannister was not a one-race wonder.

It was an epic race. Off the final bend Landy was leading, Bannister moved out to launch his attack. In that moment Landy glanced inside to check on Bannister. The Englishman saw his chance and went for the line. He won in 3:58.8, eight-tenths ahead of Landy. Bannister's time was half a second faster than his Iffley Road time but nearly a second slower than Landy's world record.

Bannister reinforced the fact that he could win races, as well as break records, at the European Championships in Berne, three weeks later. He added a 1500 metre gold medal to the bronze he had won in 1950. It was his last race.

- Bannister's colleagues, Chataway and Brasher, had their own moments of glory. Chataway held the three miles and 5000 metres world records and had a wonderful series of confrontations with the Soviet athlete, Vladimir Kuts, while Brasher won the Olympic title that eluded his two illustrious colleagues, the 3000-metres steeplechase in Melbourne, in 1956.

- Bannister had ambitions to row in the Boat Race but was too skinny.

- He was knighted in 1975. In the same year he had a bad car accident breaking seven ribs and injuring his foot. It took forty-five minutes to cut him from the wreckage.

- He later admitted that had he won an Olympic Gold medal in Helsinki, in 1952, he may well have retired there and then.

'Roger Bannister will always be remembered as the first man to break the 4 minute barrier over the blue ribbon distance of the mile. The barrier had become as much a psychological one as a physical one. After years of attempts by the world's best middle distance runners, they had always been beaten by the clock. Whatever else is said about Bannister he was first to finally break the barrier. He also won the Mile of the Century against John Landy to prove he could race as well. His career at the top was short even for his era but he was one of the first amateurs to adopt a professional approach to his training, which meant that, at least before his world record, he was not an establishment favourite. I've also heard it said that he preferred peace and the countryside to crowds and fame.'

KEN BARRINGTON

KENNETH FRANK BARRINGTON
CRICKET – BATSMAN
BORN: READING, 24 NOVEMBER 1930
DIED: BARBADOS, 14 MARCH 1980

Facts about Ken Barrington

- He was the son of a soldier, and spent his early years living in an army barracks at Reading.

- He was dropped against New Zealand in 1965 for slow scoring after crawling to 137. On his return, he hit twenty-six fours in an innings of 163.

- He refused to face West Indian pace bowler Charlie Griffith, convinced he was a 'chucker'. However, this caused antagonism between himself and the West Indians, and he suffered a nervous breakdown on the 1966 tour because of the stress.

Diligence and hard work summed up the life of Ken Barrington. Never a player to stand out, he was a model of consistency, and his Test average of 58.67 was greater than all of his peers in eighty-two Tests. Only Herbert Sutcliffe, in fifty-four Tests, and Eddie Paynter, in twenty, rank higher. He was the first player to score a century at each of England's six home Test venues, but such dedication took its toll. He suffered terribly from the anxieties of the modern game, and died tragically early.

Barrington joined Surrey at the age of seventeen, initially showing promise as a bowler, but wishing to become a top-order batsmen. After National Service, he blended seamlessly into the team that won a record seven consecutive championships under the captaincy of Surridge and May. After a successful season in the second XI in 1952, he made his first-class debut the next year. In 1955, he was selected for England against South Africa, but it was not a successful transition, and poor performances led to him being dropped. It was something he was determined would not happen again, and he took his dedication to the game to new levels. He sought to eliminate all faults in his technique. Previously, he had been largely an off-side player. Now, he played chiefly off the back foot, with an impeccable defensive technique he now scored his runs more on the on side. Together with his courage against pace, this made him a close to impregnable batsman, although it did make his batting appear over-cautious. In 1959, he scored 2499 runs and was selected for the tour of the West Indies. He seized his second England chance with both hands. He scored 1329 runs on the tour of India and Pakistan in 1961–62, and the next winter scored 1765 at an

Ken Barrington's Career

Tests	82
Test runs scored	6806
Average	58.67
Centuries	20
First class runs	31,714
Average	45.63
Centuries	76
County Championships (1953–58) with Surrey	6
Season's best batting average	1964, 1967

Test centuries in England (6)
256 v Australia at Old Trafford 1964 (highest first-class score)
137 v New Zealand at Edgbaston 1965
163 v New Zealand at Headingley 1965
148 v Pakistan at Lord's 1967
109 v Pakistan at Trent Bridge 1967
142 v Pakistan at The Ova 1967

average of over eighty in Australia and New Zealand. Indeed, Barrington was probably a better player for England on tour than at home. He played thirty-six Tests abroad, as opposed to forty-six in England, but they included fourteen of his twenty Test centuries. However, he was England's leading batsman in the 1964 home series against Australia, when he took 256 off their bowlers in the Fourth Test, his highest first-class score.

In 1967, Barrington topped the season's first-class averages for the second time, and had an

Playing with a straight bat. Barrington in his prime, doing what he did best.

excellent series against Pakistan, scoring three centuries, but he had a poor 1968, scoring less than a thousand runs, and failing to notch up a single century. It was also to be his last season. That winter, he was playing in a double wicket competition in Melbourne when he complained of chest pains. It turned out to have been a mild heart attack. He decided to retire from first-class cricket at that point.

Barrington could handle all types of bowling. As a former leg-spinner, he relished that form of bowling, and Richie Benaud was a special favourite. Although he was less at home against pace, he scored three centuries in the West Indies. He was a useful occasional bowler himself, taking twenty-nine Test wickets. In the field, too, he was an outstanding performer, both as slip and as an outfielder with a powerful arm.

After his retirement from play, Barrington continued to give much to the game. He became an England selector in 1975. He also went on several tours in a managerial capacity. In 1981, he was assistant manager on the West Indies tour. It was a particularly torrid tour, unsuccessful on the field and controversial off it, with the Jackman affair resulting in the Guyana Test being cancelled, and Barrington was a man prone to suffer from anxiety. He suffered a fatal heart attack in his hotel room in Bridgetown, Barbados, after the second day of the Third Test. The many warm tributes that poured in were a measure of the stature of the man cricket had lost.

Far from being the most flamboyant of English batsmen, he was, like Geoff Boycott, that essential requirement in a well-balanced team, the inexorable gatherer of runs. His Test Match average is remarkable by any standards. He ranks seventh on the all-time list behind Bradman, Lara, Pollock, Headley, Sutcliffe and Paynter.

'Not blessed with the natural talent of some, Barrington was a man already playing international cricket when he decided that to reach the next level he would have to work hard to rectify his faults as a batsman. This, in itself, should be a lesson to us all.'

PHIL BENNETT

**PHILIP BENNETT
RUGBY UNION – FLY-HALF
BORN: FELINFOEL, LLANELLI, 24 OCTOBER 1948**

**Facts about
Phil Bennett**

- His nickname was 'Benny'.

- He was awarded the MBE in 1978.

- The correct sequence in the famous try was: Bennett, JPR Williams, Pullin, Davies, David, Quinnell, Edwards.

- 1973 was also the year when the Scarlets beat the All-Blacks as Bennett's Llanelli beat New Zealand 9–3 at Stradey Park. It was Llanelli's centenary year.

- He was only the second Welshman to Captain the British Lions.

- He was rugby's first international 'sub' when he replaced an injured Gerald Davies in 1969

Phil Bennett did several remarkable things in his career but none more indicative of his talent than to replace Barry John, the great fly-half, when all Welsh fans thought 'the King' had retired too early, and still win the hearts of the passionate fans. Most players would have paled into insignificance in stepping into such a player's illustrious shoes. Not Bennett. And this despite not having John's will-o'-the-wisp charisma or his extrovert personality.

In the long wait for John to vacate the number ten jersey, Bennett played on the wing and at centre after winning his first cap in 1969. Before that he had the classic upbringing: the grit and determination of Welsh schools rugby and the vital ingredient of flair and panache to impress the selectors at a higher level.

Bennett played twenty-nine internationals for Wales and eight times for the British Lions. In all, he scored 166 points for his country. His scoring for the Lions was even more prodigious. In South Africa in 1974 he scored 103 points, and was top scorer in New Zealand in 1977 with more than 100 points.

Bennett performed several feats of brilliance on the rugby field, many of them involving his trademark, the Bennett side-step. He's not the only player to have used the technique in the history of the game, but no one left it so late, did it so ostentatiously, or repeated it as arrogantly as Phil Bennett. The perfect illustration of his art will be talked about, replayed and drooled over for as long as the game is played.

The occasion was grand enough: the New Zealanders' end-of-tour fixture against the Barbarians at a packed Cardiff Arms Park, in 1973. Bennett caught a deep ball underneath his own posts in only the second minute. Convention and

Phil Bennett's Career

Captain of Llanelli, 1973–79

**Captain of British Isles, 1977
New Zealand**

103 points on British Isles tour to South Africa 1974

International appearances:
   29 1969–78 (8 as Captain)
   4 tries, 18 conversions, 2 dropped goals, 36 penalty goals: 166 points

wisdom demanded a kick to touch – especially with a posse of black jerseys bearing down on him.

Bennett's audacity in side-stepping not one but three Kiwis before passing to JPR Williams began a length-of-the-field try by Gareth Edwards which is still regarded as one of the finest ever seen and heralded a match which is one of the finest ever played.

But Phil Bennett's achievements numbered many more than 'The Try' in Cardiff. He scored a memorable one in South Africa, in 1974, from sixty yards out, weaving and side-stepping through the Springboks' defence in the second test.

He was also a vital part of the great Llanelli and Welsh teams of the 1970s, the most glorious era of his nation's rugby.

There were a few raised eyebrows at Bennett's captaincy credentials, but he proved the doubters wrong at all levels. In particular, he led the Lions especially well on their tour in 1977 and he had the great distinction of leading his country to a Grand

On a typical run, making good ground. The problems came later for defenders, in predicting what he would do next.

- Gareth Edwards, the great scrum-half who played 25 of his Welsh internationals with Bennett, said of him, 'He could catch the worst rubbish you might throw at him, he could almost bewitch opponents with his footwork and has there been a better cover-tackler to play fly-half? ... A true all-time "great", absolutely no doubt about it.'

- Carwyn James, the great Welsh coach, may well have inspired Bennett's wonderful triple side-step against the All-Blacks, when he said to the nervous fly-half just before the kick-off, 'You're not in the shadows anymore Phil bach, go and show the world what Stradey knows.'

- Carwyn James later wrote about the try in the Guardian, 'Rare and unforgettable, when you can play at a level outside the conscious, when everything is instinct ... that unique moment when sport, lovely sport, not only achieves, but assumes, an art form.'

Slam in 1978. It was a hard campaign and Bennett's leadership was crucial.

After his retirement Bennett became a journalist and commentator.

'To captain your nation at a sport that is worshipped by your countrymen and to replace a man who the nation calls 'King' is pressure. To do both these things and prove yourself an artist on the field is beyond mere talent. His scores for style and fortitude are right up there with the best and if Gareth Edwards says Bennett is an all-time great, then I believe him.'

GEORGE BEST

**GEORGE BEST
FOOTBALL – FORWARD
BORN: BELFAST, 22 MAY 1946**

TOP 20

There are probably more column inches written about George Best than any other figure in British sport. Most of the copy focuses on two subjects: how good he was and what a waste of talent he came to represent. He seemed to do it all with the panache of a living legend and yet he was an unfulfilled engima: how much better could he have been if his waywardness had not intervened? If he'd been born English or German – he could have played with Moore and Charlton for England or Beckenbauer and Müller for Germany! If he'd been a Brazilian, he could have played in the great Brazilian team of 1970 – but then Jairzinho would have had to play centre-half!

Best's talents were obvious from his boyhood on the streets of Belfast. As he delights in recalling, 'no matter how hard they tried, no one could get the ball off me'.

He made his debut for Manchester United at the age of seventeen in 1963 and was a Northern Ireland international seven months later. He looked frail and certainly appeared to lack the muscular low centre of gravity of a Pele or a Maradona. But he was quick, tough and had a superb sense of balance and timing. He always seemed to be able to ride tackles and his speed in the challenge meant he invariably won balls that never should have been his.

Many insiders at Old Trafford thought his more eccentric skills needed coaching out of him – such is the way in English football – but Matt Busby, true to his beliefs, let Best express himself freely. His reward was seven or eight years of the most exciting talent ever seen in British football.

Most importantly, he was the final piece in the Manchester United jigsaw that Busby had been looking for to complete the team he had been

George Best's Career	
Football league appearances	411
Football league goals	147
FA Cup appearances	41
FA Cup goals	21
League Cup appearances	15
League Cup goals	8
International appearances	37
International goals	9
Football league championship	1965
	1967
Leading scorer (jointly)	1968
(28 goals)	
European Cup	1968
European Footballer of the Year	1968
Footballer of the Year	1968

building since the Munich tragedy five years earlier. Charlton was the lynchpin of the team; Best and Denis Law, the lethal strikers.

Wisely, Busby rested Best after his debut, in 1963, for a full three months, sensing that he wasn't ready. But after a Christmas holiday drubbing against Burnley, Busby saw his chance to 'blood' the boy from Belfast in front of an Old Trafford crowd baying for revenge in the return

Best as he will always be remembered, beautifully balanced, beguilingly vulnerable and immensely talented.

Facts about George Best

- Best's talent even won over the fanatical Portuguese crowd on the famous European Cup night in 1966 in Lisbon. After he had scored twice in the first twelve minutes the crowd chanted 'El Beatle' every time he touched the ball.

- At the end of the same game, someone from the crowd ran onto the pitch with a knife – but it wasn't to threaten Best, they wanted a lock of his hair.

- He scored six times against Northampton, in 1970, in the fifth round of the Cup. United won 8–2.

- Sir Matt Busby had these prophetic words about United's victory in the European Cup Final in 1968, 'The moment when Bobby took the Cup, it cleansed me. It eased the pain of the guilt of going into Europe. It was my justification.'

- Best withdrew from an international match, in 1971, after threats on his life.

match a few days later. The timing was perfect. This time United handed out the drubbing, 5–1. Best scored; a star was born.

The league championship came at the end of the following season, as United's team gelled: a solid defence; Stiles and Crerend aggressive and creative in equal measure; Best, Law and Charlton the match-winning superstars. Everyone wanted to see United, 'Georgie' Best in particular.

It was the era of the Beatles, the swinging 1960s; George became a central character and a piece of public property. But he was still the consummate player. He trained hard and constantly tried to improve his already immense skills.

In 1966 his talent exploded onto the international scene when 'El Beatle' destroyed Benfica in the Stadium of Light, in Lisbon, as United won 5–1 in the European Cup. Best scored twice in the first twelve minutes.

United won the championship again in 1967; Best played every game. The following season he missed only one match and was the leading scorer in the First Division with twenty-eight goals. He was at his peak and he was still only twenty-two.

On 29 May of that year, came Best's and Manchester United's finest hour. The pursuit of the European Cup had been Matt Busby's dream since his early days at Old Trafford. The Munich air disaster and the destruction of his famous 'Babes', while travelling in pursuit of the prize, had added a terrible burden to the quest. The European Cup became Busby's Holy Grail.

It was appropriate that Wembley should be the setting – almost inevitable that United would win. Even the gods intervened when Eusebio, inexplicably, shot straight at Stepney in United's goal in the dying minutes of normal time when it would have been easier to score. Best scored the crucial goal to put United 2–1 ahead at the beginning of extra time; they went on to win 4–1. Busby's journey was over.

That night at Wembley was the zenith of Best's career. Despite his not playing on the same international stage as his great contemporaries, the fact that Best was mentioned in the same breath as Pele, Beckenbauer and Cruyff is a reflection of the sheer brilliance of his playing style. Eamon Dunphy, a contemporary at Manchester United

and a much respected author, wrote of him, 'His genius was to retain the joyous innocence of the streets and impose it on the professional game in a way that only the greatest footballers have done.'

Accolades were bestowed in abundance in 1968, including Footballer of the Year and European Footballer of the Year. For at least three years after the great days of 1968 Best continued to give everything for United.

But Wembley had been a watershed. Busby retired and nothing would be quite the same again – at least until Alex Ferguson's United started to re-live the dream twenty-five years later. Best suffered more than most as United slowly went into

- Best's first international appearance was against Wales in Swansea in 1964, his last was against Holland in Belfast in October 1977 at the age of thirty-one.

- He scored a hat-trick for Northern Ireland against Cyprus in Belfast, in 1971.

- Best's tricks on the field became legendary. They included backside traps, juggling on his thigh and audacious attempts at lobbing Pat Jennings in the Spurs goal – sometimes successfully.

- His final game was at Bournemouth, in 1983, against Wigan. The attendance was 4528.

The young idol, flanked by Manchester United colleagues and England heroes Nobby Stiles and Bobby Charlton.

decline. The pressures became too much and, as the 1970s wore on, the George Best saga became more and more lurid.

A glorious career lasted about half as long as it might have done. Broken relationships, heavy drinking and a sorry plight in his business affairs conspired to make it all too much for him. It ended with a series of retirements and degrading comebacks until a veil was drawn at Bournemouth in 1983.

George Best's personal problems worsened for several years, until recently, when a modicum of stability returned to his life. He now makes personal appearances and is a popular football pundit.

'I watched George as a kid and, like just about everyone else in the country, was simply in awe of him. He was right up there with the Beatles, only he had more fun than all four of them put together! He seemed to have it all: kick with both feet; good in the air and could handle himself when the occasion called for it. But sometimes, those who burn brightest burn the shortest. George seemed to be able to take football back to the people in that he did all the things we wished we could do with a ball and looked like he was enjoying himself at the same time. I've met George a few times in my travels and he's great company, but I was too embarrassed to tell him I had a pair of his signed boots. He is the only footballer from these islands to be spoken of in the same breath as Pele and Cruyff. George scores well in most sections, but I'd ask questions about length of career, self control and coping with pressure.'

BILLY BOSTON

WILLIAM JOHN BOSTON
RUGBY LEAGUE – WINGER
BORN: CARDIFF, 6 AUGUST 1934

Facts about Billy Boston

- He was the first black player to tour with Great Britain.

- He was nicknamed (in a clever reversal of the name of the town's literary landmark) the 'Peer of Wigan'.

- Boston made his last international appearance for Britain against France on home turf at Central Park. Britain won handsomely 42–4 with Boston scoring a try.

- In the 1956–57 season Boston scored sixty tries.

- He was allowed, through the generosity of various captains, to kick four goals during his long career despite being known to have, 'two left feet'.

- In his youth he played rugby union with the great Welsh captain, Cliff Morgan.

Billy Boston's Career

Challenge Cup winner

1958 v Workington Town	13–9	
1959 v Hull KR	30–13	
1965 v Hunslet	20–16	

Challenge Cup runner-up

1961 v St Helens	6–12	
1962 v Wakefield Trinity	10–25	
1966 v St Helens	2–21	

Championship
1958–59, 1961–62

Championship play-off
1960

477 Career tries
4 Career goals
31 Test appearances for Great Britain
24 Test tries for Great Britain

Billy Boston came from Tiger Bay, in Cardiff, the sixth of eleven children. His father was from Sierra Leone, his mother from Ireland. Naturally, as a Welshman, his first rugby code was union. As an eighteen-year-old youth he played for the Welsh Boys Club and later for Cardiff Internationals Athletic Club.

He did his National Service in 1952 in the Royal Corps of Signals at Catterick Camp, where he joined an illustrious group of talented players including Phil Horrocks-Taylor, the future England Rugby Union fly-half. There, the already obvious rugby talent of the young Welsh winger attracted the scouts from the northern rugby league teams like bees to a honey pot. In the Army Cup Final he scored six tries against the Welsh Guards in front of four visiting directors from Wigan. He scored 126 tries in one season and in 1953 was signed by Wigan for the then handsome sum of £3000, to the chagrin of Hunslet who had been chasing him for three years.

He played only five games in the famous cherry hoops of Central Park before he was chosen to tour Australia and New Zealand in the Great Britain team. He was a phenomenal success, scoring a record-breaking thirty-six tries in eighteen games on tour, including two tries on his Test debut in the Second Test against Australia in Brisbane, and a record-equalling four tries in the Second Test against New Zealand in Auckland. He toured again in 1962, when he scored twenty-two tries in seventeen games, and played in the World Cup tournaments in 1957 and 1960. His long-term partnership with Eric Ashton was effective and deadly and became legendary in the history of rugby league.

In Wigan he became a folk-hero. More than 8000 people turned up to watch him make his A-team debut. By the time he left Wigan, fifteen years later, he had scored 477 tries, including a haul of seven tries on two occasions, against Dewsbury in 1955 and Salford in 1962.

Wembley became, almost literally, an annual outing. He appeared in six Challenge Cup finals in eight years, from 1958 to 1966, taking a winner's medal back to Lancashire in 1958, 1959 and 1965 against Workington Town, Hull and Hunslet respectively. He played his last match for Wigan against Wakefield Trinity in April 1968. In the twilight of his career he occasionally played for Blackpool Borough, as a second row

Boston at his best, powering over the line for a try on tour against Australia in 1962.

forward, until, on Easter Monday 1970, he sustained a bad arm injury which forced him into retirement, but only back to Central Park Wigan where he became landlord of the Griffin Hotel which stands not more than the length of the pitch from the famous ground he graced so majestically.

Billy Boston was a great ambassador for rugby league. He was big, strong and fearless and, despite the steady acquisition of thirty pounds from callow youth to seasoned professional, he retained an awesome turn of speed. This momentum, allied to his considerable bulk and coupled with his famous hand-off, supposedly reminiscent of a kick from the rear-end of a mule, made him an exhilarating sight for colleagues and supporters and a frightening one for opponents.

He was the complete all-rounder. He often played out of position and at all times read the game well and was able to create opportunities for others. His bone-jarring tackling became legendary, both for its ferocity and the precision of its timing. Off the field he was friendly and well-respected but firm enough to stand up to his club directors when in 1956 he was suspended for his 'general attitude'. He claimed his problems were caused by an ankle injury. He also coped well with the inevitable racial prejudice that came his way. To the shame of the British game he had to travel home alone at the end of the 1957 World Cup Series in Australia when the team stopped off in South Africa. His presence would have been an embarassment to South Africa's Apartheid policy.

'Billy was a scoring machine who could also play just about anywhere on the pitch, and often did. He was also a big man in a man's game. He must have had an uncanny ability to cope with pressure, because even now in the 1990s it is hard to play sport as a black man. In the '50s it must have been purgatory for him. This is highlighted by his treatment by the establishment when Great Britain visited South Africa in 1957.'

IAN BOTHAM

IAN TERRENCE BOTHAM
CRICKET – ALL-ROUNDER
BORN: HESWALL, 24 NOVEMBER 1955

Ian Botham is arguably the greatest all-round cricketer England has ever produced. The statistics say that. But his career was about much more than statistics. Controversy courted him both on and off the field, but the abiding image of the man perhaps dates from 1985, and the Fifth Test against Australia. His took his first ball from Craig McDermott, the opposition's fastest bowler, and drove it high back over his head for six. Nothing was impossible for Ian Botham.

Botham joined the MCC groundstaff from school, and then entered first-class cricket with Somerset, a county without a single trophy to their credit in over eighty years of play. Along with a new West Indian recruit, Viv Richards, Somerset soon became one of the top one-day teams in the country. They won the Gillette Cup and Sunday League in 1979, and, over the next five years, took the Benson & Hedges Cup twice, and the NatWest Trophy. These triumphs with a small county were impressive enough, but where Botham really excelled was at international level.

Botham was called up for England duty in 1977, more for his fast-medium bowling, and he took five wickets against the Australians in his first Test. That winter, he showed signs of things to come, becoming only the second England player to score a century and take five wickets in an innings with 103 and 5–73 against New Zealand in Christchurch. With cricket convulsed by the Kerry Packer World Series upheaval, English cricket needed a new hero. Now it had one.

The England captain at the time was Mike Brearley, an astute judge of character, and a man who had the ability to enable Botham to achieve his best. Botham flourished under his leadership,

Ian Botham's Career

Tests	102		
Test runs scored	5200	First Class runs	18,983
Average	33.54	Average	34.20
Centuries	14	Centuries	37
Test wickets	383	wickets	1159
Average	28.40	Average	27.08

He scored a century and took five wickets in an innings five times in Tests:

103 & 5–73	v New Zealand at Christchurch	1977–78
108 & 8–34	v Pakistan at Lord's	1978
114 & 6–58 & 7–48	v India at Bombay	1979–80
149 n/o & 6–95	v Australia at Headingley	1981
138 & 5–59	v New Zealand at Wellington	1983–84

County Championship wins
1988, 1989 (with Worcestershire)

NatWest Trophy wins
1979, 1983 (with Somerset)

Benson & Hedges Cup wins
1981, 1982 (with Somerset), 1991 (with Worcestershire)

Sunday League wins
1979 (with Somerset), 1987, 1988 (with Worcestershire)

A cricketing cavalier. England's greatest all-rounder.

Facts about Ian Botham

- He played football for Scunthorpe United and Yeovil Town.

- He holds a private pilot's licence.

- He was the first player to play for England while playing for three different counties (Somerset, Worcestershire and Durham).

- He is well known for his appearances in pantomime, in a stage show with Viv Richards, and on TV as a team captain on *A Question of Sport*.

- He once said, 'Cricket is full of theorists, who can ruin your game in no time.'

- He scored 208 against India in 1982, his double-century coming up off 220 balls, the fastest on terms of balls received

- He took 120 catches in his 102 Tests, equalling Colin Cowdrey's record

taking his 100th Test wicket only two years and nine days after his debut, a record, and passing the mark of 1000 runs and 100 wickets in only twenty-one Tests. When Brearley decided to retire from England duty after the 1979–80 tour, his protégé was elevated into his place.

It was a disastrous move. Botham found it difficult to take on the dual responsibility of performing at the highest level while motivating others. He was not helped by having to face the West Indies at their peak both home and away, and by extremely negative press coverage. After losing the first Test to Australia at home in 1981, Botham got a pair in the second at Lord's. He walked back up the pavilion steps in complete silence and on out of the England captaincy. And, within two weeks, he was England's greatest sporting hero.

Mike Brearley was recalled as captain for the Third Test at Headingley, and almost immediately Botham appeared recharged. He took 6–95 in the Australian first innings, and then top-scored with fifty when England batted. However, England had been forced to follow on, and when their seventh wicket fell second time around, they were still

Botham brought athleticism and determination to English cricket in its hour of need.

evening the Australians, after a first innings that saw them all out for 130 in a fraction more than thirty overs, had fought their way back into contention. Coming in with England at 104–5, Botham hit 118 in 123 minutes, his century coming off eighty-six balls, and including six sixes. England won by 103 runs, and the Ashes were safe.

Botham's achievements for England did not end that summer. He scored 208, his highest Test score, against India in 1982, and he went on to become the highest Test wicket taker of all time, with 383, a record since exceeded by Richard Hadlee and Kapil Dev. He was the first player to score over 4000 runs and take 300 wickets in Test cricket, and while his bowling lost pace over the years, it always had enough to surprise the batsman and take wickets. He was still a valued England member in the 1992 World Cup, taking 4–31 to upset Australia at one point.

Botham was no stranger to controversy. He was banned from cricket for a while after admitting to taking marijuana, and he was frequently a target in the popular press. He also walked out on Somerset after they decided to dispense with the services of his friends Viv Richards and Joel Garner. He moved on to Worcestershire and finally Durham, but was not the potent force of before. However, Botham was always more than just a cricketer. He dabbled in football, playing part time for Scunthorpe United, and more recently has raised funds for leukaemia sufferers by undertaking marathon walks. He was a great cricketer, but to merely call him that does not do the man justice.

ninety-two runs behind. At that point, Botham decided on attack. He hit an undefeated 149, reaching his century off eighty-seven balls, and Australia were suddenly required to score 130 to win. Then fast bowler Bob Willis, in the spell of his life, took eight wickets, and England had won by eighteen runs, only the second time a team has won a Test after following on.

The next Test at Edgbaston again seemed to be going Australia's way. A low-scoring encounter had left Australia requiring 150 to win. At 105–4, Border was removed by a ball from Emburey that exploded off a length, and Brearley decided to call on Botham. In twenty-eight balls, he took the last five Australian wickets at the cost of one run.

England now needed a win in the fifth Test at Old Trafford to retain the Ashes, and by the third

'Ian Botham arrived in the nick of time for cricket, because it needed someone to perform miracles and be larger than life. He could do both with lots to spare. Never a man to sit on his ample bottom, 'Beefy' burned the candle at both ends... and the middle! He tried it all, Hollywood fashion; walks in the Alps, panto, golf; and all this before lunch. In the afternoon, after a nap there would be time for the odd fracas, fishing, football and the occasional speech tour. If he had been born in a different age he would have been an adventurer or a pirate (and probably both). However, his numbers do him no justice because it was how he got them that counts.'

GEOFF BOYCOTT

GEOFFREY BOYCOTT
CRICKET – BATSMAN
BORN: FITZWILLIAM, 21 OCTOBER 1940

Geoff Boycott was the most dedicated and most controversial cricketer of his generation. No one could have been more devoted to the game of cricket, and after representing Hemsworth Grammar School from the age of twelve, no one could have been more sure of eventual success.

Boycott was a master craftsman. Nobody paid more attention to the art of batsmanship. He joined Yorkshire in 1962 with barely a ripple. He could bat (although Yorkshire already had plenty of talent in that department, such as John Hampshire and Phil Sharpe) he was nothing special as a fielder and no one knew if he could bowl outside the nets. In short, little was expected. Yet within two years, he was in the England team to face Australia.

The early Boycott, while hardly a swashbuckler, could attack if necessary. In 1965, he scored a thrilling 146 in the Gillette Cup final against Surrey to give Yorkshire their first one-day title. He was more dedicated to the accumulation of big scores, though, and in an era that saw Yorkshire fall from being cricket's finest county to almost permanent also-rans, Boycott's performance never faltered. Between 1967 and 1985, he averaged over sixty eleven times, and between fifty and sixty on six further occasions. However, he was essentially a single-minded performer, and when he became Yorkshire captain in 1971 he found it hard to subordinate his own tendencies to the needs of the team. As an illustration, that year he became the first English batsman ever to average over 100, scoring 2503 and hitting thirteen centuries, but Yorkshire finished thirteenth in the County Championship, and were nowhere in the one day competitions.

Textbook Boycott; textbook stroke; textbook cricket.

**Facts about
Geoff Boycott**

- He was an under-
eighteen football
trialist with Leeds
United, but failed to
make the grade.

- His highest Test score
was 246 against India
in 1967. However, it
took him almost ten
hours, and he was
dropped from the next
Test for slow scoring.

- He refused to play
under Mike Denness
from 1974 on, calling
him 'the worst England
captain I have played
under'.

- He was sent home from
India in 1981 after the
Calcutta Test. He had
been unable to field
because of an upset
stomach, but had then
gone to play a game of
golf.

- After a particularly
slow fifty in a Test at
Perth he received a
telegram saying, 'You
have done for
Australian cricket what
the Boston Strangler
did for door-to-door
salesmen.'

- He is keen on Chinese
astrology, and was
born under the sign of
the Dragon

Geoff Boycott's Career

Tests	**108**
Test runs scored	**8114**
Average	**47.72**
Centuries	**22**
First class runs scored	**48,426**
Average	**56.83**
Centuries	**151**

**Averaged over 100 in a first-class
season twice:**

1971	100.12
1979	102.53

**He topped the averages on two
further occasions**
   1968, 1972

County Championships	**1962, 1963, 1966, 1967, 1968**
Gillette Cups	**1965, 1969**
Sunday League	**1983**

He was a permanent fixture in the England team as a safe, and very consistent opening batsman. However, he was thwarted in his ambition of becoming England captain, and he was not selected for his country between 1974 and 1977.

He returned to the Test scene in 1977 to possibly his finest hour. In the Headingley Test, he hit 191 in front of many of his most loyal supporters. It was his 100th first-class hundred and, just incidentally, it happened to be in the match that England regained the Ashes.

That winter, he achieved his ambition to captain England when Mike Brearley broke his arm against Pakistan. Sadly, his four tests in charge contained little to cheer English fans: a draw in Pakistan, and a 1–1 tie in a three-match series in New Zealand. The defeat in Wellington was the first time New Zealand had ever beaten England in

a test, forty-eight years after the first meeting.

Boycott was still never far from controversy in his later years. His captaincy of Yorkshire was terminated in 1978, and in 1982 in Calcutta his Test career came to an end in the match that saw him break Sobers' Test career run record. He flew back to England claiming health reasons. In fact, he had helped to organise the first rebel tour of South Africa. It was an unhappy way to end his international career.

Boycott's career was not without its lighter moments. In the 1979 World Cup, he beat Australia with the ball, not the bat. He scored only one run, but took two vital wickets against a startled Australian top order and England went on to an easy victory.

Boycott finally retired after the 1986 season, again amid controversy, when the Yorkshire committee refused to renew his contract. Sadly, he only scored 992 runs in his final year, ending a sequence of twenty-three successive seasons over a thousand runs.

His batting will be remembered as immaculate. Not necessarily the most exciting player, he was immensely difficult to remove, and was rarely bowled. His own bowling was occasionally seen in limited overs cricket, and sometimes at Test level. He took 3–47 against the South Africans at Cape Town on the 1964–65 tour. His fielding also, while never spectacular, was safe, and he had a strong arm from the deep. He could make enemies as easily as make runs, but, for a quarter of a century, no one had a bigger impact on the English game.

He is now a television commentator, where his immense knowledge of the game is put to good use.

'Boycott was an individual who played a team game. But, when you think about it, cricket is really a game played by individuals playing as a team in name only. It is probably true to say that Boycott, while near the top as a batsman, is in a league of his own when it comes to determination and dedication to his own game.'

FRANK BRUNO

FRANK BRUNO
BOXING – HEAVYWEIGHT
BORN: HAMMERSMITH, 16 NOVEMBER 1961

The last fifteen years have seen an explosion of boxing authorities. That means that the opportunities to become a World Champion are now much greater than they once were. When Frank Bruno beat Oliver McCall to win the World Boxing Council (WBC) Heavyweight Championship he was the third British boxer to win a share of boxing's most coveted prize in less than three years. But there was not a single fight fan in the country who would begrudge him the honour.

At six feet four inches, and with a wonderful, muscular physique, Frank Bruno looks the ideal boxer. Allied to that is an explosive left jab, and a right of awesome power. It was clear from his early days in the ring that, for the first time, Britain had a boxer who could, just possibly, become Heavyweight Champion of the world.

Bruno's childhood was not easy. He was the youngest of six children, always large for his age and, with a lot of natural aggression, was often in trouble. At the age of twelve, he was sent to Oak Hall School in Sussex, an establishment for 'problem children' where, in between schoolwork, he learned to box. He channelled his aggression to such good effect that, by the age of eighteen, he was already the Amateur Boxing Association (ABA) Heavyweight Champion. However, he had to undergo a series of eye operations before he was awarded a professional licence. Once he was certified as ready, he was launched on the British boxing scene under the wing of manager Terry Lawless. Lawless was determined to protect his star recruit from being pushed too far too soon. As he pointed out, Bruno had probably not boxed more than forty rounds in his amateur career.

His first fight was in 1982 when, aged twenty-

one, he disposed of Lupe Guerra with one punch. There followed, over the next thirteen months, a string of opponents who seemed to freeze the moment they saw Bruno head across the ring. His

The big right is cocked and ready- an awesome thought if you're Oliver McCall and are about to be on the receiving end.

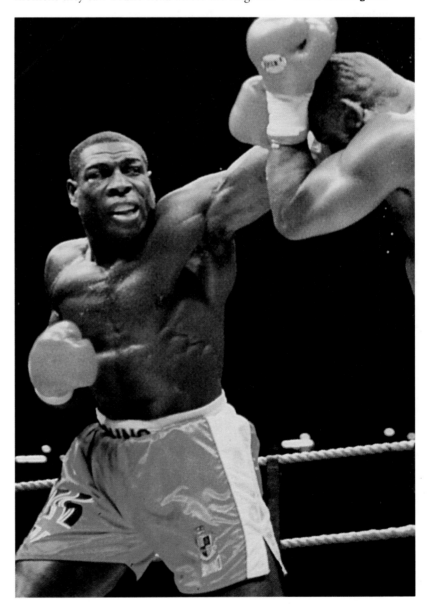

Frank Bruno's Career

Fights 44 (Won 40 Lost 4)

World Title Fights

1986	WBA v Tim Witherspoon	L RSC* 11 rounds	Wembley
1989	WBC v Mike Tyson	L RSC 5 rounds	Las Vegas
1993	WBC v Lennox Lewis	L RSC 7 rounds	Cardiff
1995	WBC v Oliver McCall	W points 12 rounds	Wembley

* Referee stopped contest

Facts about Frank Bruno

- Outside the boxing ring, Bruno is best known for his stints in pantomime, which began when he acted as a dame opposite Lenny Henry for Comic Relief.

- He had a good relationship with commentator Harry Carpenter, and 'Where's Harry' became something of a catchphrase.

- His marriage, to long-time girlfriend Laura, was a media event.

- His long-time manager, Terry Lawless, said of him, 'Frank is one of the Lord's chosen. Whatever happens to him he always comes sunny side up.'

first fourteen fights lasted an average of little more than two rounds. There was clamour for him to meet sterner opposition, but Lawless insisted that Bruno still had to learn. Some were impressed by him. Former champion Floyd Patterson thought Bruno had what it took to go all the way, but wanted to see what he would do if he got hurt.

That happened in October 1983, when a right from Floyd 'Jumbo' Cummings virtually knocked Bruno out on his feet. He was saved by the bell, and literally carried back to his corner by Lawless. He recovered, and fought Cummings to a standstill by round seven, but it was an awful warning. In May 1984, he met James 'Bonecrusher' Smith, later to win a world title himself, and after being well ahead for most of the fight walked into a left hook in the tenth. Once again, he was out on his feet, and this time there was no bell to save him. When, after a further barrage of punches he finally went down, there was no way he was going to beat the count.

Bruno's road back did not take him to the British title, by now considered an unnecessary diversion – it went straight to the European crown, which he took in 1985 with an easy four-round win over Anders Ekelund of Sweden. That put him back in the world rankings, and when he destroyed former World Boxing Association (WBA) champion Gerrie Coetzee in less than a round, he was definitely ready for a title shot.

In July 1986, he challenged Tim Witherspoon for the WBA crown at Wembley Stadium. The American was an excellent fighter, but found himself behind after seven rounds. However, his superior experience and durability told, as he took some of Bruno's best shots and started to take the fight to the British challenger. In the eleventh, he caught Bruno with a long right, and the challenge was over.

The way back was slow, but victories over the useful American James Tillis and a thirty-seven-year-old Joe Bugner gave him a shot at the seemingly invincible Mike Tyson. Some fourteen months elapsed between his win over Bugner and his meeting with 'Iron Mike' in Las Vegas, and, for many, it seemed a foregone conclusion. So it was, the record books say Tyson won in five rounds, but Bruno was not disgraced. Indeed, in the first round he seemed on the verdict of a major upset. A crashing right hurt Tyson and, momentarily, left him disoriented but instead of stepping back and taking advantage Bruno chose to cling on, and the moment was gone.

Almost three years later, in November 1991, Bruno returned again, starting out with an easy win over John Emmen of Holland. This time there was a British boxer to challenge, Lennox Lewis. After seeing off another former title contender, Carl Williams, in ten rounds, Bruno challenged Lewis in Cardiff for the WBC crown . It was the first time two British boxers had fought for a World Heavyweight title, and Bruno, the older by almost four years, had to give second best to a man who had yet to be defeated. After seven rounds, the contest was brought to a close. It seemed that Bruno would miss out on his dream.

Certainly when he announced he was still after the title, few considered him a serious challenger. However, the labyrinthine world of boxing politics came to his aid. Lewis was defeated by a relatively unknown American, Oliver McCall. Bruno, still a big name, and still a big draw, was also a ranked contender. Therefore, a match between the two was made for Wembley in September 1995. The fight went all twelve rounds and Bruno, in the most determined mood of his career, made sure his fourth title shot didn't pass him by. He won on points, and the boxing fraternity rejoiced.

'Frank, like Henry before him is a big hit with the public. He is also a good model in terms of perseverance, as can be seen from the 9 years separating his first world title fight from his fourth and winning one.'

KEN BUCHANAN

KENNETH BUCHANAN
BOXING – LIGHTWEIGHT
BORN: EDINBURGH, 28 JANUARY 1945

Ken Buchanan was one of Britain's most skilful and accomplished boxers. In the early 1970s, his talents graced the world stage and he became a hugely respected fighter. He was part of a great tradition in Scottish and British boxing: stylish, but hard.

He had a powerful left jab and an outstanding right hand and put himself to the ultimate test on several occasions in places where it is notoriously difficult to win, including New York, Tokyo, San Juan and Los Angeles.

Buchanan set off on the road to the toughest arena in sport when his father, Tom Buchanan, gave him a pair of boxing gloves for Christmas. He joined a local club at the age of eight and started to learn the craft that would lead many Americans to call him a 'gentleman boxer' – one of the old school, proud of his ring craft. The Americans

generally prefer boxers who 'fight', but they still admire the classic boxer, full of cunning, guile and counter-punches. Buchanan had all these qualities, but when it came to it, he proved he could take a good punch and he could 'fight' if he needed to.

He turned professional in 1965 at the age of twenty, and won his first four fights within three rounds. By the time he knocked out Maurice Cullen in the eleventh round in London, in February 1968, for the British Lightweight title, he had disposed of twenty-three men in almost as many months.

But then came a hiatus in Buchanan's career, in 1969, after he alleged he had been mismanaged. Eventually, the dispute was settled, but it heralded his first defeat, at the hands of Miguel Velasquez in Madrid. In January 1970, Buchanan fought him

Facts about Ken Buchanan

- Jim Watt, who lost to Buchanan in their British title fight in 1973, went on to become World Lightweight Champion in 1979.

- Shimatsu Suzuki, who beat Buchanan in their world title fight, later changed his name to 'Guts' Ishimatsu.

- Buchanan's defeat by Duran at the end of the thirteenth round was his only defeat inside the distance in seventy fights.

- Of his eight career defeats, five came after his post-retirement return to the ring.

- He always wore his own bright yellow and red tartan shorts for his fights.

- Duran nearly provoked Buchanan into a fight at the weigh-in for their Madison Square Garden battle by calling him 'Marcon' which, loosely translated, means 'Gay Libber'.

Adopting the pose in 1973. A Scottish hardman, proud of his craft and proud of his Country.

Ken Buchanan's Career

Key bouts

Year	Opponent	Title	Result	Details
1967	John McMillan	Scottish	Won	points 10 rounds
1968	Maurice Gillen	British	Won	knock-out 11 rounds
1970 (Jan)	Miguel Velasquez	European	Lost	points 15 rounds
1970 (May)	Brian Hudson	British	Won	knock-out 5 rounds
1970 (Sept)	Ismael Laguna	World	Won	points 15 rounds
1971 (Feb)	Ruban Navarro	World	Won	points 15 rounds
1971 (Sept)	Ismael Laguna	World	Won	points 15 rounds
1972	Roberto Duran	World	Lost	technical knock-out 13 rounds
1973	Jim Watt	British	Won	points 15 rounds
1974 (May)	Antonio Puddu	European	Won	knock-out 6 rounds
1974 (Dec)	Leonard Tavarez	European	Won	technical knock-out 14 rounds
1975 (Feb)	Ishimatsu Suzuki	World	Lost	points 15 rounds
1975 (July)	Giancarlo Usai	European	Won	technical knock-out 12 rounds
1979	Charlie Nash	European	Lost	points 12 rounds

- The pre-fight betting for the Duran fight was eight to five on Buchanan to win.

- The gate for the Duran fight was a Lightweight record at $223,901.

- Buchanan was not accepted as World Champion by the British Boxing Board of Control (BBBC) after his victory against Laguna in 1970 because it was a WBA fight, which the BBBC didn't recognise. They finally accepted him as Champion when he beat Navarro six months later.

for the vacant European Lightweight title and lost on points, although British opinion suggested that the decision was a harsh one.

Not in the slightest deterred, Buchanan retained his British title against Brian Hudson, at Wembley, in May of the same year, by knocking him out in round five, and then travelled to San Juan, in Puerto Rico, in September, to win the World Lightweight title, from Ismael Laguna of Panama. At five feet eight inches and 135 pounds, Buchanan was a classic Lightweight. He boxed superbly and won a split decision, 5–2 after fifteen rounds.

He defended his title twice within a year, on both occasions in foreign rings. First, he took on Ruben Navarro in Los Angeles, and won on points after fifteen rounds, and then, in September 1971, he fought a re-match against Laguna, in New York, and won in a unanimous points decision, despite suffering a bad cut above his eye.

In June 1972, Buchanan defended his world title in Madison Square Garden, New York, against a twenty-one year-old Panamanian. It was a rough, tough and hugely controversial fight. Buchanan's opponent was the up and coming Roberto Duran.

The boxing world had rarely seen a fighting machine like Duran. He seemed impervious to punishment and just rolled forward using fists, elbows, head, shoulder and knees to bludgeon his opponent. Buchanan struggled throughout the fight to use his skills to keep Duran at bay. Eventually, Buchanan succumbed and they stood toe to toe to slug it out. Buchanan was eventually stopped at the end of the thirteenth round following what seemed to be a blow directly to the groin. He got little sympathy from the referee, or the crowd, who were enthralled by the new boxing juggernaut from Panama. However, film evidence later suggested that Buchanan had been hit below the belt.

Roberto Duran went on to defend the title fourteen times and become one of the great Lightweights of all time, before moving up to Welterweight and even Middleweight; but he wouldn't give Buchanan a re-match and admitted that it was the toughest Lightweight bout he ever had.

Buchanan was far from finished after the Duran fight. In fact, he fought in all kinds of venues, dispensing with fighter after fighter. He won a Lonsdale belt outright when he outpointed Jim Watt in Glasgow in 1973 for the British title and he won the European title in Cagliari in 1974, when he knocked out Antonio Puddu in the fifth round.

He had one last attempt to win the world title, but lost to Ishimatsu Suzuki on points in Tokyo in 1975.

Buchanan retired in 1976 after defending his European title against, Giancarlo Usai, but to everyone's disappointment came back in 1979. He lost his European title to Charlie Nash on points after twelve rounds in Copenhagen, and boxed on until 1983 when he finally retired at the age of thirty-seven.

'Ken Buchanan could give or take a punch, and was one of the most skilful lightweights seen. In boxing there seems to be a huge advantage to 'playing' at home, but Ken did it the hard way, by beating people where it hurt even more, in front of their home crowds.'

JOHN CHARLES

WILLIAM JOHN CHARLES
FOOTBALL – CENTRE FORWARD
BORN: CWMDU, 27 DECEMBER 1931

'Il Buon Gigante' one of football's most impressive athletes and nicest guys.

John Charles' Career

Second Division Championship	Leeds 1956	League appearances	543
Club record goalscorer (52)	Leeds 1954	Career goals	260
First division leading goalscorer (38)	Leeds 1957	Welsh International appearances	38
Serie A Championship Italy	Juventus 1958		
Serie A Championship Italy	Juventus 1960	Welsh International goals	15
Serie A Championship Italy	Juventus 1961		
Italian Cup	Juventus 1959		
Italian Cup	Juventus 1960		

John Charles had a remarkable footballing career, a remarkable temperament and a remarkable physique. All in all, he was quite a guy.

At six feet two inches and fourteen stones, he was a giant, on the football field. But his extraordinary temperament, sufficient to allow him to survive the worst Italian football could offer for many years, led to his being known as the 'Gentle Giant'. As a player, he was widely acknowledged as the finest Welsh footballer since Billy Meredith. His touch was excellent and, although he spent most of his career playing at centre-forward, he could play anywhere he liked, and played at the highest level at centre-half.

He started his career at Swansea but was signed by Leeds at the age of fifteen. By the time he was seventeen he was in the first team and within a year had won his first cap for Wales.

He switched to centre-forward in 1952 and scored twenty seven goals in thirty matches. The following season he was the league's leading scorer with forty-two goals, a Leeds club record. Leeds won the Second Division championship in 1956, but soon his exploits had alerted the Italian scouts and Juventus sent shock waves through the British game by enticing Charles to Italy. They doubled the record British transfer fee by paying £70,000 and offered Charles a £10,000 signing-on fee.

Few British exports to Italy did well, but Charles was an exception. He joined an outstanding team which included Argentina's Omar Sivori and the Golden Boy himself, Giampiero Boniperti. The big Welshman's goals were vital, the fans loved him. It was they who christened him, 'Il Buon Gigante', the gentle giant. He helped Juve to three Serie A Championships and two Italian Cups, and he scored ninety-three goals in 155 league games – an amazing scoring rate against the world's toughest defences.

He made thirty-eight appearances for Wales and scored fifteen goals and was part of the great Welsh team in the 1958 World Cup which included Jack Kelsey and Ivor Allchurch. Wales drew all their games in group three with Charles scoring a crucial goal in the 1–1 draw against Hungary. They then had to beat Hungary again in a play-off match in the group and came from behind to win 2–1.

Unfortunately, they met Brazil and the seventeen-year-old Pele in the quarter-finals, without the injured Charles, and lost 1–0.

Charles made a brief return to Leeds in 1962, and then equally brief visits to Roma and Cardiff before retiring to become player-manager of Hereford and Merthyr. Later, he became a publican in Leeds.

'William J Charles is living proof that sometimes nice guys do finish first. Everything you read about the man, even from opponents, testifies to what a nice man he was, even while playing! His record of nearly a goal every other game is very impressive when you take into account the Italian years; what an adventure that must have been with all that money and every girl looking like Sofia Loren!'

BOBBY CHARLTON

SIR ROBERT CHARLTON
FOOTBALL – FORWARD
BORN: ASHINGTON, 11 OCTOBER 1937

Facts about Bobby Charlton

- Charlton always felt that United's courageous 3–3 draw in the second leg of the European Cup semi-final against Real Madrid, in the Bernabeau Stadium in 1968, was the most important victory in United's victorious campaign to take the Champions' trophy to Old Trafford.

- He had only one booking in 644 league appearances.

- He scored four hat-tricks for England – against Mexico, Switzerland, USA and Luxembourg.

- Charlton once said, 'Every day is like Christmas Day for me. Everywhere I go in the world I see children playing football. That's the best present anyone could have.'

Not a dry eye in the shed! Bobby's final game for United, against Chelsea at Stamford Bridge in 1973.

- He was a leading member of Manchester's bid team for the 2000 Olympic Games.

- Charlton was awarded the OBE in 1969.

- He came out of retirement for a brief period to try and help his ailing Preston North End out of trouble. He played his final game at Port Vale on 29 March 1975.

- His retirement from Manchester United was a very emotional good-bye at Stamford Bridge in April 1973. Even the battle-hardened Chelsea fans in the notorious 'shed' chanted his name every time he touched the ball. No other modern English player would have received such a generous tribute.

- Coincidentally, Bobby's brother, Jack, retired on the same day.

Bobby Charlton achieved everything in football on the field of play, but in many ways achieved even more off it. Universally liked and admired for his sportsmanship and quiet dignity, he became the perfect ambassador for his club, his country and his sport. His knighthood, in 1995, was the final richly deserved accolade in a glittering career. Sir Bobby became living proof that nice guys don't always finish last. Charlton's modest temperament and unhurried calm often disguised his qualities as an athlete. He was superbly balanced and moved with a flowing, graceful stride that would glide past opponents with a change of direction that seemed to come from no more than a slight drop of the shoulders. His passing was exemplary and his left foot was explosive from up to thirty yards.

Charlton hailed from that famous hotbed of football, the northeast. His uncle was 'Wor Jackie'

Milburn, the idol of St James' Park, and his brother Jack duplicated most of the honours won by Bobby, including the one on that most famous day in English football history when England won the World Cup in 1966.

Bobby's talent was obvious at an early age and he became one of the few boys to make it to senior level from England schoolboys.

Manchester United were at the front of a very

Sir Bobby Charlton's Career

League Cup Championship
Manchester United
1957, 1958, 1965, 1967

FA Cup
Manchester United 1963

European Cup
Manchester United 1968

World Cup
England 1966

Football league appearances	648
Football league goals	206
International appearances	106
International goals	49
European Footballer of the Year	1966
Footballer of the Year	1966
OBE	1969
Knighted	1995

long queue of clubs eager for his signature in 1954. He made his debut two years later, at the age of nineteen, against Charlton Athletic and scored twice. During that season he scored ten goals in thirteen matches and played in his first FA Cup Final when United lost 2–1 to Aston Villa, a final marred by the injury to United's goalkeeper, Ray Wood, after six minutes, reducing United to ten men.

United returned to European competition in 1957; they had entered the European Cup the year before, against the wishes of the Football league, and lost only to the might of Real Madrid in the semifinal. It was typical that Busby – a Scot after all – should know better than the English Football League where the future of English football should be!

But Busby's dream turned to tragedy. Manchester United were returning from Belgrade, in February 1958, where a 3–3 draw against Red Star had earned them another European Cup

One of Bobby's many emotion-laden days; playing at Wembley against Bolton Wanderers in 1958 in the aftermath of Munich.

- Helmut Schoen's decision to have Beckenbauer mark Charlton in the 1966 World Cup Final probably spiked Germany's most powerful weapon. The two great players cancelled one another out, but it allowed England's Alan Ball the freedom to run the German defence ragged.

- Alf Ramsey's decision to substitute Charlton in the stiffling heat of Leon in the 1970 World Cup quarter-final, when England were leading 2–0, may well have been crucial in allowing Germany back into the game. England eventually lost 3–2.

semi-final place. The plane refuelled in Munich, and tried three times to take off in appalling conditions before crashing. The 'Busby Babes' were no more. Seven players were among the twenty-two who died instantly, two more never played again. Bobby Charlton and Matt Busby were among the survivors, but Busby's life was in the balance for weeks afterwards. Duncan Edwards, probably the greatest of the 'Babes', whom Charlton still refers to as the greatest player he's ever seen, died two weeks later.

Charlton and Busby became the tragic heroes as Busby recovered and began the task of rebuilding his team around a man who was still only twenty-one years old.

Charlton played in the emotional Cup Final in May of that year. Bolton Wanderers won but United's makeshift team had already won the hearts of the nation. From that year onwards the tragedy of greatness snatched away from a team not much older than teenagers would make Manchester United a team apart in British football. Bobby Charlton came to embody everyone's hopes as he and Busby tried to make United great again.

It took ten years. But United's quest was only part of the Charlton story, for he also became England's hero.

He played 106 times for his country, a record at that time, and scored forty-nine goals, still a record. He became so synonymous with his country that, thoughout the world, 'Bobby Charlton' became the most oft-repeated English name as foreigners, without any grasp of the language, tried to communicate with their English visitors.

He scored on his debut for England, against Scotland, in April 1958, just two months after the horror of Munich. His England career became littered with spectacular goals, especially in his and England's finest hour in the 1966 World Cup. His long-range missile that broke the deadlock against Mexico, and his two goals in the semi-final against Portugal, were the key to England making it to their date with destiny.

When the day was won all the England players were heroes: Jack Charlton fell to the ground, head in hands, in disbelief; Nobby Stiles danced a jig with a toothless grin; Alan Ball ran himself 'daft', as commentator Ken Wolstenholme said he had done

throughout the game; Bobby Moore proudly held the trophy aloft; and Bobby Charlton cried.

Matt Busby's and Manchester United's journey was also nearing its end. Busby had created another great team at Old Trafford: Stepney, Foulkes, Crerand, Stiles, and the legendary trio – Best, Law and Charlton. They had won the Cup in 1963 and the league in 1965 and 1967. The first European campaign, in 1966, ended disappointingly against Partizan Belgrade in the semi-final after they had demolished Benfica at the quarter-final stage, but two years later it would be a different story.

The final against Benfica at Wembley in front of 100,000 fans – most of them Mancunians – was one of English football's most magical occasions. At last, the gods looked kindly on United. The game came alive in a dramatic period of extra time. Graca had equalised for Benfica fifteen minutes from time, after Charlton had put United ahead early in the second half, but United scored three times in the first nine minutes of extra time to turn the occasion into an amazing night of celebration. Busby's life's work was over; Charlton had completed his set of honours; United had laid the ghost of Munich.

Charlton made his final appearance for United in 1973 against Chelsea before retiring to manage Preston North End. Management wasn't for him and he returned to United as a member of the board in 1984. He now revels in watching the latest crop of talent under Alec Ferguson's wing at Old Trafford, runs a successful soccer training school for youngsters from around the world and still travels the globe as a soccer ambassador.

'What can I say about Bobby Charlton that hasn't already been said, except perhaps that most if it is probably true. Every time I've met him over the past 15 years he has always had a smile, a good word and great knowledge about current sport. But you can still see the competitive gleam in his eye when the talk comes round to football or Manchester United. I would like to admit here and now, that, as a kid, when we chose teams and my side was United I never wanted to be Bobby. He wasn't flash enough nor animated enough for me, but now that I'm more mature (only a little), I can see his qualities.'

LINFORD CHRISTIE

LINFORD CHRISTIE
ATHLETICS – SPRINTER
BORN: ST ANDREWS, JAMAICA, 2 APRIL 1960

The power and the glory. Linford knows he's the best.

Jamaica has been a fertile island for runners. Olympic champions such as Herb McKinley, Arthur Wint and Don Quarrie came from the Caribbean island. Linford Christie was also born there, but the finest British sprinter of all time came to London as a small boy, and learnt to run on cold evenings at the West London Stadium.

It was obvious that he had great physical ability. A powerfully built man at over six feet tall, he ran under eleven seconds for the 100 metres in 1984 and came close to selection for the Los Angeles Olympic squad. Only one thing stood between him and greatness, his attitude. Christie had a lackadaisical approach to training, and enjoyed the good life – not an attitude conducive to sporting success. It caught up with him, and he wasn't selected for the British squad for the 1985 European Cup. He protested to the director of coaching Frank Dick, but he had really left the British selectors little option. He was told that he had the talent to become Europe's best sprinter, but it was being wasted. Christie's attitude changed

Sealed with a kiss; World Champion 1993, following the Olympic title in 1992 in Barcelona.

Linford Christie's Career

Olympic Games
1988 (Seoul)	100 metres (2nd)
	4 x 100 metres (2nd)
1992 (Barcelona)	100 metres (1st)
	4 x 100 metres (4th)

World Championships
1987 (Rome)	100 metres (3rd)
1991 (Tokyo)	100 metres (4th)
	4 x 100 metres (3rd)
1993 (Stuttgart)	100 metres (1st)
	4 x 100 metres (2nd)
1995 (Gothenburg)	100 metres (8th)

European Championships
1986 (Stuttgart)	100 metres (1st)
	4 x 100 metres (3rd)
1990 (Split)	100 metres (1st)
	4 x 100 metres (2nd)
1994 (Helsinki)	100 metres (1st)

Facts about Linford Christie

- He wore a Union Jack draped around his shoulders to receive the 1986 European Championships 100 metres gold. He was reprimanded by the European authorities.

- Two of Christie's medals, his bronze from Rome in 1987 and silver from Seoul in 1988, were awarded away from the rostrum after the Ben Johnson affair.

- His old training ground, West London Stadium, was renamed Linford Christie Stadium in 1993.

- He once said the International Stadium in Gateshead was his favourite stadium.

- He was the men's team captain at the Barcelona Olympics and the Stuttgart and Helsinki World Championships, and collected the European Cup on behalf of the British team in 1989.

overnight.

In 1986, he suddenly became Britain's top sprinter. He had trained hard the previous winter under his coach Rod Roddan. At the European Indoor Championships he won the gold over 200 metres, and ran 10.04 in a 100 metres race in Seville. That compared to 10.42, his best from the previous season. Only a muscular Canadian called Ben Johnson pipped him for the 100 metres at the Commonwealth Games. Then, in the European Championships in Stuttgart, he proved he was Europe's best sprinter, storming to victory in the 100 metres with Allan Wells the previous number one trailing in fifth.

Having proved himself the best in Europe, Christie now had to overcome the rest of the world. His first chance was at the Rome World Championships the next year, but this was the first major confrontation of Ben Johnson and Carl Lewis. Christie crossed the line in fourth place. At the Seoul Olympics, Christie did better. He finished third, and his time of 9.97 seconds was the first time a European had broken the ten-second barrier. Of course, the bronze medal was later upgraded to a silver after the Ben Johnson drug scandal, but Christie had his own problems with chemicals. He had been taking ginseng and other vitamin supplements. One contained a stimulant, pseudoephedrine, which showed up in his urine sample as just over the allowable limit. After questioning by the IOC's Medical Committee, he was cleared of cheating, and went out to anchor the relay squad to a silver medal.

For Christie, beating the Americans, and especially Carl Lewis, became an obsession. His European results still kept him way ahead of any competition at home, but during the Grand Prix season, Christie was often second best. It seemed

that he was going to have to settle for that position in 1991, when, at the Tokyo World Championships his time of 9.92 seconds was only good enough for fourth place. His preparations for Barcelona were even more strenuous.

Christie was sure that 1992 would see him overcome Lewis once and for all. The American, although Christie's junior by almost a year, had had almost a decade at the top, and was finally being overhauled. Eventually, he failed through illness to qualify for the American 100 metres team, and Christie took his chance. Few who saw that final can forget how complete Christie's concentration was before and during the race. He heard nothing except the gun, and saw nothing except the finishing line. He completed the race in 9.96 seconds, and he was Olympic champion. At thirty-two, he was the oldest Olympic sprint champion of all time. He was also the first Briton to win in twelve years.

Some critics pointed out that he hadn't faced Lewis in the final. That was still a cause for disappointment, although Christie had a much better season overall than the American. In 1993, the two met in a much-hyped and very lucrative meeting at Gateshead, with Christie an easy winner. Less than a month later, in August, Christie finally proved beyond doubt that the title of world's best sprinter now belonged to him. At Stuttgart, Christie became World Champion in a time of 9.87 seconds. It was the second fastest legal time ever, only a hundredth of a second outside Lewis's Tokyo mark in 1991. Lewis was a distant fourth.

In 1994, he became only the second man to win the European Championship 100 metres three times after Valery Borzov, and also took the Commonwealth Games title, continuing a career long past the age when most sprinters in previous times had given up. However, the rewards are much greater these days and, although his 1995 season was blighted by outbursts against the press and failure in the World Championships, Christie was still dominant on the Grand Prix circuit. Indeed, only ten days after losing his world title, he beat the new champion, Donovan Bailey of Canada, quite convincingly. Only Christie himself will know when he has finally come to the end of the road.

'Linford is without doubt the best sprinter to have come from these islands. He could also, in my book, lay claim to the world record as the current record was set on that very fast (maybe illegal) track in Tokyo. It's also a pity that when Linford was at his best Lewis was passed his, because that would have sorted a few things out between them. I would also like to say a little about the rumour that I used to beat him regularly in the sprints when we were both young. It is very true and it's also true that I'm the one who's spreading the rumour. I think he can win in Atlanta and finish '96 as the World's No.1 sprinter.'

JIM CLARK

JAMES CLARK
MOTOR-RACING DRIVER
BORN: KILMANY, 4 MARCH 1936
DIED: HOCKENHEIM, GERMANY,
7 APRIL 1968

Colin Chapman, lotus team boss, listening intently as Clark tells him how it is, at Brands Hatch in 1964.

Among motor-racing aficionados Jim Clark is usually spoken of as being in the same league as Fangio and Senna, among the all-time greats. That is the measure of his stature within his sport. He was certainly the greatest driver of his generation when, in the 1960s, he and Colin Chapman's Lotus reigned supreme.

Clark was a Border Scot and proud of it. He was the reasonably well-off son of a farmer and throughout his life was always able to switch between the glamorous Jim Clark of the Grand Prix circuit and the down-to-earth 'Jimmy' Clark of his local farming community. He was held in great affection by everyone who knew him for his self-contained dignity and his calm, quiet modesty.

His flamboyance came from his driving reputation. He was lionised by racing enthusiasts through stories of his being able to drive anything with wheels.

He was fortunate enough to be able to drive fast cars from his youth and it was soon obvious that he had a rare talent. A local racing team was soon formed around him called 'Border Reivers' (the ancient name of a band of border raiders) and Clark's road to motor-racing immortality had begun.

Clark soon came to the attention of Colin Chapman, at his newly formed Lotus company. He had his first Formula One drive in 1960, at the Dutch Grand Prix, as a replacement for John Surtees who was still fulfilling some outstanding motor-cycling commitments. It was an impressive debut, he was in fourth place when he had to retire. In only his second race, two weeks later, at Spa-Francorchamps in the Belgian Grand Prix, he had to face the full, awesome reality of his chosen sport. In an event full of tragedy, a good friend was killed, Stirling Moss suffered serious injuries during practice and Michael Taylor crashed when his steering broke. Then, Clark was flagged down by a marshall as he turned a bend during the race, because of a crash involving Chris Bristow's car. He later described what he encountered: 'The Marshall bent down and grabbed this thing by the side of the road. It looked like a rag doll. I'll never forget the sight of his mangled body being dragged to the side.

Facts about Jim Clark

- Clark drove at Le Mans in 1960 for Aston Martin. He finished third.

- He was a very compact man and stood only five feet seven inches tall.

- Clark never won at Monaco despite the fact that it was his favourite race.

- There is a museum of Clark's achievements and memorabilia in his home town of Duns in the Borders.

- Clark's prize-money at Indianapolis in 1965 was a huge $170,000.

- Off the track he was prone to shyness and nervousness. He hated making speeches and bit his finger-nails relentlessly.

- Clark stayed single. He once said, 'I couldn't ask any woman to share this kind of life.'

Facts about Jim Clark

World Drivers Championship 1963
1965
Winner Indianapolis 500 1965

Grands Prix Summary:
Wins – 25 from 72 races
Total points – 274
Pole positions – 33
Fastest laps – 28

Grands Prix victories: (25)
1962	Belgian, British, United States
1963	Belgian, French, British, Dutch, Italian, Mexican, South African
1964	Belgian, British, Dutch
1965	Belgian, French, German, British, Dutch, South African
1966	United States
1967	British, Dutch, Mexican, United States
1968	South African

I remember at the end of the race finding that my car was splattered with blood. Towards the end of the race, my team-mate, Alan Stacey, was also killed. A bird flew into his face and his car went off the road. Thankfully, I didn't see the accident or the car. Had I done so, I'm convinced I would have given up motor-racing for good.'

1961 was not an auspicious year either. At the Italian Grand Prix, Clark pulled alongside Wolfgang Von Trips, their wheels touched and Von Trips' Ferrari crashed into a fence killing him and fourteen spectators. His introduction to Formula

'Jim Clark was never going to win prizes for public speaking, or being the life and soul of the party. But, give the man a steering wheel and four road wheels, and he could get just that bit more out of any machine. And he would drive anything. He was a natural who combined consistency with great technique. Obviously, his career was tragically short, but his 25 wins in 72 races shows the magnitude of his greatness.'

One driving could not have been more horrifying.

The following year was a far less harrowing one and was also his breakthrough year as a top driver. He had a new car, the Lotus 25, with a revolutionary monocoque body. After two mechanical failures, at Zandvoort and Monaco, Clark drove superbly to win his first Grand Prix at Spa. He won twice more that year, in the United States and at home in Britain, and collected thirty points to come second in the Drivers' Championship behind Graham Hill.

Three glorious years followed. In 1963 he became World Champion with a record breaking seven wins from ten starts, and came second in the Indianapolis 500. In 1964 he won three races and came third in the Drivers' Championship, and in 1965 he won his second championship with six wins from nine starts. He also won the Indy 500 that year and earned the respect and admiration of the American motor-sport audience.

The Formula One specification changed from 1.5 litres to 3 litres in 1966. Lotus didn't have the engine to be seriously competitive at first and in that year won only one Grand Prix. But in 1967 they introduced the Cosworth DFV and Clark was again the man to beat. He won at Zandvoort, on the car's debut, and pushed Denny Hulme all the way that year before finishing third in the championship with four wins and forty-one points.

He started 1968 with a victory in the first race at Kyalami, in South Africa. It was Clark's twenty-fifth victory and broke the record of the great Juan Manuel Fangio. It seemed highly likely that 1968 would bring him his third championship.

On 7 April he appeared in a Formula Two race at Hockenheim. It was a relatively unimportant race and Clark was lying in eighth place on the sixth lap. He was under no pressure, but coming out of a gentle right-hand bend at high speed, he slid sideways off the track and into the trees. He was killed instantly. It is thought he must have had a sudden tyre problem causing him to lose control.

The world of motor-racing was stunned. Clark was thirty-two years old and at his peak. Chris Amon spoke for everyone in the sport, 'Beyond the grief, there was also a fear which we all felt. If it could happen to him, what chance did the rest of us have? It seemed we'd lost our leader.'

SEBASTIAN COE

SEBASTIAN NEWBOLD COE
ATHLETICS – MIDDLE-DISTANCE RUNNER
BORN: CHISWICK, 29 SEPTEMBER 1956

Seb had a lot to prove in LA and did so in emphatic fashion.

Facts about Seb Coe

- He is an avid supporter of Chelsea.

- His first race against Steve Ovett was in the intermediate section of the English Schools Championships in 1972. Coe was tenth, Ovett second; the winner was Kirk Dumplington who became a club runner in St Albans.

- He ran his first sub four-minute mile at the age of nineteen in the Emsley Carr Mile on 30 August 1976 while finishing seventh. His mile personal best at the beginning of that season had been 4.07.6. Less than three years later he broke the world mile record with a time of 3.48.95.

• In 1988 Coe and Steve Cram attempted 'The Great Court Run' at Trinity College, Cambridge, made famous in the film *Chariots of Fire*. Coe won and just beat the clock chimes.

The 1500 metres is one of the great Olympic events. Its position in the Olympic programme, on the last day, as the final individual event, emphasises its importance. It has probably produced more thrilling contests than any other Olympic track event. Only one man has ever won it twice.

Sebastian Coe was born in London, but grew up in Sheffield. He started as a sprinter, experimented with 3000 metres and cross-country before finally finding his destiny at middle distance. From the start, the most profound influence on his career was his father, Peter. An engineer by profession, Peter saw athletics as an intellectual challenge as much as a physical one. He taught himself training techniques, biomechanics and physiology from

scratch. He then applied that knowledge to his son.

Coe first came to prominence in 1977. He became European Indoor champion in March over 800 metres, and, just to emphasise his versatility, won the Emsley Carr mile ahead of world 1500 metres record holder, Filbert Bayi, of Tanzania. A new era of British middle-distance running was emerging. Coe's arrival was to challenge another young runner who had already proved himself on the world stage, Steve Ovett.

Their rivalry would dominate British athletics for the next four years. They met in the 800 metres final in the 1978 European Championships in Prague, only for both to finish behind Olaf Beyer of East Germany, Coe in third place. One year further on, and Coe would shatter all opposition. In the space of forty-one days, three world marks fell to him: he took a second off Alberto Juantorena's 800 metres record in Oslo. Two weeks later, in the same Bislett Stadium, he erased John Walker's mark for the mile, and finally he shaved a tenth of a second off Filbert Bayi's 1500 metres time.

1980 was an Olympic year, and, although the Moscow Games were marred by the America-led boycott, the middle-distance races were amongst the events that emerged largely unscathed. Coe against Ovett over both 800 and 1500 metres, with the Sheffield runner favoured for the former and Ovett for the latter were the highlights of the athletics programme. As with all great Olympic stories there were to be many twists in the plot.

The 800 metres came first. Coe had not been beaten over the distance since his failure at the European Championships almost two years previously. He won his heat and semi-final easily, and then lined up against Ovett as a strong favourite. Then he ran the worst race of his life.

Coe was normally a positive front-runner, but this time he dawdled, let others take the initiative, and drifted to the outside lanes. Then, when Ovett kicked for home, with 200 metres to go, Coe was in no position to challenge. While his sprint took him past almost all his rivals, he was still five metres behind when Ovett crossed the line.

Coe had to wait six days for his revenge. He courageously put the massive disappointment behind him, and, after a slow couple of laps,

Seb Coe's Career

Olympic Games:
Gold (2):	1500 metres (1980, 1984)
Silver (2):	800 metres (1980, 1984)

European Championships:
Gold (1):	800 metres (1986)
Silver (2):	800 metres (1982), 1500 metres (1986)
Bronze (1):	800 metres (1978)

World Records:
800 metres	1:42.33	Oslo	3/7/79
	1:41.73	Florence	10/6/81
1000 metres	2:13.40	Oslo	1/7/80
	2:12.18	Oslo	11/7/81
1500 metres	3:32.03	Zurich	15/8/79
Mile	3:48.95	Oslo	17/7/79
	3:48.53	Zurich	19/8/81
	3:47.33	Brussels	28/8/81

Other achievements:
Economics graduate of Loughborough University
Vice-Chairman of Sports Council 1986–89
Awarded MBE in 1982
Awarded OBE in 1990
Member – International Olympic Committee (IOC) Athletes Commission
Member – Health Education Authority

followed the East German, Jurgen Straub, who had broken away at 800 metres. Coe kicked for home, with 80 metres to go, and won with ease. Ovett was never in serious contention. It was an astonishing comeback.

With no major championships the next year, the season was devoted to record breaking. In June, he lowered his own 800 metres mark to 1:41.73. It still stands today. Then, in the space of eight days, he broke the mile record twice, reducing it by over a second and a half.

However, his star then appeared to be on the wane. A silver medal in the European Championships in 1982 was all he had to show for the next two seasons. He was diagnosed as suffering from a blood disorder, and, to some, his time had ended. Coe thought otherwise. His mental determination was one of his greatest assets throughout his career, and he was still only twenty-seven. He was after another Olympic gold.

1984 in Los Angeles had many echoes of Moscow for Coe. Once more there was a boycott, which did not seriously devalue his events; once more he was second best in the 800 metres, this time to Joaquim Cruz of Brazil; and once more he took the 1500 metres, this time with a new Olympic record.

Coe's career was by no means over. In 1986, he finally won a major gold at his favourite distance of 800 metres at the Stuttgart European Championships. That was followed by a 1500 metres silver behind Steve Cram. It was to be his last major triumph, though. He was controversially not selected for the 1988 Olympics after failing in the trials, although his performances at several Grand Prix meetings that summer suggested that he could well have won a medal.

In early 1990, aged thirty-three, he went to the Commonwealth Games in Auckland to try to add another medal to his collection. However, age had finally caught up with him. He finished sixth, and his sporting career was over.

Seb Coe was a remarkable athlete by any standards. Herb Elliott, whom most people would regard as one of the best three or four middle-distance runners of all-time, had no hesitation in saying that Coe was the finest runner he'd ever seen. Steve Ovett described him in his foreword to

The ecstasy after the agony. Coe's dramatic 1500m victory in Moscow after defeat behind Steve Ovett in the 800m.

his great rival's authorised biography as, 'The Renaissance Man'. International Olympic Committee (IOC) President, Juan Antonio Samaranch, committed a rare diplomatic indiscretion by trying to interfere in Britain's decision not to select Coe for the Seoul Olympics in 1988 because he was so concerned that a runner he admired so much would not be able to appear at the Games.

Coe was fiercely determined, and a prodigious trainer. He had a physique designed in heaven for middle-distance running, and a beautiful, flowing, economic style. His performance record is second to none: his two trios of world records in 1979 and 1981 are breathtaking, especially the 1.41.73 for

The advent of the great British trio in Moscow in 1980 with Coe leading Ovett and the young Steve Cram.

'There are a handful of people in this list that I know personally – not just met but know a little. These few I have seen both socially and under pressure in competition. Even in this rarefied company, Seb stands head and shoulders above all but a couple. His marks in all categories are exemplary. If there are any average marks (foolish to call them weaknesses), I would have said that his personality/image wasn't to everyone's taste (but I like him). His dominance over peers wasn't supreme but with rivals like Ovett and Cram around it was never going to be a total dominance. Maybe a title or two more at 800 metres, for which he still holds the world record would have helped. When you look at things like impact, he took the whole of his sport and put it both on the front and back pages. In fact, Seb with the help of Ovett, so captured the imagination and took athletics to such heights, that it enabled a young boy who competed in an event within athletics that no one had ever heard of, to have enough of a career to end up writing this book!'

800 metres set in Florence in June 1981, and his unique 1500 metre Olympic double, a performance made yet more remarkable by the circumstances of adversity which surrounded both triumphs.

Another career opened up for Coe in 1992, when he was elected Conservative MP for Falmouth. Within two years he reached the first rung on the government ladder, as a Parliamentary Private Secretary. Given the vagaries of politics, it may be a long time before he reaches the top rung, but then, all through his sporting career, there was never any doubt that Coe would find success.

DENIS COMPTON

DENIS CHARLES SCOTT COMPTON
CRICKET – BATSMAN, FOOTBALL – FORWARD
BORN: HENDON, 23 MAY 1918

Denis Compton was one of those rare men, someone with the natural ability to succeed in more than one sport. He is, of course, most famous for his outstanding cricketing exploits, yet he was also an excellent footballer who would certainly have represented his country on numerous occasions had injury, war and cricket not intervened. In the immediate post-war years, Compton was colourful, unorthodox, and played both games with a showman's flair. Few sportsmen have made such an impression on the public in any era.

Compton was born in Hendon, north London. In 1936, aged just eighteen, he played his first game for Middlesex, batting at number eleven. He didn't stay in that position long, and within a month had made the first of his 123 first-class centuries. He impressed so much in that first season that some felt he should have been included on the tour of Australia that winter. If he had, though, he may have missed out on the other part of his sporting career.

Compton had joined Arsenal in 1935 from the Hampstead amateur club, the route taken by his elder brother Leslie, and in September 1936, instead of preparing to go 'Down Under' he made his League debut against Derby County. The teenage outside-left made fourteen appearances, and scored four goals that first season, and showed enough to indicate a profitable future in football beckoned.

Facts about Denis Compton

- He was known for his bad time-keeping, and was known to turn up for a game directly from the night outbefore still wearing full evening dress.

- His 100th century came up in 552 innings, the fewest innings of any batsman except Bradman

- Compton was known as the 'Brylcreem Boy', becoming almost synonymous with their hair products.

- Compton was probably the worst judge of a run of any great player His team-mate, John Warr said, 'He was the only player to call his partner for a run, and wish him good luck at the same time.'

Another boundary for Compton in his magnificent series against South Africa in 1947. Not much point setting off for a run when you're sure it's a four!

- John Arlott wrote a poem entitled *On a Great Batsman* suggested by an innings of Compton's:
*As the gull conceals in easeful glide
The inborn gift to curb and ride
The gale, merging the sea wind's force
With lovely movement on a chosen course,
So, in timed swoop, he moves to charm
The ball down-swirling from the bowler's arm
Along some glissade of his own creation,
Beyond the figure's black and white rotation.
Recorded centuries leave no trace,
On memory of that timeless grace.*

- He gave a marvellous performance on the wing in the 1950 FA Cup final, setting up one of the goals as Arsenal beat Liverpool 2-0. It was also his last but one match for Arsenal; he retired from the Winter Game at the end of that season.

- He was awarded the CBE in 1958.

Denis Compton's Career

Cricket

Tests	78
Test runs scored	5807
Average	50.06
Centuries	17
First-class runs	38,942
Average	51.85
Centuries	123
County Championships	1947, 1949 (shared with Yorkshire)

Football

Football league appearances	54
Goals	15
Unofficial and Victory Internationals	14
League Championship	1948
FA Cup	1950

He was to have little time for that in the years leading up to the war as his cricket career took off. In 1937, he made his Test debut against New Zealand. The next year, he played in all four Tests (one was rained off) against Australia, scoring 102 in the Trent Bridge match. That innings, coming nineteen days after his twentieth birthday, still makes him the youngest Englishman to have scored a Test century.

When war clouds descended across Europe, Compton had the cricket world at his feet, a twenty-one-year-old regular in the Test team, playing for Middlesex, who were runners-up in the County Championship for the third year running. But most of his wartime exploits were on the football field. In April 1940, he represented England against Wales at Wembley, the first eleven appearances in wartime internationals, established in a forward line that included Stanley Matthews, Tommy Lawton and Raich Carter. He also played regularly for Arsenal, and in the 1942-43 season

helped them to win the League South and the League South Cup which they won with a 7-1 victory over Charlton in the final. In 1944 though, he was posted to India with the Army, and his football career came to a temporary close.

Oddly enough, the posting enabled him to get back into first-class cricket, turning out for Holkar, then one of the major domestic teams, and he returned to Middlesex and England in 1946 in excellent form. Football now went on the back-burner (although he did appear for England in a Victory International against Scotland) as his batting developed to its full potential. In 1947, he had possibly the best season any batsmen has ever had, scoring no less than 3816 first-class runs, an untouchable record. He was part of a wonderful Middlesex line-up, and his partnerships with Bill Edrich (they were known as the 'Terrible Twins') were always spectacular. He scored eighteen centuries, also a record, including six against the touring South Africans. Middlesex were County Champions, inundating all opponents in a deluge of runs, so many and scored so fast that there was usually enough time for their rather unspectacular bowling attack to seal victory.

However, Compton injured his knee in the last match of that year and was never wholly free of discomfort for the rest of his career, although that did not stop him from making several noteworthy performances for England. Perhaps his finest innings came against the all-powerful 1948 Australians at Old Trafford when he was knocked out and retired hurt early in his innings but came back to score an undefeated 145 against Lindwall at his finest. The next winter, he scored 300 in only three hours in a tour match at Benoni, South Africa, by far the fastest triple-century ever made.

In between times, he still turned out occasionally for Arsenal, playing fourteen times in their championship winning team of 1947-48, and playing for them in the 1950 Cup final, when they beat Liverpool 2-0. However, after that he required an operation to remove a fragment of bone from his knee. It caused him to miss most of the 1950 cricket season and his career in top-class football was over.

He never fully recovered from the injury, but

still gave great value to the cricketing public. It was his sweep shot at the Oval in 1953 that won the Test to give England the Ashes. The next year, he flayed the Pakistan attack to score 278 in less than five hours. His injury grew worse, though, and in November 1955 Compton finally had to have his knee-cap removed. Typically, he returned to the Middlesex team with a century and played in the final Test of 1956 against Australia, scoring a brilliant ninety-four. He failed to do himself justice on the tour to South Africa that winter, though, and retired after the 1957 season.

Compton is best remembered, of course, for his batting. At first glance it appeared to have little to do with the coaching manual, but technically he was very sound. He was, of course, chiefly associated with the sweep. It brought him many runs, even if it is associated with peril, but he could play just about any shot to which he put his mind. Perhaps the cover-drive was his best shot,

brilliantly placed and perfectly executed. In fact, the only thing he didn't seem to be able to do was judge a run. Any non-striker answering his call was taking his life in his hands. He was also a more than competent leg-spinner, with twenty-five Test wickets to his name. His good looks and charm gave him a huge following all round the world. The post-war world was a drab and austere place, and statistics alone do not do justice to the marvellous entertainment he gave so many people in that time.

Dissecting first and second stump, the art of a great batsman.

'Denis Compton is one of those people you know about before you know what they do – their legend goes before them. He was the first sportsman in my memory to do commercials. Compton obviously had plenty of style and was a showman at heart, and was able to do more with a bat and ball than the merely talented could imagine, and if his only weakness was in judging a run, then I'd have him in my team any day. With those gifts just think what he could be doing if he was plying his trade today?'

JOHN CONTEH

JOHN CONTEH
BOXING – LIGHTHEAVYWEIGHT
BORN: LIVERPOOL, 25 MAY 1951

Facts about John Conteh

- Conteh got involved in a failed movie venture with former boxers, Terry Marsh and Jimmy Batten, called 'Tank Malling'. Jason Connery played the villain. Jimmy Batten was philosophical about it: 'If you put Kevin Costner on at the Albert Hall you wouldn't get it half full. Generally, people want to see actors acting and boxers boxing.'

John Conteh was one of boxing's glamour boys. He had the wit and charm of a streetwise scouser and a body men envied and women would die for: six feet and 180 pounds of perfectly proportioned fighting muscle. Sadly, he became one of boxing's many examples of a glittering career which turned, after retirement, into a life of failed business ventures, women problems and alcoholism.

He was an outstanding amateur boxer who won Amateur Boxing Association (ABA) titles at Middleweight and Lightweight before he decided to turn professional in 1971 as a twenty year-old. His arrival on the professional scene led to early predictions of a stunning career. He had a very correct, upright stance, but moved forward with deadly intent. He had lightning-quick hands and his combination punching was a delight to watch. Not that his opponents could see it, nor did they have long to enjoy it. He despatched fifteen of the

first eighteen of them inside the distance. He fought only once a month for the first two years of his career, until his first big fight in March 1973.

It was against Rudi Schmidtke in London for the European Lightheavyweight title. Schmidtke made it to the twelfth round but then Conteh caught him. The career that so many had predicted for him was beginning to open up.

Two months later he had the first of two outstanding fights against the courageous London Irishman, Chris Finnegan. They were classic British contests and Conteh's performances brought the boy from Liverpool a new London fan club. He won both contests and in doing so added the British and Commonwealth titles to his European crown.

The world title beckoned. Bob Foster, the great American Lightheavyweight champion, had announced his retirement at the age of thirty-four in September 1974. Conteh's fight at the Wembley Arena on 1 October, against Argentinian Jorge Ahumada, was recognised as a contest for the world title by the WBC. Ahumada was a tough opponent, typical of his countrymen. He took an excellent punch and would stand his ground and fight.

Ahumada fought bravely, conceding both height and reach to Conteh, but the Liverpudlian was too strong for him and too quick. Conteh won on points and Britain had a new World Champion. The press got to work and 'Big John' was a star. He fell for the lot; hook, line and

John Conteh's Career

Key bouts

1973 (March)	Rudiger Schmidtke	European		Won	technical knock-out	12 rounds
1973 (May)	Chris Finnegan	European, British & Commonwealth		Won	points	15 rounds
1973 (Oct)	'Baby Boy' Rolle	Commonwealth		Won	points	15 rounds
1974 (March)	Tom Bods	European		Won	technical knock-out	6 rounds
1974 (May)	Chris Finnegan	European, British & Commonwealth		Won	technical knock-out	6 rounds
1974 (Oct)	Jorge Ahumada	World		Won	points	15 rounds
1975	Lonnie Bennett	World		Won	technical knock-out	5 rounds
1976	Jaqui Lopez	World		Won	points	15 rounds
1977	Len Hutchins	World		Won	technical knock-out	3 rounds
	(vacated WBC Lightheavyweight World Title)					
1978	Mate Parlov	World		Lost	points	15 rounds
1979	Saad Muhammad	World		Lost	points	15 rounds
1980	Saad Muhammad	World		Lost	technical knock-out	4 rounds

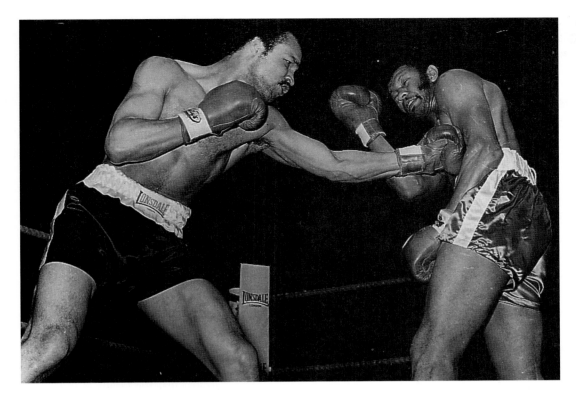

Conteh preparing for his fateful encounter with Mate Parlov, defeating Joe Coke in Islington in 1978 over 10 rounds.

- Conteh wrote the following about his drinking problems: 'Everyone, it seemed, wanted to have a drink with the Champion of the world. But, whether or not the Champion could handle his liquor was his problem, not theirs.'

- His World Lightheavyweight title was the first British victory since Freddie Mills in 1950.

- Although there was much expectation and speculation about what would have been a great fight, Conteh never fought Victor Galindez, the WBA (World Boxing Association) Champion.

- Conteh had an unfortunate confrontation with a total of six cars while driving a Rolls Royce down Oxford Street. During the incident, he damaged his right hand so badly he could never again make a fist with it.

sinker and became the man about town.

He made three successful defences of his world title. The first was against the American, Lonnie Bennett, in London. Conteh stopped him after one minute and ten seconds of the fifth round and was led to his corner with blood pouring from a cut eye. His second defence was a points victory against Alvaro 'Vaqui' Lopez in Copenhagen, and the third was a three-round victory against American, Len Hutchins, in Liverpool.

This was all commendable work, but it wasn't good enough for the WBC. The three defences were spread over a period of two and a half years. Conteh had been having all kinds of problems, the most severe of which were constant injuries to his hands which required surgery and long periods of recuperation. He also became involved in contractual and financial disputes with his management.

The World Boxing Council (WBC) stripped him of his title in 1977, when he refused to defend it against Miguel Angel Cuello of Argentina. Cuello proceeded to win the vacant title by beating Jesse Burnett in Monte Carlo. However, when Cuello in turn lost the title to Mate Parlov of Yugoslavia in 1978, Conteh had the chance to win his title back. The chance came in Belgrade in June.

After a fierce fifteen-round contest, Conteh lost a controversial decision on points and Parlov retained his title.

Parlov didn't keep the title for long and it changed twice more before it fell into the gloves of Matt Franklin of Philadelphia – better known by his adopted name, Matthew Saad Muhammad. His first defence was against Conteh in Atlantic City in August 1979. It was another stunningly exciting fight and turned out to be Conteh's last great bid for the title. Unfortunately, he narrowly lost on points.

However, it was discovered that Muhammad's corner had used an illegal substance to stem the blood from a bad cut on his eye during the fight. A rematch was ordered. The fight took place in March 1980, again in Atlantic City. But Conteh wasn't the fighter he had been, it seemed that the talent had gone in a matter of months. He was put down five times before the fight was stopped in round four.

Conteh fought and won a farewell contest against James Dixon in Liverpool two months later and then retired from the ring.

'John loved being the champion of the world, he lived it to the full. As someone said, 'there's always a price to pay'. I was a teenager when John was champion and he had some great fights, I remember thinking that when they got dirty, John could dish the dirt with the best.'

HENRY COOPER

HENRY COOPER
BOXING – HEAVYWEIGHT
BORN: WESTMINSTER, 3 MAY 1934

Facts about
Henry Cooper

- Henry's identical twin brother, George, was also a boxer who fought professionally as 'Jim'.

- Cooper was a Lance Corporal in the Royal Ordnance Corps # 22698686.

Henry Cooper was brought up near Lewisham in South London. Although not a true cockney, he carried his South London origins around proudly like a badge of honour. After a dignified and courageous career, his natural charm and good humour endeared him to the British public in a quite remarkable way.

When he retired, Reg Gutteridge, the boxing commentator, said that Cooper 'had stolen the affection of the public for a longer spell than any other sportsman. He had indestructable dignity.'

He started his career with an ABA title at light-heavyweight, in 1952, at the age of eighteen. He then fought at the Helsinki Olympics but lost in the first round to the eventual bronze medallist, Anatoly Perov of the Soviet Union. He won a second ABA title in 1953. After his National

Service in the army, he went to trainer Jim Wicks, the 'Bishop', and formed the partnership that would prove to be crucial to his development as a boxer. He turned professional in 1954.

Cooper's first three title fights all ended in defeat in 1957. He lost to Joe Bygraves following a ninth round knock-out for the British Empire title, to Ingemar Johansson after a fifth round knock-out for the European title, and to Joe Erskine on points after fifteen rounds for the British title. Wise observers suggested that the twenty-four-year-old Cooper should call it a day.

But he kept going and in 1958 he came of age. He fought the highly fancied Welsh hope, Dick Richardson, in Porthcawl, and in the fifth round unleashed what would become 'Enery's 'ammer – the best left hook in the business. Cooper then

Henry Cooper's Career

55 Professional fights		Wins 40	Draws 1	
		Defeats 14	Wins inside the distance 29	
Key victories				
1959	Brian London	British and Empire	points	15 rounds
1959	Gawle De Klerk	British and Empire	stopped	5 rounds
1959	Joe Erskine	British and Empire	knock-out	12 rounds
1961	Joe Erskine	British and Empire	retired	5 rounds
1963	Dick Richaroundson	British and Empire	knock-out	5 rounds
1964	Brian London	British, Empire and European	points	15 rounds
1965	Johnny Prescott	British and Empire	retired	10 rounds
1967	Jack Bodell	British and Empire	stopped	2 rounds
1967	Billy Walker	British and Empire	stopped	6 rounds
1968	Karl Mildenberger	European	disqualified	8 rounds
1969	Piero Tomasini	European	knock-out	5 rounds
1970	Jack Bodell	British and Commonwealth	points	15 rounds
1970	Jose Urtain	European	stopped	9 rounds

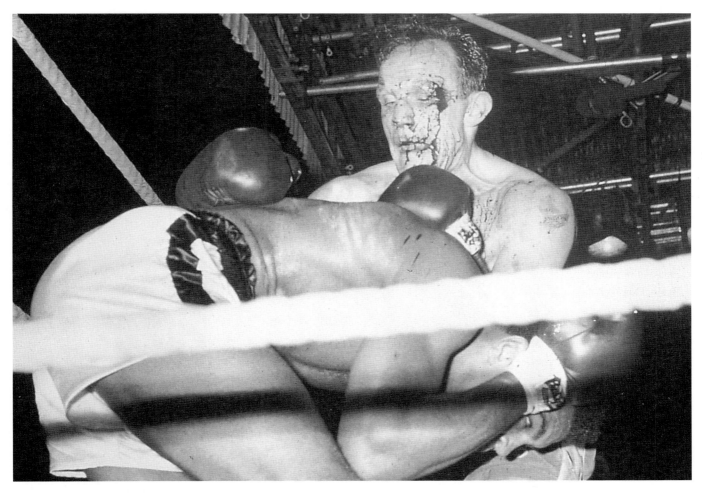

outpointed the American Zora Folley at Wembley, and suddenly he was a contender.

The following year the British and Empire titles were his when he beat Brian London on points over fifteen rounds. His subsequent reign as champion was outstanding and he went on to win three Lonsdale belts.

Cooper's popularity was enhanced by the arrival of television and its ability to bring the drama of the fight into the living-room. There were many famous encounters throughout the 1960s: Dick Richardson, Johnny Prescott, Brian London, Billy Walker and Jack Bodell twice. There were also two European defences in 1968 and 1969 against Karl Mildenberger and Piero Tomasini.

However, beyond all the other epic encounters, it will be for a famous fight and a famous moment that Henry Cooper will always be remembered. It was in 1963, at Wembley Stadium, the opponent a young, brash American called Cassius Clay. Clay's main claims to fame at that time were an Olympic title from Rome, three years earlier, and the ability to talk a good fight like no one had ever heard before. What no one realised at the time, except perhaps Angelo Dundee his trainer, was that Cooper was to face a man who could not only talk a good fight but would leave his mark on sport, let alone boxing, like nobody else.

Clay boasted that Cooper would fall in five, but in the fourth round Cooper caught him with his famous left hook and Clay went down. There were only four seconds left of the round and Clay staggered to the corner. There was little doubt that Clay would struggle to survive the next round, but in one of boxing's most talked about incidents, Angelo Dundee, in Clay's corner, embellished a slit in his glove with a razor-blade to buy the young American time to recover. The ploy worked and Clay recovered sufficiently to pummel Cooper's already cut left eye to win in the next round as the fight was stopped.

Clay's prediction came to pass. However, one of

Henry's date with destiny against Cassius Clay in 1966. His eyes were always his Achilles heel - and a graphic illustration of the rigours of sport's hardest game.

Handsome Henry in his prime.

- He had lots of home-made remedies sent to him for his cut-eyes dilemma. 'People meant well' he said. 'They would send me pickled onions, vinegar and herbs – shame it didn't work.'

- Cooper got the OBE in 1969 and was voted 'Boxer of the Year' by the Italian press after he defeated their champion, Piero Tomasini, in March of that year

- He was twice voted BBC Sports Personality of the year, in 1967 and 1970.

- The BBC also made him a resident captain of its long-running TV series, *A Question of Sport*.

- He played John Gully, a former bare-knuckle pugilist, in the film, *Royal Flash* and had to fight Oliver Reed.

- He also released a record, 'Knock Me Down With a Feather', and did the famous 'Splash it all ova' Brut commercial. He said, 'They chose me because no one can call me a poof.'

the great 'ifs' of British sport was left hanging that night – what if the bell hadn't intervened and Angelo Dundee hadn't used his subterfuge to protect his young fighter?

Muhammed Ali, as Clay later became known, developed a great respect for Cooper, and showed it when they met again, in 1966, at Highbury Stadium. This time Ali put his world title on the line. The fight lasted six rounds but, sadly for Cooper, a cut was again his undoing.

Cooper continued fighting until 1971 when he lost what he, and many other people, thought was a monstrous decision against Joe Bugner on points. He was thirty-seven and decided to retire. He had only just won back all his titles after injury forced him to give up one, his European crown, and a

dispute with the British Boxing Board of Control over their refusal to sanction a world title fight against American Jimmy Ellis, led him to relinquish the other two, his British and Commonwealth titles. He felt he had been badly treated twice and said, 'That's me lot!'

'Our 'Enery' was immediately taken to the bosom of the British people and became a national institution. He has remained there ever since.

'Henry has made his way on to this list more for the way the public has taken him to their hearts than for achievement. His honours are mostly domestic and European but the affection of his public is world class.'

HENRY COTTON

THOMAS HENRY COTTON
GOLFER
BORN: HOLMES CHAPEL, 26 JANUARY 1907
DIED: LONDON, 22 DECEMBER 1987

Henry Cotton was born into a well-off family. He went to public school and may well have chosen the traditional path of talented young men from his background – amateur golf, university and a well-paid job in commerce or the law. However, he chose to leave school early and devote himself to a full-time golf career. This meant adopting a professional mantle, not quite the 'done thing' at the time, and associating more with the tradesmen of the game than its gentlemen. In doing so, Cotton, with his prodigious talent, probably did more for the contemporary professional golfer than any other player.

He was outspoken and ruffled many feathers, especially the fine feathers of the game's establishment. He admitted he was controversial. 'I was a rebel, but not much of one really,' he once said.

Cotton became a professional in 1924, first as assistant at Fulwell and then, at the age of nineteen, as the senior pro at Langley Park, Beckenham, in 1926. Within three years he was selected for the winning Ryder Cup team against the Americans, in 1929. He played in six Ryder Cups in all between 1929 and 1947; in 1947 as captain. He was also non-playing captain in 1953.

His first tournament win was about as far from home as possible, at Mar del Plata, in Argentina. It soon became a country close to his heart, especially after he subsequently met 'Toots' there, his future wife.

It wasn't long before he won his first tournament in Europe, the Belgian Open, in 1930, a success he was to repeat in 1934 and

The elegant rebel. Henry Cotton in 1927 at St Andrews.

Facts about Henry Cotton

- He was one of the first professionals, with Bobby Locke and Walter Hagen, to be elected as honorary member of the Royal and Ancient.

- Henry Cotton had a bet with Fred Perry that he would win the Open before Perry won Wimbledon. Cotton won the bet, in 1934, by six weeks.

- His sixty-five in the Open, at Sandwich, gave birth to the famous 'Dunlop 65' golf ball.

- His victory at Muirfield, in 1948, was watched by King George VI – the first time a reigning monarch had been to the Open.

- He was a founder of the 'Golf Foundation', formed to encourage youngsters to take up the game.

- He instituted the 'Henry Cotton Rookie of the Year Award', in 1960, for the most promising young professional.

- He was awarded the MBE, in 1946, for his fund-raising for the Red Cross.

Henry Cotton's Career

British Open Champion	1934, 1937, 1948
British Professional Matchplay Champion	1932, 1940, 1946
Six Ryder Cup matches (Captain in 1947)	1929–47
Ryder Cup non-playing Captain	1953
Belgian Open	1930, 1934, 1938
Italian Open	1936
German Open	1937, 1938, 1939
French Open	1946, 1947

1938. From his early days he was committed to developing golf as a world game. He travelled extensively, partly to guarantee his income and partly to spread the gospel of golf; a message he preached to the Europeans in particular. He became a professional at Waterloo, in Belgium, and had by the end of his career done as much as anyone to lay the foundations for the modern European game. In fact, in the early part of his career Cotton got far more praise and even hero-worship in continental Europe than he did in Britain, largely because professionalism didn't carry the same stigma there that it did in the clubhouses at home.

His first British Open triumph was in 1934, at Sandwich. His first two rounds were magnificent: a sixty-seven followed by a sixty-five. His midway 132 was twelve under-par, and the second-round sixty-five stood as a record for over forty years. An even-par third round was followed by a nervy and tense seventy-nine, but he still won by five strokes on 283 from South African, Sid Brews. Significantly, Cotton's victory ended ten years of American domination at the Open.

A second Open Championship followed at Carnoustie, in 1937. His rounds of seventy-four, seventy-two, seventy-three and seventy-one were not spectacular, but it may well have been a victory more indicative of his true talent than the Sandwich performance because the field included the entire US Ryder Cup team. He won by two from fellow Ryder Cup player, Reg Whitcombe.

Crucially, for his status in the history of the game, the Second World War then intervened. He was thirty-two at the outbreak of war, twice Open Champion and at his peak. It is not difficult to imagine that he would have won at least two more Opens had the demands of wartime not changed everything. He became an officer in the RAF and gave up senior golf for six years.

His third and final Open victory came in 1948, at Muirfield. His first two rounds were reminiscent of 1934: a seventy-one and a sixty-six. Then followed a poor seventy-five and a seventy-two, but it was still enough to give him a five-stroke victory over defending Irish champion, Fred Daly.

Henry Cotton made only sporadic trips to the United States and won only one PGA event. Just as it is difficult to speculate about his potential for more Open championships, it is difficult to know what he could have achieved in the American game had he been able to travel there as often as modern players can, and had it not been for the intrusion of war.

Cotton carried on playing into his forties but began to devote more and more time to teaching and course design and later moved into commentating and tournament organisation. He even had an Open 'swansong' in 1956, in his fiftieth year, when he came sixth at Hoylake.

He learned that he was to be knighted in the 1988 New Year's Honours list just before his death in December 1987.

'Henry Cotton was a pioneer in the game of golf. One of the few ever to turn from gentleman to player at a time when most sports still had 50 or so years to go before they would be open to everyone, regardless of background. His professional attitude did nothing to endear him to golfs' rulers, a common problem faced by many of the people in our list.'

COLIN COWDREY

SIR MICHAEL COLIN COWDREY
CRICKET – BATSMAN
BORN: PUTUMALA, INDIA, 24 DECEMBER 1932

Proud, upright and quintessentially the English batsman.

It is one of cricket's most famous stories that Colin Cowdrey's father christened him Michael Colin in order to bestow the initials 'MCC' (Marylebone Cricket Club) on his son. The son exceeded his father's wildest dreams, captaining his country, becoming England's top Test run scorer, going on to chair cricket's premier body the ICC (International Cricket Conference), and, in his turn, having a son who would lead England.

Steeped in cricket from his early years in India, Cowdrey was sent to school in England, and represented Tonbridge at the age of thirteen. From then, it was an imperious progression. He represented his school at Lord's that first season, scoring seventy-five against Clifton, and also distinguished himself as a left-arm spinner. He remains the youngest player ever to appear in a

- His highest score was 307, for the MCC against South Australia on the 1962–63 tour.

- He so infuriated Garry Sobers with his go-slow tactics in the Trinidad Test of 1968, that the West Indian captain declared, setting England a meagre run chase, just to see if Cowdrey would accept. He did, and England won.

- Cowdrey toured Australia six times with England, between 1954–55 and 1974–75, and never once captained his team in a Test there. He served under six different captains (Hutton, May, Dexter, Smith, Illingworth and Denness).

- He was in no doubt as to his favourite shot, and why. He once said, 'The cover drive is the most beautiful stroke in batsmanship. Does that throw any light on why I am a self-admitted lover of all things British and traditional?'

school match at Lord's. He scored a century for the Public Schools against a powerful Combined Services, and after spending three years as an Oxford Blue he was selected for the 1954–55 tour of Australia aged only twenty-two.

He made his debut in the First Test, and England lost by an innings and 154 runs, though Cowdrey's batting (he made forty in the first innings) was creditable. He scored his first century in the third Test, and England went on to win the series, the first they had won in Australia for two decades. He was clearly a major force and over the next twenty years he developed into a permanent fixture in the England team. Among his many great performances was his share of the 411-run partnership with Peter May that helped England save the match against the West Indies in 1957 and, in doing so, finally dispel the threat of the West Indian spinners. In 1960, he hit 155 against South Africa at The Oval in a superb exhibition of attacking batting to save the Test. Perhaps though, his most remarkable appearance at the wicket was an occasion when he didn't even face a ball. His wrist broken by a ball from Wes Hall, he appeared at the crease as a non-striker as England saved the Lord's Test against the West Indies in 1963. He became the first player to play in a century of Tests (114 in all), and scored twenty-two centuries, equalling Hammond's record.

Injury meant that he did not captain England as often as he might have. Among his triumphs was in England's last series win in the West Indies in 1967–68. He played his last Test at home against Pakistan in 1971. However, when England needed a dependable replacement on the tour of Australia in 1974–75, they sent once more for Cowdrey. This time though, the pace attack of Lillee and Thomson finally proved too much for a man in his forties.

He was sometimes not the most spectacular of batsmen, and did show a marked tendency to drift into uncertainty against the best bowling. It may have been that he could simply not believe how much better he was than those around him, as his technique was impeccable, he was equally as good on the front and back foot, and, as well as being a masterful driver, he was superb when the ball was pitched to leg. However, his use to the team was

Colin Cowdrey's Career

Test match runs	7624
Average	44.06
Tests	114
Centuries	22
First-class runs	42,719
Average	42.89
Centuries	107
County Championship	1970
Gillette Cup	1967, 1974
Benson & Hedges Cup	1973, 1976
Sunday League	1972, 1973, 1976

not solely confined to his batting. Although he abandoned his youthful flirtation with leg spin, he was also an excellent slip fielder, and his record of 120 catches has only been equalled by Ian Botham.

At domestic level, he played for Kent for twenty-seven years, and captained them between 1954 and 1971. Never a powerful county, he helped to transform them and in 1970 they won their first County Championship since 1913. They also became a powerful one-day side, winning the Gillette Cup in 1967, and, after Cowdrey had passed on the baton of captaincy, winning the Gillette Cup once more, the Benson & Hedges Cup in 1973, and the Sunday League three times.

After retiring from playing, Cowdrey became a noted administrator, and he was awarded a CBE and then a knighthood in 1992. He also saw his son Christopher captain England, although perhaps not under the happiest of circumstances, against the West Indies in 1988. Perhaps his finest accolade was his appointment as MCC President in its bicentennial season. His father would have been proud.

'Colin exemplified the Bulldog British Spirit of his day and who knows what his figures might have been if his confidence had been as good as his technique?'

STEVE CRAM

STEVE CRAM
ATHLETICS – MIDDLE-DISTANCE RUNNER
BORN: GATESHEAD, 14 OCTOBER 1960

Steve Cram joined Jarrow and Hebburn Athletics Club at the age of twelve where he came under the influence of Jimmy Hedley who was to become his coach. Cram went on to make the most dynamic duo in British middle-distance running into a phenomenal trio. To have two athletes like Coe and Ovett to enjoy could be regarded as exceptionally fortunate, to have three can only be described as miraculous.

Cram's promise was obvious as early as 1975 when he came third in the English Schools Junior Cross Country and fourth in the 1500 metres. He set a 1500 metres UK age best for a sixteen year-old in 1977, and a world age best for a seventeen year-old in the Emsley Carr mile in 1978, when finishing fourth.

In 1979 Cram ran in the 3000 metres in the European Junior Championships in Bydoszcz, in Poland, and came home with the gold medal. He was starting to be noticed and was soon rewarded with the third place in the British trio for the 1500 metres at the Moscow Olympics in 1980. The first two places were, of course, for Coe and Ovett who were already established at the forefront of world athletics.

Cram made it to the final but finished eighth, as Seb Coe reversed his earlier defeat at the hands of Ovett in the 800 metres to take gold.

Cram was finally able to step forward as an equal with his two great rivals in 1982 when he won the 1500 metres at both the European Championships and the Commonwealth Games. He later said that the European victory was the most stressful of his career. 'For the first time in my life I was favourite in a major championships and I

felt the pressure a lot. I knew I should win but I still had to go out there and do it. Getting out in front with so far to go and then starting to tire – I really had to hold it together.'

The only caveat about 1982's successes were that they had been achieved without opposition from Coe and Ovett. The former had been ill, the latter injured.

The caveat was largely withdrawn in 1983 when Cram met Ovett head-to-head in the inaugural World Championships in Helsinki (though, Coe was again absent through illness). Ovett ran an unusually inept race and finished fourth, and Cram added a world title to his rapidly growing

The pressure of top-level competition. Cram in 1993 at the World Championships in Stuttgart.

Facts about Steve Cram
- He is a big football fan and keen player. His passion is Sunderland.

Steve Cram's Career

Commonwealth Games
Gold	1500 metres	1982
Gold	1500 metres	1986
Gold	800 metres	1986

European Championships
Gold	1500 metres	1982
Bronze	800 metres	1986
Gold	1500 metres	1986

World Championships
Gold	1500 metres	1983

Olympic Games
Silver	1500 metres	1984

World records
16/7/1985	Nice 1500 metres	3:29.67
27/7/1985	Oslo 1 mile	3:46.32
4/8/1985	Budapest 2000 metres	4:51.39

Also ran on the rarely attempted 4 x 800 metres world record relay team with Peter Elliott, Gary Cook and Seb Coe in 1982 at Crystal Palace in a time of 7:03.89

- His uncle, Bobby Cram, played 150 games for West Bromwich Albion and later for Colchester.

- In his teens he seriously considered taking German nationalility because of the strength of middle-distance opposition. His mother Maria was German and had met Steve's father, Bill, while he served at RAF Gutesloh in Germany.

- He was awarded the MBE in 1986.

collection. If final proof of Cram's stature were needed, it was provided by the International Athletics Council (IAC) event at Crystal Palace, in September of that season. Ovett had refound his form and reclaimed his 1500 metres world record, in Italy. A few days before the race Ovett threw down the challenge by entering the mile. Convention among track stars at the time suggested that Cram would avoid the confrontation and switch to another race, but Cram picked up the gauntlet. 'If I'm going to believe I'm the best in the world, which I'm supposed to be as world champion, then I shouldn't be frightened of anybody. And if I'm frightened of Steve Ovett then I don't believe I can beat him.'

It was a great race. Cram kicked for home with nearly a lap to go. Ovett chased him all the way, right on his heels. But Cram wouldn't yield and won by a metre.

Cram still needed the Olympic gold medal to complete his set. He also had to have his head-to-head victory against Coe. 1984 and the Los

Angeles Olympics should have been perfect, he was reaching his peak; Coe and Ovett – although not necessarily past their best – were both having problems. Perversely, it was Cram whose preparations for Los Angeles were troubled by a persistent calf injury. He recovered in time, but in a dramatic 1500 metres final, which saw Ovett drop out with severe breathing problems, a not entirely fit Cram had to be content with a silver medal as Seb Coe completed a unique 1500 metres Olympic double.

Infuriatingly for Cram's Olympic ambitions, 1985 was his greatest year. It was a year for world records. He set his first at 3:29.67 for 1500 metres in Nice, on 16 July, and simultaneously claimed the scalp of Morocco's Said Aouita. He then got the one he really wanted by beating Coe eleven days later in Oslo and taking his world mile record with a time of 3:46.32. Finally, he beat John Walker's 2000 metres world record in Budapest eight days later, by one-hundredth of a second at 4:51.39.

1986 brought more titles as he went for a double double – the 800 metres and 1500 metres in both the European championships and the Commonwealth Games. He managed three, only failing in the 800 metres in the Europeans, in Stuttgart, when he came third after Coe and Tom McKean.

Unfortunately, Cram's outstanding career became increasingly dogged by injury and disappointment from 1987 onwards and the remaining accolade he sought so much, an Olympic Gold medal, finally eluded him.

'Crammie and I have been friends since the end of the1970s and he along with Coe and Ovett were the corner stone on which the base of athletics' golden years was laid. Genes, environment and good luck gave us the three of the best middle-distance runners the world had ever seen at the same time. Steve's only misfortune was that he was never at his best at the Olympics. But in terms of world records, quality of opposition and titles he has top marks. Unlike a lot of the top performers, he had a high work ethic, but also found the time to enjoy himself.'

JOHN CURRY

JOHN ANTHONY CURRY
ICE SKATER
BORN: BIRMINGHAM, 9 SEPTEMBER 1949
DIED: STRATFORD-ON-AVON, 15 APRIL 1994

John Curry always wanted to be a ballet dancer. Those who saw him skate may consider he fulfilled that ambition, because no one combined the athleticism and grace needed as well as he.

His father refused to entertain that possibility so Curry turned instead to skating. He started at the age of twelve at the Summerhill Road rink in Birmingham, but moved to London in 1965 after the death of his father. Here he was able to train with Arnold Gerschwiler, the coach at the Richmond rink. He was a strict disciplinarian, and although Curry's skating improved he found his relationship with Gerschwiler a difficult one. Curry could at least begin ballet classes, and he was able to use these to bolster his skating.

Curry became British junior champion in 1967, and won the senior title three years later. However, he was a long way from the finished article. While his routines were marvelously graceful, he had a real problem with jumps, so much so that when his routine at the 1971 World Championships in Lyon went disastrously wrong he left the ice by a side entrance rather than face Gerschwiler. However, his performances did improve steadily, and at the 1972 Winter Olympics in Sapporo he finished in eleventh position. In 1974, he won a bronze medal in the European Championships but after a disastrous performance in the Worlds he was ready to walk away from skating altogether.

However, at those championships in Munich he met Ed Mosler, an American millionaire. He had sponsored many athletes, including most of the US team. Now he wanted to take Curry to America. Mosler's sponsorship gave Curry freedom from financial worries, access to superb facilities in Denver, Colorado, and excellent coaching. Curry

met Gus Lussi, who worked on his jumping. Lussi insisted that Curry was spinning on the wrong foot, and made him learn to spin all over again, starting with the basics. It worked, because spinning in the same direction in which he jumped enabled Curry to improve the speed of his airborne revolutions. Then he worked on his routine with Carlo Fassi and, in 1976, soared right to the top.

He competed in the European Championships in Geneva with his free programme, to the music of Minkus's Don Quixote. However, Fassi had advised him to withdraw from the tournament, as five of the nine judges came from the Communist bloc and Fassi was not blind to the importance of politics in sport. He did not believe the Briton could beat the Russian Vladimir Kovalev. But the Czech judge voted against the other Eastern European judges, and Curry had the gold.

There was no such doubt about the Olympics. He was far ahead of the other competitors in Innsbruck, and even though the Russian and Canadian judges voted for their own skaters, he was an easy winner. After a ten-day lay-off, he went for the Grand Slam at the World Championship at Gothenburg. Despite a relatively poor showing in the compulsory figures and a mistake in the short

John Curry's Career

Olympic Games

1972 (Sapporo)	11th
1976 (Innsbruck)	1st

World Championships

1975 (Colorado Springs)	3rd
1976 (Helsinki)	1st

European Championships

1974 (Zagreb)	3rd
1975 (Copenhagen)	2nd
1976 (Geneva)	1st

Also won the British Championships in 1970, 1972-75

Poetry in motion in embryo. A young John Curry in 1971 at the European Championships in Zurich.

Facts about John Curry

- Curry had an unusually low double lutz technique (normally to complete the jump requires a lot of height), which he attributed to having to watch for other skaters at Richmond Ice Rink.

- Curry took a course of positive thinking in autumn 1975, which he considered helped him become the champion of 1976.

- He became an actor, frequently appearing in the provinces, but never in the West End or on Broadway.

- He was awarded the OBE in 1976.

- In early 1976, Curry very nearly lost the British championship to Robin Cousins, who replaced him as Olympic champion in Lake Placid four years later.

programme, his magnificent free routine gave him a third gold medal.

He turned professional at the end of the season, and was able to negotiate a huge contract. He also brought a huge ice show to London in an effort to capitalise on the popularity he had brought to his sport. Sadly, he was diagnosed HIV positive in 1987, his later years were marred by illness, and he died in 1994.

Curry helped to turn ice skating into a mainstream sport, one that is now followed with interest by the British public. He was also one of the most graceful skaters his sport has ever produced, using his ballet training to great effect. Curry's programmes had jumps, spreadeagles and spins co-ordinated perfectly to the music. He was a great champion.

'John was a ballet dancer on ice. He thrilled the nation back in 1976, and took his sport into homes with no interest in skating whatsoever. I remember thinking that it wasn't really me – but that I'd watch it anyway (but I never told my mates).'

KENNY DALGLISH

KENNETH MATHIESON DALGLISH
FOOTBALL – FORWARD
BORN: GLASGOW, 4 MARCH 1951

Kenny Dalglish has many claims to fame. He was a forward of rare quality, of whom it has been said, that, with his back to goal, there's never been a better player, anywhere in the world, at any time. He also had the ability to drift away from close markers, as if he could make himself transparent, to create space for himself. He could turn defenders at will, and his close control was as good as anybody's in the modern British game. He had that rare gift, given only to a few people in any

In full-flight for Scotland against the East Germans.

**Facts about
Kenny Dalglish**

- 'Dalglish's life-long friend who began his career with Celtic at the same time as Dalglish was the great Scottish full-back, Danny McGraen.

- To Bill Shankly's subsequent horror, because he didn't know about it at the time, Dalglish had been to Liverpool for a trial before Celtic signed him in 1968. He wasn't picked out and nobody bothered to contact him after he returned to Glasgow.

- He was awarded the MBE in 1985.

- His transfer fee, when he signed for Liverpool from Celtic was £440,000, a British record.

- Dalglish is notoriously difficult to interview or to get close to. This is one journalist's view from the Mail on Sunday:

- Ten Modern Labours of Hercules:
  1. Make Kenny Dalglish laugh uncontrollably.

- Bob Paisley on Dalglish: 'Kevin [Keegan] was quicker off the mark, but Kenny runs the first five yards in his head.'

Kenny Dalglish's Career

For Celtic

League Championship:	1972, 1973, 1974, 1976, 1977
Scottish Cup:	1972, 1974, 1975, 1977
Scottish League Cup:	1975
Appearances	313
Goals	167

For Liverpool as a player

League Championships:	1979, 1980, 1982, 1983, 1984
League Cup:	1981, 1982, 1983, 1984
European Cup:	1978, 1981, 1984
European Super-Cup:	1978

For Liverpool as a player-manager (achievements as a manager only not included)

League Championship:	1986, 1988
FA Cup:	1986
Appearances	482
Goals	168

For Scotland

Appearances	102 (National record)
Goals	30 (National record, jointly with Denis Law)

Thirteen appearances as a schoolboy, youth and U.23 international

sport, of appearing to operate according to his own rules of time and space. He always seemed to have time, he always seemed to be able to make space.

Astonishingly, it is not any of these qualities that represents Dalglish's main claim to fame in British sport, despite their impressive collective weight. It is rather a simple matter of statistics. Kenny Dalglish has accumulated a mountain of honours in British football that is unlikely ever to be equalled. He has a record of achievement at Club, European and International level that is incomparable. Even a simple summary is awesome: 102 international caps, thirty international goals; twelve League titles, five Cup-Winners medals, five League Cup-Winners medals; three European Cup-Winners medals, one European Super-Cup-Winners medal; 795 Club appearances, 335 goals. He is a legend on both sides of Hadrian's wall and is revered throughout British football, especially in Glasgow and Liverpool.

Dalglish was brought up the Glaswegian protestant way: Sunday School, Boys Brigade and Ibrox on Saturdays to watch Rangers. He started to play for Possil YMCA, a well-known breeding ground for soccer talent. He played for Glasgow Schools in 1966 when they won the Scottish Schools Cup and was soon playing for Scotland Schoolboys. He scored twice on his debut against Northern Ireland in Belfast, in May 1966, while still only fifteen.

For reasons known only within the walls of Ibrox, Dalglish was overlooked by Rangers and was signed instead by Celtic, in 1968. He couldn't have joined a finer nursery, the bulk of the 'Lisbon Lions', Celtic's European Cup winning team from 1965, were still there – McNeill, Auld, Lennox, Johnstone, Gemmell and Murdoch. Dalglish quickly became a part of a local Glasgow legend, the Celtic Reserve team. They were so good, they were nicknamed the 'Quality Street Gang' and included Danny McGrain, Lou Macari, Paul Wilson, George Connelly and David Hay.

He became a first team player in 1971 while still only twenty. Then followed six seasons of Celtic magic at Parkhead; little wonder the fans called it 'paradise' – five Championships, four Scottish Cups, a League Cup and 167 goals. It was a fine period for Celtic and one during which Dalglish established himself as one of Scotland's all-time greats.

It was inevitable that he would 'go south'. Shankly had wanted him at Liverpool and Bob Paisley, his successor, maintained the interest. What's more, Dalglish wanted to move, he yearned for a bigger challenge. He went to Anfield to fill the huge boots of Kevin Keegan. He did it with ease and established a record at Liverpool even more impressive than the one at Parkhead. He made his debut at Wembley in the Charity Shield in August and scored within seven minutes on his league debut.

After two years in English football, he had scored fifty-five goals in only 111 games and was voted Footballer of the Year.

By the end of the 1983 season, Dalglish was winning trophies several times over. He had won the European Cup, in 1978, at Wembley against Brugge (when he scored the winning goal) and a second one, in 1981, in Paris against Real Madrid, and he had won four league titles in 1979, 1980, 1982 and 1983. These marvellous achievements were doubly recognised in 1983 when he was voted Footballer of the Year for a second time, and the Professional Footballers Association Player of the Year.

Dalglish had become the central character in a wonderful era at Liverpool Football Club. He was surrounded by other great players like Hansen, Souness and Rush, and in 1984 he won his third European Cup-Winners medal, as Liverpool won their fourth, in the Stadio Olimpico in Rome against Roma.

But Liverpool's success story went tragically wrong in 1985. The awful loss of life in the Heysel Stadium in Brussels before the start of that season's European Cup Final, between Liverpool and Juventus, was a sad turning point in the history of English football. Dalglish impressed everyone with the dignified way in which he handled the sad circumstances of Heysel, and when Joe Fagan

departed as manager of Liverpool, Kenny Dalglish began his second career at Liverpool, as player-manager. But it would be as mentor of a team without the challenge of Europe. Liverpool supporters were blamed for the crush which led to the deaths of thirty-nine Juventus fans at Heysel and English teams were banned from Europe as a consequence of the tragedy.

Dalglish continued his rich vein of success and coached Liverpool to yet more triumphs from his usual position on the field of play for several years before eventually he permanently confined himself to the manager's bench. The success went on and he was voted Manager of the Year in 1986 and 1988 (while still playing) and again in 1990. 1990 was a very special year as Liverpool won the League and Cup double, only the third team to achieve the feat this century.

But in 1991 he shocked the world of football by resigning as manager at the height of his success. He said that the stress and the expectations had become too great and that, for the first time in his life, he was putting himself first, rather than Liverpool Football Club. He took a long break, got his sanity back and was relaxed and happy. Then the telephone rang. It was Jack Walker, the multi-millionaire owner of Blackburn Rovers. Dalglish had resigned in February of 1991, and Walker, shrewdly, had given Dalglish a few months to get itchy about football. Walker's hunch was right and Dalglish became manager of Blackburn on 12 October 1991.

In four years, Dalglish took Blackburn from a moderate Endsleigh League team to the Premiership title, before moving behind the scenes at the Club and relinquishing first team management to his assistant, Ray Harford, in 1995.

Dalglish was forty-four and stepped into the background with only one question remaining: What will be the great Scot's next challenge?

'Kenny had the talent to make up his own rules as to how the game should be played. He has won and done it all in football. He was a great player who could make others around him play better. A quiet (most of the time) man who led by example.'

- Alan Hansen on Dalglish: 'I used to think all that stuff about him running the first five yards in his head was rubbish until I'd played with him for a while.'

- John Smith on Dalglish: 'The best player this Club has signed this century.'

- Tommie Smith on Dalglish: 'Dalglish was the best player I ever lined up with. He was a complete one-off, a football genius.'

- Bob Paisley (again) on Dalglish: 'Of all the players I have played alongside, managed and coached in more than forty years at Anfield, he is the most talented. When Kenny shines, the whole team shines.'

- 1986 must have been a very special year for Dalglish. It was his first full year of management. Liverpool won the double and he was named Manager of the Year. But he was still playing. He made seventeen appearances for his Club and scored three goals (including the vital winner in the final game of the season at Chelsea), and he won his 100th cap for Scotland.

LAURA DAVIES

**LAURA DAVIES
GOLFER
BORN: COVENTRY, 10 MAY 1963**

Facts about Laura Davies

- She was awarded the MBE in 1988.

- She is entirely self-taught, has never had a lesson and doesn't employ a coach.

- Her fluent style and what she considers her instinctive 'feel' for the game came from watching her role models, Ballesteros and Langer, and copying what they do.

- Davies started playing golf because her brother Tony did. She was fourteen. She also played football and cricket.

- Her headmaster's advice was not prophetic. He advised against golf, saying she would never make any money out of it.

- She declined an American Collegiate scholarship, preferring the comforts of home instead.

- She had to borrow £1000

Laura Davies' best years may yet lie ahead of her. She is still only in her early thirties and in the kind of form that could dominate women's golf for several years. To date she has already achieved enough to be regarded as Britain's finest woman player. She has accumulated over a million and a half dollars in career earnings and was ranked as world number one for 1994.

Davies is renowned as a big-hitter and has been known to propel the ball over 350 yards. Her drives lead to gasps of admiration from around the tee wherever she plays, but she regards her short-game as her best asset. Her stature and strength give her an in-built power advantage over most of her colleagues but, as any golfer knows, distance comes from good technique, not brute strength. None the less, at five feet ten inches tall, with a shock of blonde hair and striking blue eyes atop a considerable frame, she is an imposing sight for her opponents.

She had a very successful amateur career. She won the 1983 English Intermediate Championship and the South Eastern Championship, and in the following year repeated the South Eastern Championship victory and won the Welsh Open

Laura Davies' Career

WPGET victories	22
LPGA victories	8
Winning team:	
Solheim Cup	1992
Majors:	
US Women's Open	1987
LPGA Championship	1994

Stroke Play Championship. She was also a member of the Great Britain and Ireland Curtis Cup Team in 1984.

After turning professional she quickly came to prominence in Europe by leading the WPGET Order of Merit in 1985 and 1986. Then, in 1987, she took America by storm. She won the US Women's Open when not even a member of the LPGA Tour. It was a little like winning the local club championship without being a member of the club – and a foreigner to boot! The shock caused the organisation to amend its constitution in order to give her an exemption from the qualification procedure necessary to join the Tour.

Strangely, therefore, the Open champion played her rookie year in 1988, and won twice, in the Circle K LPGA Tucson Open and in the Jamie Farr Toledo Classic. She also won the Lady Keystone Open, in 1989, by birdying the last three holes.

The early 1990s presented a few problems and she didn't play her best golf. Her LPGA ranking went to sixty-fourth in 1990, improved to twentieth in 1991 but went down to thirty-ninth in 1992. But there were a few highlights: in 1991 she won her fourth title on the LPGA Tour and scored the lowest round of her career, a sixty-two in the first round of the Rail Charity Golf Classic; in 1992, she was a member of the victorious European team in the Solheim Cup, against the Americans.

Things took a considerable turn for the better from 1993 onwards. The McDonalds' Championship came in that year and then in 1994 all hell broke loose. She was victorious on all five continents, a feat never achieved by anyone before, man or woman, by winning three times in the

The most powerful shot in the women's game.

USA, twice in Europe and once in Thailand, Japan and Australia. What's more, one of the US victories was the McDonalds' LPGA Championship, one of women's golf's four major championships. It was a truly great year. She had twelve top-ten finishes, scored twenty-eight rounds in the sixties and had a scoring average of 70.91.

'Laura suffers a bit in this list because she is only just starting the summer of her career. In terms of achievement and dominance she is going to be a little short because of her lack of years. But any female who can make that most chauvinist of clubs, the male fraternity of golf, sit up and take note must be doing something right.'

from her parents to turn pro. She had won £4000 by the time of her second tournament.

- Her view of professional golf: 'Playing golf for a living isn't a real job, it's a privilege.'

81

LYNN DAVIES

LYNN DAVIES
ATHLETICS – LONG JUMPER
BORN: NANT-Y-MOEL, 20 MAY 1942

Lynn Davies's Career

Olympic Games

1964 (Tokyo)	1st	
1968 (Mexico City)	9th	
1972 (Munich)	did not qualify	

European Championships

1962 (Belgrade)	11th
1966 (Budapest)	1st
1969 (Athens)	2nd
1971 (Helsinki)	4th

Commonwealth Games

1962 (Perth)	4th
1966 (Kingston)	1st
1970 (Edinburgh)	1st

Facts about Lynn Davies

- He was on the books of Cardiff City as an amateur footballer

- He became technical director of the Canadian athletics programme leading up to the 1976 Montreal Olympics.

- His British record long jump of 8.23 metres set in 1968 still stands (as at the end of 1995).

A lot of firsts accrued to Lynn Davies. He was the first Welsh Olympic champion, he was the first athlete to win Olympic, European and Commonwealth gold, and he was the first British winner of a field event since the 1908 London Games.

Davies was a natural sportsman. He was a good footballer and rugby player, but he turned to athletics after a chance meeting with the Welsh national athletics coach Ron Pickering who persuaded him that he could achieve great things in that discipline. In the 1962 Commonwealth Games, Pickering's opinion was borne out, when Davies finished fourth in the long jump with a new British record of 7.72 metres.

In 1963, with no major championships to aim for, he experimented by changing his 'hang' style of jumping to the 'hitchkick'. As well as becoming technically more proficient, Pickering coached him to be both faster, with a time of 9.5 seconds over 100 yards, and, with an intense weight training programme, stronger. When the 1964 season began, he had become a world-class jumper, and opened the year with a jump of 8.01 metres, a new Commonwealth record. He improved that by a centimetre in July. However, he was still a long way behind American jumpers such as defending Olympic champion Ralph Boston, and when he took part in the US Championships he could finish no better than sixth. The trip to America had given him the experience of high-level competition that was to prove invaluable in Tokyo.

The Olympic long jump competition was held on a foul day. The runway was waterlogged, it was cold and there was a swirling wind which resulted in many jumpers performing way below their best.

Davies, however, was inspired. He had only qualified for the final with his last jump but, entering the fifth round, he was in third place. He had been told by Pickering that if he saw the flag in the Tokyo stadium drop, it was a good indication that the wind within the stadium was about to fade. On the runway, he looked at the flag, and it dropped. He broke the British record with a leap of 8.07 metres, and took the lead. It was late in the competition, and no one could summon up the energy or willpower to surpass it. Davies had the gold medal.

Despite his Olympic title, Davies could never call himself the undisputed world number one. In 1965, he lost to Boston, and to the Russian Igor Ter-Ovanesyan, but in 1966 he was back to his best, improving his British and Commonwealth record to 8.18 metres, and then taking Commonwealth title in Kingston, Jamaica, and the European gold in Budapest, clinching that with his very last jump. When he broke the twenty-seven-foot barrier with a leap of 8.23 metres (27 feet 0 inches) at the start of 1968, he seemed to be in the sort of form to retain the Olympic crown. Sadly for him, Mexico City was the site of Bob Beamon's legendary achievement.

Davies had no intention of retiring, though,

and set his sights on 1972. He achieved immense personal satisfaction by beating Beamon at a meeting in Stuttgart in 1969, and was a close second to Ter-Ovanesyan in that year's European Championship in Athens. He won his second Commonwealth title in Edinburgh but by the time the 1972 Munich Games came around he was no longer the force he had been, and dogged by injury he failed even to make the final. The next year, he decided that enough was enough. Britain has never found a long jumper to match him.

'Lynn is one of the most competitive men I have ever come across. He is so bad that whenever I know I'm going to be seeing him I have to get into shape for a press-ups contest or a back wrestle match! I know he was great at rugby, tennis and football as a youth because Lynn told me. That cold wet day in Tokyo, he also told me that facing the wind and water logged runway, was just like being back home in Wales. He is proof that hard work and the will to win can take you to the top.'

'Lynn the leap' . The supreme competitor.

JOE DAVIS

JOSEPH DAVIS
SNOOKER PLAYER
BORN: WHITWELL, 15 APRIL 1901, DIED: LONDON, 10 JULY 1978

Facts about Joe Davis

- His father was a bookmaker and publican who used to manage local boxers.

- As the first world snooker champion, Davis won six pounds and ten shillings.

- The 1928 World Billiards Championship match against Tom Newman took two weeks to complete.

- In 1963, he became the first snooker player to receive the OBE.

- His books, *How I Play Snooker* and *Advanced Snooker*, introduced Steve Davis, John Parrott and many other professionals to the game.

Snooker is now one of Britain's most popular sports. Its top players are household names, and millionaires. Its major championships are televised at length, and all this has happened only within the last twenty-five years. The current position of snooker can be traced back to the exploits of one man, Joe Davis.

Davis was born in a small mining village, but at a very young age, his parents managed to take over a small pub outside Chesterfield. Through scrimping and saving, they eventually took over a larger establishment, the Queen's Hotel, that contained a billiard table and it was here, from the age of eleven, that young Joe learnt his skill with a cue. At the age of thirteen, he won the Chesterfield Championship, and from then on he was only interested in taking up the game professionally. In 1926, he reached the World Professional Billiards

Joe in 1950. The father of the game, setting the standard for all who followed him.

title, only to lose to Tom Newman, but when he beat the same player two years later all of Chesterfield turned out to meet him off the train.

Davis had also developed an interest in billiards' poor relation, snooker. By the mid-1920s it had become a popular game in billiard halls, although professionals tended to look down on it as being an inferior knock-about game only fit for those without much skill. Davis saw snooker as the game of the future. Billiards was played with only three balls, so usually not a great deal was happening on the table, and when professionals played the occasional game of snooker spectators tended to be at least as interested in the outcome. In 1925, Davis made a break of ninety-six against Tom Newman in a quick frame thrown in after an early finish to a billiards match, and it caused a minor sensation. Davis therefore suggested the foundation of a World Snooker Championship and in 1927, in Nottingham, he defeated Tom Dennis by twenty frames to eleven to become the first champion.

The next year Davis won both the billiards and snooker titles, and he retained the former until 1933, when he lost to the legendary Australian, Walter Lindrum. Unfortunately for Davis, two important factors were now conspiring against his profession. The first was the Depression. Davis was forced to tour not only Britain, but also South Africa and Australia, continuously giving exhibitions just to make ends meet. Davis's repertoire of trick shots was especially famous. The second was that billiards players were simply too good. The breaks got longer and more tedious, until the paying public simply didn't want to pay anymore. Lindrum beat Davis in the 1934 final and returned to Australia. He didn't want to come back to defend his title, no one wanted to go to Australia to challenge him, and the championship fell into abeyance for seventeen years.

That meant that snooker now held centre stage, and the finest exponent was Davis. He was World Champion for twenty years until he abdicated undefeated in 1946. The only time he was even remotely challenged was when his younger brother Fred succumbed 37–36 in 1940. Even after his withdrawal from the championship, he was still regarded as the best player, still winning many

Joe Davis's Career

World Snooker Championship wins

1927	beat Tom Dennis	20–11
1928	beat Fred Lawrence	16–13
1929	beat Tom Dennis	19–14
1930	beat Tom Dennis	25–12
1931	beat Tom Dennis	25–21
1932	beat Clark McConaghy	30–19
1933	beat Willie Smith	25–18
1934	beat Tom Newman	25–23
1935	beat Willie Smith	25–20
1936	beat Horace Lindrum	34–27
1937	beat Horace Lindrum	32–29
1938	beat Sidney Smith	37–24
1939	beat Sidney Smith	43-30
1940	beat Fred Davis	37–36
1941–45	No contests	
1946	beat Horace Lindrum	78–67

World Billiards Championship wins

1928	beat Tom Newman	16,000–14,874
1929	beat Tom Newman	18,000–17,219
1930	beat Tom Newman	20,198–20,117
1931	No contest	
1932	beat Clark McConaghy	25,161–19,259

tournaments after conceding a substantial handicap, and whenever he gave exhibitions he drew a large crowd. He was co-leaseholder of the Leicester Square Hall in London, the sport's premier venue, and in 1955 it was here that he became the first player to make a 147 break, in an exhibition against Willie Smith.

Davis finally retired from active play in 1964. He had scored 687 century breaks, and had only been beaten three times in level play, each time by brother Fred. He died peacefully in July 1978, at the age of seventy-seven, having finally seen his game establish itself as a major spectacle.

'The only man to have held the snooker and billiards world title at the same time is accolade enough, but to be unbeaten for 29 years or only been beaten 3 times in 40 years, is unbelievable. If he is responsible for taking his sport from smokey halls into millions of homes, then he must be a genius.'

STEVE DAVIS

**STEVEN DAVIS
SNOOKER PLAYER
BORN: PLUMSTEAD, 22 AUGUST 1957**

Facts about Steve Davis

- He was christened 'Interesting' Davis by the satirical TV programme *Spitting Image*. Davis did not resent the nickname, and in 1988 published a book called *How to be Really Interesting*,

- He compiled the first televised 147 break against John Spencer at the Lada Classic in 1982.

- He sang, with the other members of Barry Hearn's Matchroom stable, on the Chas 'n' Dave record 'Snooker Loopy', which reached number five in the charts.

- John McCririck, the racing pundit said, 'Steve Davis is acknowledged by his peers to be a peerless master.'

Steve Davis was the first superstar of snooker's television age. At his peak, he was an awesome potting machine, capable of wearing down any opponent. If his play sometimes lacked the emotion of other performers he was always a well-respected figure and, as his star has waned in recent years, he has become even more popular with the snooker-watching public.

Davis's snooker career began on the tables of the Plumstead Working Men's Club. Encouraged by his father, he studied the instruction books of his illustrious namesake Joe Davis, and he improved rapidly with his enormous dedication and analytical approach to any mistakes. In particular, he developed a textbook cueing action and his natural talent turned into something altogether more consistent.

Davis was something of a late developer. He never won the British junior snooker title, but he accrued a lot of experience as an amateur, travelling all round the country and winning a number of pro-am tournaments before finally turning professional in September 1978. However, life as a snooker amateur had not been too hard. There was no restriction on accepting prize money, or taking fees for exhibitions, and Davis had effectively been a professional since leaving school. After his 'A' Levels, he had been seen by Barry Hearn, owner of the Romford Snooker Club, who became his manager.

It took Davis some time to get used to the more rarefied atmosphere of the professional circuit. Although he had a wonderful technique, he did not yet have the experience or temperament required to win big matches. In 1980, that started to change. He beat Terry Griffiths, the defending champion, in the second round of the World

Steve Davis's Career

World Championship wins

Year	Opponent	Score
1981	beat Doug Mountjoy	18–12
1983	beat Cliff Thorburn	18–6
1984	beat Jimmy White	18–16
1987	beat Joe Johnson	18–14
1988	beat Terry Griffiths	18–11
1989	beat John Parrott	18–3

British Open wins
1981, 1982, 1984, 1986

United Kingdom Open wins
1980, 1981, 1984, 1985, 1986, 1987

Benson & Hedges Masters wins
1982, 1988

Championship. Later that year, he made the breakthrough, winning the UK title in style. He whitewashed Griffiths 9–0 in the semi-final, and destroyed Alex Higgins 16–6 to take a £6000 first prize. He followed that by taking his first World title at the end of the season, beating Doug Mountjoy 18–12.

His manager, Hearn, now developed Davis into snooker's first superstar. He was sponsored by the brewers Courage for a six-figure fee, and appeared on television and in commercials. That did not mean to say he was free of flaws, though. His first world title defence in 1982 ended after eleven embarrassing frames when he capitulated 10–1 to Tony Knowles. It seemed that he was being distracted by matters away from the table, as on the day of the match he was promoting a new video. That mistake would not be made twice.

Davis still kept a busy schedule of assignments outside snooker in 1983. Hearn was quoted as saying Davis would earn £350,000 for the year before he took his cue out of the case, but retaining the World Championship was his priority, and he defeated Thorburn 18–6 in the final. The next year, he became the first player to retain the

The most famous stare in snooker. Davis in classic potting position.

- He is a keen collector of R & B and soul music, and publishes a quarterly magazine, *Voices from the Shadows* dedicated to soul music.

- Early in his career, he used to relax away from the table with a video console playing *Space Invaders*.

tournament at the Crucible Theatre, Sheffield, beating Jimmy White 18–16 in an altogether more interesting match.

He did not retain his title for a third year, but the manner of his defeat has gone down in sporting history. His opponent in the 1985 final was Dennis Taylor and Davis, as only he could, raced into an 8–0 lead. This time, his opponent refused to buckle and, over the course of a bewitching two days, drew level. The match went to the last frame. It was after midnight and 18.5 million people watched for the sixty-eight minutes it took to complete. Davis missed a cut into the bottom pocket on the last black and Taylor was the champion by eighteen frames to seventeen. Perhaps this was the first time snooker could count itself a truly mainstream sport.

Davis lost the final the next year, far more surprisingly, to a rank outsider, Joe Johnson, but he secured his fourth title a year later against the same opponent, and retained it against Terry Griffiths

the next year. In 1989 he won his sixth World Championship, and his third in a row, with a complete destruction of John Parrott. His 18–3 win was the most comprehensive in World Championship history.

Since then, though, Davis has been overshadowed by the rise of Stephen Hendry. His 16–15 defeat in the final of the 1990 UK Open to the young Scot was highly symbolic. Davis, while still an opponent to be feared, has definitely been overtaken by a new generation of talent. But the new generation has still got a long way to go to beat his achievements.

'He is called "Interesting" because when he is at the table his only concern is winning and it's impossible to tell how he's feeling from the look on his face. Like Joe Davis, snooker players owe Steve a huge debt of thanks for taking their sport closer to the hearts of the public.'

DIXIE DEAN

WILLIAM RALPH DEAN
FOOTBALL – FORWARD
BORN: BIRKENHEAD, 22 JANUARY 1907
DIED: LIVERPOOL, 1 MARCH 1980

Facts about Dixie Dean

- Dean's father was an engine driver, and his mother was in domestic service.

- Dean was christened 'Dixie' by Tranmere Rovers supporters in 1924, possibly because of his black, curly hair. At first, he resented the nickname, and preferred to be called Bill.

- In the spirit of Eric Cantona, Dean once attacked a fan at Tottenham who had been subjecting him to particularly nasty abuse. A policeman witnessed the incident and allegedly said, 'I saw nothing, but it was a fine punch.'

- He scored 349 goals in 399 matches for Everton, an all-time record for any one club.

- He scored thirty-seven hat-tricks in his career, a record.

Dixie Dean was a peerless goal-scoring machine. In his case, the statistics do not lie. Sixty League goals in a season, and 310 in only eleven First Division seasons are records that will stand for ever. Dean could score with either foot, and was a peerless header of the ball. His name is almost as well known on Merseyside now as when he was playing.

Dean was born in Birkenhead, on the opposite side of the Mersey. Like many of his contemporaries, he grew up thinking about little else but playing football. His father was an Everton fan and, when Dean was eight, took him to see a game at Goodison Park. From that point, his path was set. He would become a professional footballer.

In 1923 his local club, Tranmere Rovers, signed him as an amateur. They were then a lowly club in the newly formed Third Division North, without too many ambitions. They suddenly saw Dean's worth in his second season. He scored twenty-eight goals in twenty-eight games, and Everton were suddenly interested. They paid £2500 to bring the eighteen year-old to Goodison for the 1925–26 season.

He was not an immediate selection, but after scoring seven goals for the reserves in a game against Bradford, he could not be ignored for long. That season was a good one for forwards. The offside rule had been changed and forwards had a field day. Everton could not ignore the potential of their new star recruit, and he was thrown into the first team, scoring thirty-two goals in thirty-eight games. The Everton fans looked forward to the coming season with confidence.

Unfortunately, Dean was involved in a serious motorbike accident that summer. He was

unconscious for thirty-six hours, and he suffered a broken jawbone and a fractured skull. At first, it was announced that his football days were over. Dean had a strong constitution, though. He astounded doctors with his progress, and by October was back in the Everton team. By the end of the season, he had also made his England debut, scoring twice in a 3–3 draw with Wales, and then netting both goals as England won 2–1 in Glasgow, their first victory on Scottish soil for twenty-three years.

The next season, 1927–28, saw Dean at his very best. Everton had become a very good team, definitely title material, and they started the season in magnificent form. Dean scored thirty goals in Everton's first nineteen matches as they led the table by five points, and by 7 January, his thirty-ninth goal had already broken the Everton record by a forward in one season. They were already champions by the time of their final match with Arsenal but Dean, with fifty-seven

The goal-scoring juggernaut on his way to another encounter for Everton against Arsenal at Highbury in 1936.

goals, was still two goals behind the record set by George Camsell, of Second Division Middlesbrough the previous season. The game finished in a 3–3 draw, and Dean scored all of his team's goals. When he completed his hat-trick, with a trademark header, he broke Camsell's records. In all matches that season, including representative games, he played fifty-six times, and scored exactly 100 goals.

Dean stayed with Everton for ten more seasons, helping them to the championship again in 1932, scoring forty-five goals, and the FA Cup the next year, scoring in the final at Wembley in an easy 3–0 win over Manchester City. However, injuries started to take their toll and he spent most of the 1937–38 season in the reserves. Everton had also discovered another talented young striker in Tommy Lawton and in March 1938 he was sold to Third Division Notts County for £3000. The decision caused uproar on Merseyside, but Dean barely played for his new club as injuries grew increasingly more frequent. However, he ended the 1938–39 season in Ireland, with Sligo Rovers, and a losing appearance in the FAI Cup final. The war then brought his career to its conclusion.

Dean maintained his interest in football and Everton, concerned that their treatment of Dean at the end of his career could have been better, gave him a testimonial match in 1964, twenty-six years after his last appearance in their colours. However, his final years saw him in declining health. He had a leg amputated because of thrombosis in 1976, and died in 1980, appropriately enough at Goodison Park, after an Everton–Liverpool match.

'There have been many greats who have played on Merseyside, but nobody was held in greater affection than William Ralph Dean. The best centre-forward and goal scorer of his and maybe any generation – it will be a good man indeed who beats his 60 goals in a season or betters his goal-a-game for England. This man was 'Roy of the Rovers' 30 years before the great comic hero was first drawn.'

GEOFF DUKE

**GEOFFREY DUKE
MOTOR-CYCLIST
BORN: ST HELENS, 29 MARCH 1923**

Facts about Geoff Duke

- He flirted briefly, but unsuccessfully, with four-wheel racing for Aston Martin, in 1958, but soon returned to the saddle.

- He was awarded the OBE in 1951 after his remarkable World Championship double.

Geoff Duke is regarded as the father of modern British motor-cycling. His record was impressive enough but, most importantly, he brought style and panache to the track and to the image of the rider.

Duke visited the Isle of Man in 1939 and the famous TT Races became his inspiration. During the Second World War he rode army despatch bikes and became an instructor. He started riding in moto-cross and trails events after the war and was soon introduced to the Norton team by Artie Bell, one of the best riders of his day. Duke made his debut on a 350cc Norton at the Manx Grand Prix, in 1948. He was twenty-five years old. It was nearly a sensational debut. He was leading at the half-way stage, but had to pull out with oil failure. Only a year later he won the Senior Clubman's TT and the Senior Manx Grand Prix, and in 1950 won

the Senior TT for his first World Championship race. He eventually won three 500cc and one 350cc races that year and missed the World Championship by only one point behind Umberto Masetti of Italy. It had been an astonishingly quick rise to prominence.

1951 was a very special year. He became the first man to win both the 350cc and 500cc titles in the same year, as well as the Junior and Senior TT races in record times. In an amazing twelve months he won five 500cc races and four 350cc races.

Unfortunately, his Norton became uncompetitive in 1952. He held on to his 350cc title but came a distant seventh in the 500cc class. At the end of the season he switched to the Italian manufacturer, Gilera. It was a shrewd move. He won the 500cc class for the next three years in 1953, 1954 and 1955, winning thirteen races in all.

Things started to go significantly less well for him in 1956. His International Federation banned him for six months after he supported an unofficial riders' boycott during the 1955 Dutch TT. Then, injuries severely restricted his season in 1957 following an accident in the Italian Grand Prix. Finally, after a brief marriage with BMW, he returned to Norton in 1958, but achieved only a single victory in each of the 350cc and 500cc classes in a season that would see Duke's final victories on the circuit.

By the end of a remarkably distinguished career, Duke had left his mark as the first of the modern giants of the sport – soon to be followed by Hailwood, Surtees and the great Giacomo Agostini.

Geoff Duke settled on his beloved Isle of Man and briefly returned to the circuit, in 1963, as boss of the Scuderia Duke racing team, but without much success.

'Geoff was the first to bring both success and flair to the sport of motor cycling. As well as his many victories he was the first to wear the all-in-one leather suits which he had a local tailor make for him.'

Proudly on the winners' podium yet again, this time at the Swiss Grand Prix in Berne in 1953.

Geoff Duke's Career

Total Grands Prix wins	33 (11 – 350cc, 22 – 500cc)	
World Championships		
350cc	1951	(Norton)
	1952	(Norton)
500cc	1951	(Norton)
	1953	(Gilera)
	1954	(Gilera)
	1955	(Gilera)
TT Wins		
1948	Senior Clubman	(Norton)
1950	Senior	(Norton)
1951	Senior and Junior	(Norton)
1952	Junior	(Norton)
1955	Senior	(Gilera)

GARETH EDWARDS

GARETH OWEN EDWARDS
RUGBY UNION – SCRUM-HALF
BORN: GWAEN-CAE-GURWEN, 12 JULY 1947

Facts about
Gareth Edwards

- Edwards was on the end of the famous move started by Phil Bennet and scored 'the try' for the Barbarians against the All-Blacks in Cardiff, in 1973.

- When he realised that he'd been picked to partner Barry John for the first time he rang him to discuss tactics. John cut him short to announce 'Don't worry. You throw it, I'll catch it!'

- On the two occasions Edwards was substituted, through injury, he was replaced by 'Chico' Hopkins against England, in 1971, and by Clive Shell against Australia, in 1973.

Gareth Edwards was and is a renaissance Welshman. Much loved, and even revered, in the rugby world, it seems that the young Edwards could have chosen several sports. In later life he became a successful businessman, author and commentator.

He was born into a mining community in South Wales and, like most boys, dreamed of playing for Wales. At secondary school he was fortunate to have a PE teacher who recognised his many talents and persuaded Millfield School in Somerset, the sports specialists, to accept him. It can't have been difficult. He played full-back for Glamorgan Schools, in 1963, and at centre for Welsh Schools, in 1966 and also had a final trial for

the Welsh Youth Soccer Team. In 1964 the Welsh Games Committee selected him as the 'most promising athlete of 1964' and while at Millfield he won the English Schools 200 yards hurdles title.

Rugby won the battle for his talents and he joined Cardiff. He went on tour with them in 1967, and people began to hear of a versatile new talent who could play anywhere on the back line. His international career began before he was twenty and seemed to go on forever. In fact it was ten years, but in rugby terms, especially for a scrum-half, it was an eternity. During the entire time he never missed a game, but had to be carried off twice, and once played when he shouldn't have, when injured, in order to bolster the team – such

Edwards in the thick of things as usual; for the British Lions against the All-Blacks in 1971.

Gareth Edwards's Career

Home International Honours

1969	International Championship and Triple Crown
1970	International Championship (shared)
1971	International Championship and Triple Crown
1972	International Championship (shared)
1975	International Championship
1976	International Championship, Triple Crown and Grand Slam
1977	Triple Crown
1978	International Championship, Triple Crown and Grand Slam

British Lions

1968	South Africa
1971	New Zealand
1974	South Africa

Welsh Internationalappearances: 53

British Lions appearances:	10
Welsh tries:	20
Welsh Captain:	13

was the beating meted out to a scrum-half!

Edwards's physical courage, strength and aggression, perhaps coupled with his amazing turn of speed over ten yards, were his greatest assests. Many of his twenty tries for Wales followed a quick burst to the line with opposition players hanging off him trying to bring him down.

He was a dominant personality on the field and his legendary partnerships with Barry John, and then with Phil Bennett, exemplified the finest era in Welsh rugby. In all, he played fifty-three times for his country.

He also played ten Tests for the British Lions on their tours to New Zealand in 1971 and to South Africa, in 1968 and 1974. The victorious tours of 1971 and 1974 were halcyon days for British rugby, and Edwards was a vital part of those wonderful teams. Apart from the ten Tests, Edwards made thirty-eight appearances for the Lions on tour: eight in 1968, fifteen in 1971 and fifteen in 1974.

Gareth Edwards retired at the peak of his game. He was a happy man. He had won everything there was to win and had become a Welsh hero. It was just what the little lad twenty years earlier had dreamed of.

Among the many Max Boyce stories about Gareth Edwards, these are but two. The first is a poem, set in the future, about the great man's famed longevity in the Welsh team:

'A man came home off afternoons and found his son in woe. And asked him, 'What's the matter bach, pray tell what ails you so? Your little eyes are swollen red, your hands are white and shaking.' 'Oh! Dad,' he said, 'I've got bad news, my little heart is breaking. Gareth Edwards has been dropped, 'twas on the news just now, The Welsh selectors must be mad, there's bound to be a row.' His father said, 'Now dry your eyes and don't get in a state. Let's be fair, mun, after all, the man is seventy-eight!'

The second is an apochryphal story from the England–Wales game at Twickenham, in 1978:

'A Welsh supporter was standing outside the ground in the pouring rain when he shouted up to some English supporters inside the ground. 'What's happening? What's happening?', only to be told that the entire Welsh team, other than Edwards, had been carried off injured. Minutes later there was a huge roar, whereupon the Welshman called out again, 'What's happened? What's happened? Gareth scored has he?'

- When he won the English Schools 200 metres hurdles (while at Millfield) trailing way behind was a young man called Alan Pascoe, later to become an Olympic silver medallist with the British team in the 400 metres relay in Munich, in 1972, with David Hemery, David Jenkins and Martin Reynolds.

- He was awarded the MBE in 1975.

- Edwards represented Wales at another sporting passion, angling. In 1990 he set a British record for a pike at Llandegfedd Reservoir, in Gwent. It weighed 45lb 6ozs.

- He has written several books, including his memoirs, a history of Welsh rugby and a fishing book.

'Gareth could have been any number of things and once he had chosen rugby they must have been singing in the valleys. Even amongst the best he was in a different class. Physically he had it all, and coupled with a mind working half a move ahead of the rest of the field, he was amazing. Add to this heady mixture, his reputation as a raconteur of legend and a sporting socialite, and you will know why every Welsh boy still wants to be him.'

JONATHAN EDWARDS

JONATHAN DAVID EDWARDS
ATHLETICS – TRIPLE JUMPER
BORN: LONDON, 10 MAY 1966

Facts about Jonathan Edwards

- He graduated in physics from Durham University.

- Before becoming a full-time athlete, he was a genetics research officer at Newcastle Hospital.

- In 1994, he contracted Epstein-Barr virus, a condition akin to glandular fever, which affected his performances.

- He is married with two sons, Samuel and Nathan. Nathan was born in May 1995, shortly before Edwards's record-breaking season started. Samuel was born a week before dad's bronze medal in the 1993 World Championships.

- He was awarded the MBe in the 1996 New Year's Honours list.

Just occasionally, athletics throws up a performance which overturns all previous conceptions about the discipline. The most famous, of course, is Bob Beamon's long jump in 1968. Jonathan Edwards's triple jump at the 1995 World Championships also comes into that category, and his winning smile was surely the high spot of British sport that year.

Edwards is the son of a vicar and, as a committed Christian, would not for many years jump on Sundays. He was a fairly slow developer, first jumping 16 metres in 1986. He qualified for the 1988 Olympic team but failed to qualify for the final. The next year, he was ranked Britain's number one triple jumper for the first time, and started to achieve world-class distances. In June of that year, he jumped over 17 metres for the first time, in a wind-assisted effort in Vigo, Spain. At the World Cup later in the season, he leapt 17.28 metres for a bronze medal.

Edwards, though, was very aware that there was more to life than sport. As a man of deep religious conviction he withdrew from the 1991 World Championships squad when he realised he would have to jump on a Sunday. He still remained Britain's best triple jumper and, with a personal best of 17.43 metres before that season, he would certainly have been a medal hope. In Barcelona, he had a disappointing Olympics once again, and was eliminated before reaching the final. Only at the World Championships in 1993 was he seen on top form. Although his Christianity had not wavered, he was now prepared to compete on a Sunday and with a personal best of 17.44 metres, he took the bronze

Jonathan Edwards's Career

Olympic Games

1988 (Seoul)	did not qualify
1992 (Barcelona)	did not qualify

World Championships

1993 (Stuttgart)	3rd
1995 (Gothenburg)	1st

European Championships

1994 (Helsinki)	6th

Commonwealth Games

1990 (Auckland)	2nd
1994 (Victoria)	2nd

World Record
18.29 metres set at Gothenburg, August 1995

medal behind the American Mike Conley.

1994 was a disappointing year for Edwards. He barely broke seventeen metres at any event, still lagging way behind Conley whenever the American participated. In the European Championships, the year's major event, he performed poorly to finish in sixth place almost a metre behind the winner, Kapustin of Russia. It seemed to many observers that Edwards would probably never fulfill his potential.

Yet when the 1995 season started, Edwards was a changed jumper. He was still doing the same things, only doing them much better. He carried no more muscles on his slight-looking frame, but perhaps the secret lay in his feet. His foot

In the Brussels Grand Prix in 1995. A memorable year for a modest man.

movement was considerably more rapid than his rivals, and his final jump into the pit was far superior. At the start of the year, he launched a wind-assisted jump of over eighteen metres. Then in a meeting at Santander, Spain, he jumped 17.98 metres. That was a centimetre more than Willie Banks's record, which had stood for ten years. Suddenly Edwards was favourite for the World Championships in Gothenburg.

This time, he had no trouble qualifying, and was confident and relaxed for the final. He flew down the runway for the first time and exploded off the track for the 'jump', the third component of the triple jump. He came to rest way beyond the 18 metre sign, and the crowd erupted as the scoreboard showed 18.16 metres. The wind was legal, and it was a new world record by some distance.

Edwards was not finished, though. Rather than pass, he went for his jump in the second round and, with the crowd in a state of high excitement, flew even further, to 18.29 metres. This, for those statisticians still working in imperial measurements, broke an even more important mark; the sixty foot barrier. Needless to say, none of the others came close and Edwards was world champion.

Edwards's achievement sparked more than a little interest in his discipline. He was named the IAAF (International Amateur Athletic Federation) Male Athlete of the Year, and was voted BBC Sports Personality of 1995 by the British public. It was a tribute not only to a great sporting landmark, but also to a gentle and modest man.

'There are a number of people who are in our list who are still competing. They will suffer in some categories, Jonathan is one of these. 1995 was an incredible year for him. He went from mere finalist to the No.1 man in the triple jump. The other thing that sets Jonathan apart is his modesty. I think it is every athlete's greatest dream to break the world record while winning the Olympics, well doing it at the World Championships can't be far behind.'

NICK FALDO

**NICHOLAS ALEXANDER FALDO
GOLFER
BORN: WELWYN GARDEN CITY, 18 JULY 1957**

TOP 20

Facts about Nick Faldo

- Faldo is a very keen fly-fisherman. 'The joy of casting in clear waters, where you can see the trout and the bugger can see you, is wonderful because it's a great skill and a marvellous contest.'

- He was BBC Sports Personality of the Year in 1989.

- He went to America on a golf scholarship but didn't like it. He said his studies got in the way of his golf.

- His hours and hours of practice at Welwyn became famous. 'I'd play imaginary games against Jack, Arnie and Tom Weiskopf. I'd start at eight in the morning and play until dark. Sometimes, I'd play a hole backwards – if it was a three-wood and then a five-iron to the green, I'd take a five-iron off the tee and a three-wood to the green.'

Nick Faldo is still at the peak of his career, but, on achievements so far, he is already far and away Britain's most successful golfer and has been widely regarded as the world's best player for several of the last half dozen years.

His strong, athletic physique and sporting skills pointed him in several competitive directions as a young man, but, as a fourteen year-old, he was inspired to take up golf by watching Jack Nicklaus win the Masters at Augusta. He became fanatical about the game and would practise all day, every day at his home course, in Welwyn.

Within two years he came to prominence as an amateur and in 1975 won the British Youths' Open Amateur Championship and the English Amateur before turning professional in 1976. His first tournament win came quickly, in 1977, when he won the Skol Lager in a play-off. The victories accumulated, particularly in 1983 when he won five times on the European Tour, was at the top of the Order of Merit and had an average score per round of 69.03. He was a world-class player and highly-respected. But it wasn't enough. At a point when most players would be content that they had reached the pinnacle and could look forward to many years of success, Faldo decided to dismantle his swing and start from scratch.

He went to David Leadbetter, the golf coach, and one of golf's great stories unfolded. 'It was an uncharted journey for both of us. I was a guinea pig.'

Faldo was looking for the control that would make him a legend, not just a good player. He was searching for the key to becoming the new Hogan, the next Nicklaus. To all intents and purposes he found it. But it was hard work. 'I'd hit 1500 golf balls a day. My fingers were so sore that they

Nick Faldo's Career

Major Championships: (5)

The Open	1987
The Masters	1989
The Masters	1990
The Open	1990
The Open	1992

The Ryder Cup:

10 appearances,	1977–95

PGA European Tour victories: 30

Other tournaments: 8

swelled up and I couldn't grip the club properly.'

Two years later it all came good. Leadbetter would become golf's guru extraordinaire. Faldo would become a legend. 'One day in 1987 I went to this place called Hattiesburg in America. I shot four sixty-sevens. Everything fell into place. It was like sunshine.'

He won the Spanish Open and then the big one, the 1987 Open Championship. It was as if his final round at Muirfield was justification for all his efforts to control his swing – a perfectly controlled round, in poor weather, with a par on every hole.

1987 was also the year of Europe's most famous Ryder Cup victory when Faldo was part of the greatest European team ever selected which beat the Americans 13–11. It was the first victory on US soil in the sixty-one-year history of the event. The European team included Ballesteros, Olazabal, Langer, Lyle and Woosnam, as well as Faldo.

Faldo's quest for immortality went on. America was convinced of his talent when he won the

Masters, in 1989, and fought Curtis Strange to a play-off in the US Open at Brookline, in 1988, before losing by four shots.

1990 was his finest year. First came the Masters. He scored a seventy-one, seventy-two and sixty-six to go into the final round three shots behind Ray Floyd. His outstanding sixty-nine put him in a play-off with Floyd. The American veteran put his second shot into the water on the second hole and Faldo joined Jack Nicklaus as the only players to win consecutive Masters titles. Only the edge of the cup separated him from a play-off for the US

Faldo at St Andrews in 1990 in his final round, calculating the borrows for his second Open Championship.

'The Master'. Perfect timing in the sands of victory for his first triumph at Augusta in 1989.

- He has scored three holes-in-one.

- He was awarded the MBE in 1988.

- Faldo has often been reminded of his resemblance to the Harrison Ford character in Raiders of the Lost Ark – Indiana Jones.

- He is a serious collector of wildlife paintings, especially by the English artist, Simon Combes.

- The best four holes of my life' is how he describes the recovery he made over the closing holes at Muirfield in the 1992 Open when a comfortable position went horribly wrong at the beginning of the back-nine in the last round.

- His ever-present companion on the golf course is his Swedish caddy, Fanny Sunneson, a female exception in a notoriously male world.

Open title before he went to St Andrews for what, for a while, promised to be a titanic struggle with Greg Norman. But Norman fell away with a third round seventy-six while Faldo hit an impressive sixty-seven. The next day, Faldo won his second Open, and his fourth major, by five shots.

His fifth major started with all the hallmarks of a run-away victory. In 1992 he was back at Muirfield, the scene of his first Open Championship, and his two-round aggregate of 130 led the bookmakers to make him an amazing 6–1 on for the Championship. He still led by four after three rounds and by three mid-way through the final round. He then had a disastrous eleventh, thirteenth and fourteenth. John Cook, the American playing ahead, was suddenly two shots in the lead. He should have won, but, in a nail-biting finish, Cook cracked and Faldo just held himself together. However, by the final putt – a one-footer

to win the Championship – he was visibly shaking. As soon as it went in he burst into tears and was incoherent for some time afterwards. Such are the pressures of golf.

Nick Faldo is already an all-time great but is certain there is more to come. Unpleasant headlines and constant press attention over the break-up of his marriage in 1995 will not have helped his game, but he's still two majors short of a full set and still has the burning ambition he always had.

'With 5 majors behind him and many years ahead of him, Nick is in a great position to move way up these rankings. My reasons for not having him near the top are based on the length of his career and how his majors' tally compares against other all time greats. Maybe his charisma could use a little work.'

TOM FINNEY

THOMAS FINNEY
FOOTBALL – FORWARD
BORN: PRESTON, 5 APRIL 1922

No one who saw Tom Finney play could fail to be moved by his genius. He was a supremely skilful winger, as good as, and some would say better, than his great contemporary and friendly rival Stan Matthews. Not only was he a great ball-artist, he was a prolific goalscorer. He could play equally well on either wing and is arguably the most complete England forward of all time. Yet, although Finney was respected and feared across the world, his only domestic honours were a Second Division championship, and an FA Cup runners-up medal.

Finney was Preston born and bred and, naturally, he joined his club straight from school. He joined as an inside-left, but appeared a little frail for the position. He managed to persuade the club to put him on the right wing. It was an inspired move for, although Finney was naturally left footed, he had a perfectly serviceable right, and the combination was devilish for any full-back. Finney could turn the defender either way and then fly past him down the wing. He was especially adept at getting to the by-line and taking out the entire defence with a deadly centre.

The war intervened before Preston could introduce this new jewel to the first team, but the teenager impressed with a brilliant performance as Preston beat Arsenal in the War Cup final of 1941. Shortly afterwards, he joined the Army. He returned unscathed to not only to go straight into the North End first team, but also into service with England. He made his debut in Belfast in the first post-war international. England, with Finney keeping the forward well supplied, won 7–2 with the Preston striker getting one of the goals. More controversial, though, was the fact that Finney had been selected ahead of Stan Matthews. It took ten

months for the matter to be solved. Finney, a more versatile forward, moved to the left wing, allowing Matthews in on the right. One on his own was bad enough, and the pair together were devastating. They beat the Portuguese 10–0 in Lisbon, and then Italy 4–0 in Turin. Italy were world champions at the time, although that title hadn't been defended for ten years. They were a fine team, though, based on the Torino line-up that had proved invincible in the domestic game. Finney, always a more regular goalscorer than Matthews, netted two in the second half.

At domestic level, Finney had been the star of a very small club. He had had to spend two years in the Second Division before coming back as champions in 1951. Two years on, and they lost to the title to Arsenal on goal difference. In 1954, they reached the Cup final.

Finney had inspired the team on their way to Wembley. His wing play had been inspired against Sheffield Wednesday in the semi-finals, getting to the by-line so frequently that North End had forced twenty-two corners in their 2–0 win. Just as 1953 had been the 'Matthews Final', so 1954 was expected to be the 'Finney Final'. Their opponents, West Bromwich, had other ideas. Finney went into the match troubled by a groin strain, and was

Facts about Tom Finney

- He served with the Eight Army in the Middle East during the war, and then fought in Italy. After the war, he played in an army team touring the peninsula.

- In 1952, the chairman of Italian club Cagliari offered Finney a huge fee to sign for his club, more than he could ever have earned in the English game. Finney asked the Preston chairman for permission to sign, but, not unexpectedly, the request was turned down.

- He played his last international in 1958 against the Soviet Union at Wembley. England won 5–0.

- Bill Shankly was a great admirer of Finney and said, 'Finney would have been great in any team, in any match, in any age – even wearing an overcoat.'

Tom Finney's Career

Football League appearances	431
Goals	187
International appearances	76
Goals	30

Finney in the famous
white shirt of his beloved
Preston North End in 1955.

- He was awarded an
  OBE in 1961

- He was voted Fotballer
  of the Year in 1954
  and 1957.

marked closely by the Throstles' captain, Millard. He was allowed barely a kick as North End lost 3–2 to a late goal. Finney was heartbroken, he felt he had let everybody down, but even the giants can have off-days.

Finney finally retired in 1960. He had established a profitable plumbing business, and never had the financial worries some of his contemporaries encountered. He stayed closely involved with his beloved North End, and is now their president. Despite the admiration, Finney remained a modest man throughout, and after, his career. Jimmy Greaves once described him as 'The First Gentleman of Football'.

There are those who say Finney retired too soon, that even at thirty-eight he still had years of football left in him. Preston North End have certainly never recovered. The first season without him ended in relegation, and they've never been back to the top flight since.

'Tom was always compared to Stanley Matthews. It may be fair to say that Stan had it by a touch as a winger, but that Tom was the better all-round forward. His flexibility and goal scoring point to that. Staying at one club for an entire career is unthinkable to the modern player.'

MIKE GIBSON

**CAMERON MICHAEL HENDERSON GIBSON
RUGBY UNION – FLY-HALF AND CENTRE
BORN: BELFAST, 3 DECEMBER 1942**

Mike Gibson's Career	
Irish International appearances:	69
British Lions appearances:	12
Irish International appearances:	67
International Championship:	1974

Mike Gibson's demeanour belied his great talent. He was an unassuming Irishman who became a marvellous example of the truly dedicated athlete. His position as one of the great backs of world rugby is unquestioned. Many critics regard him as the most versatile, and would thus put him at the top of the tree.

He had great courage, and on five tours with the

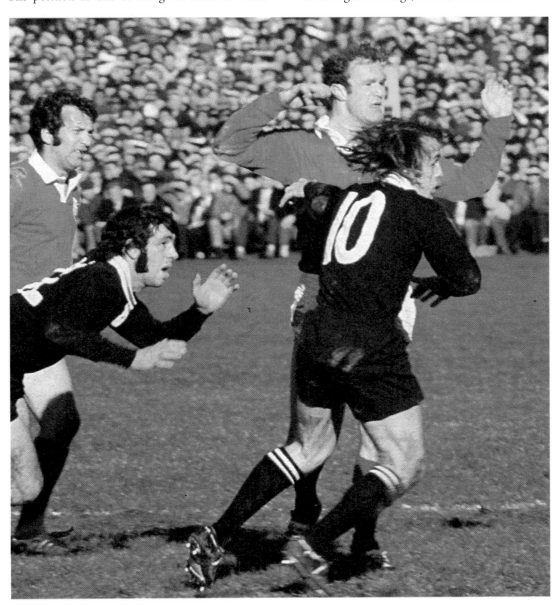

The pride of the Lions in 1971 in New Zealand. Gibson has the Kiwis in disarray.

Gibson prepares for his first Lions' tour in 1966.

Facts about Mike Gibson

- He was a Cambridge blue in 1963, 1964 and 1965.

- Although he didn't play in the Tests in New Zealand in 1977 – Fenwick and McGeechan were preferred as centres – Gibson was the only tourist to play in all the winning games.

- Gibson made history as the first player to take the field as a replacement at Test level when he came on for Barry John in the opening Test at Ellis Park, in South Africa, in 1968. John had broken a collar-bone.

- 'Gibbo' was his nickname. He was a very conscientious trainer, was always immaculately turned-out for matches and hardly ever touched alcohol.

- He was awarded the MBE for services to rugby.

British Lions he needed it. He could take a hard tackle and dish out a good one himself.

Gibson was twenty-two when he made his debut for Ireland against England, at Twickenham, in 1964. He played fly-half as Ireland beat England for the first time in sixteen years. It was an auspicious start. His attributes were noted: very quick over the first ten yards, a good side-step, excellent when required to kick and an outstanding passer of the ball.

He became a permanent fixture in the Irish team from his debut, in 1964, until his retirement in 1979. Forty of his sixty-nine caps were gained at centre, twenty-five at fly-half and four on the wing; statistics that bear testament to his versatility. When he won his sixty-ninth cap he became the most capped rugby player of his day. His final couple of appearances were among his most memorable. It was in 1979, in Australia when Ireland played the Wallabies in a two-test series. The Irish, with Gibson probing on the wing, created a major upset by winning both matches.

Mike Gibson's career for the British Lions was remarkable. He was the only player, with fellow-Ulsterman, Willie John McBride, to have gone on five Lions tours. He played in all four Tests in New Zealand, in 1966 and 1971, and South Africa in

1968. He was a stalwart of the party in South Africa, in 1974, and in New Zealand in 1977, but did not play in the Tests. In the twelve Tests he participated in, he played four as fly-half and eight as centre. In addition, he played in a further fifty-seven matches while on tour. His finest performances came in the historic victory against the All-Blacks, in 1971. Carwyn James was the coach, John Davies the captain and the team was the finest Lions team ever to visit New Zealand. Gibson was one of the players the Kiwis feared the most. At the end of the tour, and with an historic victory under his belt, Gibson was widely hailed as the best all-round player in the world in the back division.

He retired in 1979 as a world-record holder for international caps and as one of the most respected men ever to play the game. He then devoted himself to his real job as a Belfast solicitor.

'Until the first Rugby World Cup I was not really a big fan of Union (nor League) but I have known Cliff Morgan for years and he tells me that Mike is the best all-round player he has ever seen, which means more than I could ever say. I know he was a hard trainer and very meticulous, as anyone who has played a round of golf with him can verify.'

GRAHAM GOOCH

GRAHAM ALAN GOOCH
CRICKET – BATSMAN
BORN: LEYTONSTONE, JULY 23 1953

Graham Gooch is now England's all-time top run-scorer. He has led his county, Essex, from being very much outsiders to become the most successful team of the last decade, and he has captained England with great success. Yet he has been highly controversial, serving a long suspension from Test cricket for going on a rebel tour to South Africa, and his presence in the England team has upset politicians in India and the West Indies.

Gooch made his England debut against Lillee and Thomson in the summer of 1975. It was not very auspicious. A pair on his debut and a none too convincing thirty-seven scratched out of two innings in his second test led to three years back in county cricket. By 1978, he had been promoted to opener, and was ready. As partner to Boycott, though, he was still not wholly convincing, and his first Test century did not come until his twenty-second appearance. It was a superb 123 against the West Indies at Lord's in which he tamed the world's fiercest fast bowling attack with a masterful display of aggression. Indeed, two centuries against the West Indies on that winter's tour had him marked out as one of the few England batsmen with the courage to take cricket's 'world champions' on.

However, after the 1981–82 tour to India and Sri Lanka, he decided to throw in his lot with the rebels in South Africa. He was banned from Test cricket for three years. The plus side to this was that it enabled the East London boy to concentrate on domestic duties. Essex had won their first County Championship in 1979. Now, with Gooch freed from national duties, they won again in 1983, and retained the title the following year. There was success in the one-day competitions as well.

As soon as Gooch was available again, in 1985, he was selected for England, and played a full part in seeing off the Australians 3–1 in a very exciting series. In addition to scoring two centuries in the one-day internationals, he averaged 54.11 for the series, and scored 196 in the final Test.

In 1988, in the summer of chaos against the West Indies, Gooch captained England for the first time in the final Test. He was relatively successful, and was selected to lead the England tour to India that winter. Unfortunately, the Indians had neither forgotten nor forgiven what they saw as his duplicitous behaviour over the earlier rebel tour. The tour was cancelled amid much acrimony. It was made worse the next summer when the new chairman of selectors, Ted Dexter, decided to give the captaincy to David Gower and in the process described Gooch as having the personality of 'a wet fish'. This remark reflected more on Dexter than on Gooch and when the 1989 series ended in utter disaster for England the chairman ate his words and Gooch was appointed captain for the West

Graham Gooch's Career

Tests	113
Test Match runs	8655
Average	43.49
Centuries	20
County Championship	1979, 1983, 1984, 1986, 1991, 1992
NatWest Trophy	1985
Benson & Hedges Cup	1979
Sunday League	1981, 1984, 1985

Facts about Graham Gooch

- He supports West Ham United

- In his time at Essex, they have won six County Championships, one NatWest Trophy, one Benson & Hedges Cup and three Sunday Leagues. They had never won a single trophy before.

- He suffered the rare indignity of being out 'Handled the Ball' against Australia at Old Trafford in 1993, after brushing the ball away from his stumps.

- There was controversy about when Gooch scored his 100th century after one scored on the rebel tour was declared not to be first class. Officially, he scored it for Essex against Cambridge University at Cambridge on 1 May 1993, and then declared himself retired out.

• He once took 7–14 for Essex against Worcestershire in 1982.

• Gooch is an excellent one day player and his score of 198 not out for Essex against Sussex in the 1982 Benson & Hedges Cup is the highest score in a match between two first-class counties.

Gooch at the height of his considerable powers in 1992 in the third one day international against Pakistan.

Indian tour.

Gooch thrived in the captaincy. His team won a Test in the West Indies for the first time in sixteen years, and only lost the series when Gooch suffered a broken hand in the third Test. Back in England, 1990 was to be his year of miracles.

The first series of the summer was against New Zealand. Gooch started off with a duck as the first Test ended in a rain-affected draw. The Kiwis were finally seen off with a victory in the last match at Edgbaston, Gooch scoring 154. Then came the Indians, and the first Test at Lord's contained one of cricket's great achievements. In almost ten and a half hours, Gooch scored 333, the first English Test triple century in twenty years. Then, when the Indians avoided the follow on, Gooch went in again and hit 123, the only time in first-class history a player has hit a triple century and a century in the same match. England won that match, the only definite result in the series. Gooch scored 752 runs in the three matches, and 1058

over the six-Test summer. Along with his record in domestic cricket, 1990 produced 2746 runs at an average of 101.70.

Gooch went on to overtake David Gower's record of runs for England but his captaincy suffered the indignity of a 3–0 reverse in India in 1992–93, and then a 4–1 hiding to the Australians the next summer. He relinquished the leadership to Mike Atherton for the West Indies tour, but played in the two home series in 1994. Ironically, he finished his Test career against the South Africans, now no longer rebels.

'I once spent a very pleasant weekend with Graham while we were both walking the Channel Tunnel; he was very good company even when he had huge blisters, but then maybe I like wet fish. He's been hard working and professional throughout his career and whatever he has got out of the game he has earned the hard way.'

DAVID GOWER

DAVID IVON GOWER
CRICKET – BATSMAN
BORN: TUNBRIDGE WELLS,
1 APRIL 1957

David Gower played more tests than any other English cricketer and, at the end of his international career, he had scored more test runs. He did all this with an ease and style that none could match. And yet David Gower's career was dogged by controversy, his attitude was frequently questioned, and he retired, some would say, when he still had a contribution to make to English cricket.

Gower's formative years were spent in Tanganyika, where his father was in the Colonial Service. On his return, he went to school in Kent before the family moved to Loughborough. Gower went to University College, London, to study law, but the call of cricket was too great and he abandoned his academic career for Leicestershire.

He made his debut at the age of eighteen, and within three years had not only been voted Young Cricketer of the Year but he had also become the brightest batting star of a new England crop. But his first season with England in 1978 with series against Pakistan and New Zealand showed why his career would be controversial. Wonderful innings would be ended by loose shots. However, the young left-hander demolished the opposition with eyecatching brilliance, notably in his debut century, 111 against New Zealand at the Oval. He went on tour to Australia and although he failed to shine in the World Cup the next year he memorably took the Indians apart at Edgbaston later that summer with an undefeated 200.

At the age of twenty-two, he was clearly one of

Gower calling the shots in 1988.

Facts about David Gower

- He was one of England's least successful captains on paper, leading his team in thirty-two Tests, winning only five and losing eighteen. However, ten of those defeats were in his ten Tests against the West Indies.

- He once lost a hire car by driving it onto a frozen lake in St Moritz in Switzerland, where it fell through the ice.

- He scored nine centuries against the Australians, level with Wally Hammond, and behind only Jack Hobbs.

- His second domestic trophy as captain came in 1991 when he led Hampshire to the NatWest Trophy in the absence through injury of Mark Nicholas

- As well as his well publicised aerial jaunts, Gower also enjoys skiing and is an afficianado of the Cresta Run.

David Gower's Career

Tests	117		
Test Match runs	8231	First-class runs	26,339
Average	44.25	Average	40.08
Centuries	18	Centuries	53

County Championship	1975 (with Leicestershire – played three matches)
NatWest Trophy	1991 (with Hampshire)
Benson & Hedges Cup	1985 (with Leicestershire)
	1992 (with Hampshire)
Sunday League	1977 (with Leicestershire)

the finest batsmen in England. He could still be frustrating, but when he applied himself there was none better. His 154 not out against the West Indies in Jamaica in 1981 was perhaps the best example of his skill being matched to great determination.

In 1983, Gower took over the captaincy of Leicestershire and that winter took over as England captain for the first time when Bob Willis fell sick in Pakistan. It wasn't the best time to captain England, as they were swept 5–0 by the West Indies at home that summer. Gower kept the captaincy for the trip to India and here he showed that, while his captaincy may not always have been the most imaginative, his buoyant personality could get the best out of his players. India is always a tough tour, but he cajoled his team back from defeat in the first Test to take the series 2–1.

The next summer, the Australians visited and Gower, desperately out of form early in the season, led England to a 3–1 win, in the process scoring three fine centuries. The pick was probably his 215 in the fifth Test at Edgbaston, a marvellous exhibition of attacking strokeplay that pushed England to an innings victory and, in doing so, decisively turned the series. Just for good measure, he guided Leicestershire to the Benson & Hedges Cup.

That was to be to be the high point of his captaincy, though. He suffered another 'Blackwash', this time in the West Indies, when his laid-back attitude was seriously questioned, and then he was unceremoniously removed as

captain after defeat against India at Lord's the next summer.

The label of underachiever proved a tough one to remove. When he was recalled to the captaincy by Ted Dexter to face the Australians in 1989, there was widespread optimism that this heralded a change in England's fortunes. It did not. Against Allan Border's tough outfit Gower led his charges to a 4–0 defeat and did not go to the West Indies that winter.

Gower was now one of England's senior players but sometimes his attitude was questioned by his peers, notably Graham Gooch. In 1990–91, he scored two centuries in Australia, but his dismissal to the last ball before lunch in Adelaide helped to damn him in the eyes of his colleagues, and when he and John Morris hired a couple of Tiger Moths and buzzed the ground during a match against Queensland, Gower's card had been marked. Things came to a head when he was not selected to tour India in 1992–93. It was not a popular decision, and rebel members of MCC forced a vote of no confidence in the selection committee, but Gower never played for England again.

His was a more memorable career than most though, and perhaps best summed up by the award he received from a national newspaper. It simply said 'For Fun, Style and Excellence'

'David always looked to me as if he was out there having fun and if he lost his wicket ,then it was just a game.'

JIMMY GREAVES

JAMES PETER GREAVES
FOOTBALL – FORWARD
BORN: POPLAR, 20 FEBRUARY 1940

Jimmy Greaves was regarded as the best forward of his generation. He was a small, wiry player who was a superb opportunist, and his record of 357 goals in 514 League matches speaks for itself, but he is as well-known for his off-field problems with alcohol. In more recent years, he has become best known as a television pundit.

Greaves grew up playing football as a schoolboy in East London. It was clear he was a major talent and he was signed by Chelsea in 1955. He was an instant hit, and scored no fewer than 114 goals in 1956–57 as an apprentice professional. In 1958–59, while still a teenager, he scored thirty-two goals and was the First Division's joint top scorer. At the end of that season he went on a tour of South America with the England team and, not three months past his nineteenth birthday, he marked his debut with a goal against Peru in Lima. Sadly England lost that game 4–1 but Greaves soon established himself in the national team. In 1960–61, he became the first player to score 100 senior goals before his twenty-first birthday and with forty-one League goals was easily the First Division's top scorer. He also scored thirteen goals in eight England appearances that year, including a hat-trick as England beat Scotland 9–3 at Wembley. However, Chelsea decided to cash their young star in, and sold him to AC Milan for a record £80,000 in 1961. It was a disastrous move. Greaves never settled into the new circumstances and within five months he was on his way back home.

Tottenham was his new club, and he joined the double winners in time to help them to the FA Cup. The next season, Greaves scored twice as Tottenham became the first British club to win a European trophy, the Cup-winners' Cup, beating

Atletico Madrid 5–1. Hopes were therefore high when Greaves travelled to Chile with the England squad for the World Cup but sadly he had a poor tournament, scoring only one goal, and England went out to Brazil in the quarter-final.

Greaves returned to Tottenham to become England's top scorer three seasons in a row. Tottenham, though a fine team, were not as good as the 1961 Double Winners, and Greaves did not find himself in the running for honours. He was, however, an England regular and, with the 1966 World Cup approaching, a lot of people looked to him to lead the England attack. Unfortunately, in late 1965 he came down with hepatitis. He missed almost four months and, in his own words, lost half a yard of pace. However, he did start as England's centre-forward but after failing to score in England's three group matches he suffered an injury and was replaced by West Ham's Geoff Hurst. Although he was fit for the final he was not included and watched from the sidelines as England won the World Cup. He only played three more times for his country, but a record of forty-four goals in fifty-seven internationals puts him third on England's all-time scoring list.

He returned to form the next season, and scored twenty-five League goals for Tottenham. That year, Tottenham also won the Cup, beating Chelsea 2–1.

Facts about Jimmy Greaves

- He was fined £50 per day he was late for pre-season training with Milan while waiting for his baby daughter to be born. She arrived almost three weeks behind schedule.

- He played in thirteen Under-23 internationals and scored twelve goals, a record.

- During England's 1962 World Cup match against Brazil the pitch was invaded by a stray dog. As Greaves was carrying it to the touchline, it urinated on him.

Jimmy Greaves's Career

Football League appearances	516	European Cup-Winners' Cup	1963
Goals	357	FA Cup	1962, 1967
International appearances	57	Member of 1966 England World Cup	
Goals	44	winning squad	

- Bill Nicholson, Tottenham's manager, did not want to saddle Greaves with the label of football's first £100,000 player when he bought him from AC Milan, so he did the deal for £99,999.

- Greaves, with Tony Fall as co-driver, took part in the 1970 World Cup motor rally from Wembley to Mexico City. It was a 16,245 mile race and went across both Europe and South America. They finished sixth out of 71 starters and Greaves counts it amongst the most difficult things he has ever done.

- Greaves scored three or more goals for England six times in his career, and achieved the feat 27 more times at club level.

Greaves in his glorious heyday with Chelsea at Stamford Bridge.

In all, he stayed at Tottenham for almost ten years, and his 220 League goals for them remain a club record. They were never quite good enough to win the League title but, under the management of Bill Nicholson, were lauded for their attractive football.

In March 1970, he moved to West Ham in part exchange for Martin Peters, and played out his last full season for them. He scored twice on his debut against Manchester City, completing a record of having scored on his debut for Chelsea, AC Milan, Tottenham, West Ham, England and England Under-23s. It is an admirable record, and perhaps the one that best illustrates his worth, as his generation's finest goalpoacher.

'Jimmy had an extraordinary gift for scoring goals that, for 9 years, made him the most fared goal scorer in the game. He scored at every level he played in, but, where as Lineker was at his best in the 6 yard box, Greaves could also take people on and beat them all around the penalty area.'

SALLY GUNNELL

SALLY JANE JANET GUNNELL
ATHLETICS – 400 METRES HURDLER
BORN: CHIGWELL, 26 JULY 1966

Sally Gunnell emerged in the 1990s as Britain's favourite female sporting personality. She was called the 'girl next door', the 'Essex girl made good' and 'good ol' Sal'. But all these tabloid headlines were typically condescending. Like so many journalistic perceptions of female British athletes, she was defined in 'human interest' terms, rather than in terms of her athletic prowess. The geographical location of her birthplace fitted the current vogue of tarring everyone from the ancient land of the East Saxons with the same brush.

In fact, Gunnell's athletic credentials suggest that she holds a unique place in British athletics, being the first and only woman to hold an Olympic, World, European and Commonwealth title at the same time.

Sally as Britannia. Her finest moment at the Barcelona Olympics.

Britain's victorious anchor in the European Cup in Birmingham in 1994.

Facts about Sally Gunnell

- Many people are surprised, on meeting her, to find that she is only five feet five and a half inches tall.

- She has twice come second in the BBC Sports Personality of the Year awards, in 1993 and 1994.

- She was awarded the MBE in 1993.

- Gunnell made the mistake of letting her mind wander as she got down on her blocks at the start of the 100 metres hurdles in the European Championships in Stuttgart in 1986. She noticed the mutilated fingertips of her awesome Bulgarian rival, Yordanka Donkova, in the next lane. She completely lost her concentration, 'blew' the race and came sixth.

- In 1995 she designed and developed her own 'state of the art' sports bra.

Sally Gunnell's Essex origins were much more typical of the rural home counties than the fabled towns along the dreaded Fenchurch Street to Southend 'Misery Line'. Her parents, who originated in Huntingdonshire, had a 300-acre farm in south-west Essex, close to Chigwell. She was born on the farm and raised as a farmer's daughter. Both her parents were good athletes in their youth, but sport wasn't a major priority until Sally went to school.

She was encouraged at school by Patricia Kaye, a keen-eyed PE teacher, to work hard at athletics. She also persuaded her to join Essex Ladies at Woodford, a good athletics club with a fine tradition.

At Essex Ladies she met her coach, Bruce Longden, who had among others Daley Thompson under his wing in preparation for the Moscow Olympics. Longden initially moved Gunnell towards the pentathlon and then to the heptathlon. But, after narrowly missing selection for the Los Angeles Olympics as a seventeen year-old in 1984, she decided to switch to a single event, the 100 metres hurdles. Within two years she was Commonwealth Champion in Edinburgh, in a time of 13.29, but didn't make it to the final in the World Championships in Rome in 1987.

It was time to think about going for the longer distance, the 400 metres hurdles. Both she and her coach were concerned about the seemingly endless flow of East Europeans in the sprint hurdles, and so the transition began.

The first hint of real potential came with an excellent fifth place in the 1988 Olympic Games in

Seoul. The following year was a year for consolidation: second in the Europa Cup, second in the World Cup and second in the overall Grand Prix. Suddenly, she was ranked number three in the world; the transition had paid off. By way of a bonus, she had also won a gold medal in the 400 metres flat at the European Indoor Championships and in doing so had broken the British record.

Medals of all colours came fresh from the mint in 1990. First, it was the Commonwealth Games in Auckland: gold in the 400 metres hurdles in front of Debbie Flintoff-King from Australia, the Seoul Olympic Champion; a silver in her 'old' discipline, the 100 metres hurdles behind British hurdler, Kay Morley Brown; and gold with the British Team in the 4 x 400 metres relay. Later in the year, it was the European Championships in Split and another British 4 x 400 metres relay medal, this time a bronze.

1991 was a World Championship year and it started auspiciously with Gunnell's appointment as the Women's Team Captain. It also ended well, with a silver medal in Tokyo, but not quite as well as it might have done. Gunnell made a mistake and got too close to the tenth hurdle, lost her stride pattern, and with it the race. However, there was no disgrace in a silver medal and a British and Commonwealth record of 53.16.

Gunnell got her revenge on Tatyana Ledovskaya, who had beaten her in Tokyo, at the Barcelona Olympics, a year later, as she caught her and the American, Sandra Farmer-Patrick, in the last third of the race to win a gold medal for Britain. 'Good ol' Sal' really had done well. But there was more to come.

1993 was World Championships year, and they were held in Stuttgart. Again, she beat Farmer-Patrick, but this time in a stunning world record time of 52.74. The 'girl next door' was now a superstar, the sponsors queued up, and the journalists formed another line; everyone wanted to know her.

The final medal in the 'full set' came in Helsinki, in 1994, with gold in the European Championships. There was also a third gold medal in the Commonwealth Games in British Columbia. 1995 was a year plagued by injury, which forced her to miss the World Championships in Gothenburg. But this only

Sally Gunnell's Career

World Record
1993		400 metres hurdles Stuttgart 52.74

Olympic Games
1992	Gold	400 metres hurdles

World Championships
1991	Silver	400 metres hurdles
1993	Gold	400 metres hurdles

European Championships
1990	Bronze	4 x 400 metres relay
1994	Gold	400 metres hurdles

Commonwealth Games
1986	Gold	100 metres hurdles
1990	Gold	400 metres hurdles
	Silver	100 metres hurdles
	Gold	4 x 400 metres relay
1994	Gold	400 metres hurdles

strengthened her resolve to add to what is already a unique collection of medals in British athletics, at the Olympic Games in Atlanta in 1996.

She described her feelings at the end of her gold medal performance at the Barcelona Olympics in revealing terms: 'Suddenly I could hear the crowd breaking into my isolation. The sound was so loud it was almost a physical pressure … there was a sea of Union Jacks waving crazily. Everyone seemed to be jumping up and down. Everyone was smiling, hurling their arms around. Everyone was looking at me. I thought, "Is that it? Is it over?"'

Gunnell also offered an insight into British Team solidarity at the World Championships in Stuttgart in 1993. Her heats and semi-final had not gone well. Linford Christie and Colin Jackson sensed something was wrong and gave her a thirty-minute morale booster. Linford said, 'Look, when we get back to Heathrow, do you really want me to be at the front with you just hanging around in the background with everyone else?'

- To Gunnell's great surprise, Sandra Farmer-Patrick, the American, who stumbled at the same hurdle as Sally in the Tokyo World Championships, later blamed her for slowing down. The video evidence gave no credence to the American's version of events.

'Sally's 'girl next door' image hides a high work ethic and lots of talent. You only have to see what she has won; maybe not in terms of the most medals, but by far the best in terms of quality. If she is back to her best in Atlanta, we will be able to assess her true standing. Her world record was beaten easily at the World Championships, by Kim Batten, of the USA, and the outcome in Atlanta is intriguing.'

MIKE HAILWOOD

STANLEY MICHAEL BAILEY HAILWOOD
MOTOR-CYCLIST, MOTOR-RACING DRIVER
BORN: OXFORD, 22 APRIL 1940
DIED: BIRMINGHAM, 23 MARCH 1981

Facts about Mike Hailwood

- He was awarded the MBE in 1967.

- He won the European Formula Two title in 1972 (on four wheels!)

- Hailwood had a brief flirtation with four wheels early in his career when he briefly drove a Lotus for Reg Parnell.

- He was multi-talented and it was said he could have been a top golfer, boxer or musician.

- Racing took its toll on him. He once admitted that 'Racing has made me an old man before my time'.

Hailwood's nickname was too easy to contrive, but it did say it all; he was, in the eyes of the motor-cycling world, 'Mike the Bike'. The only other rider ever mentioned in the same breath as Hailwood was his great rival, the Italian maestro, Giacomo Agostini. If 'Ago' was the greatest ever, and there are plenty of Brits who would dispute it – especially the Isle of Man TT fraternity – then Hailwood was certainly close behind.

He was the son of a wealthy Oxford motor-cycle dealer, and by the age of seventeen was already winning races. His first was a 250cc race, the Cookstown 200, in Ireland. His massive potential was recognised immediately. Fans flocked to see the new sensation and, within the close and knowledgeable world of bikes, he came to be revered. One of his many exploits confirmed his talents: as early as 1958 he won the 125, 250 and 350cc titles at the ACU Star Championships. The following year he added the 500cc to make it a clean sweep; and then in 1960, he did the clean sweep again.

1961 was the dramatic beginning of his halcyon days. He became the first man to win three races at

Hailwood rides an MV Augusta in the Belgian Grand Prix in 1965, on his way to a fourth successive 500cc Championship.

the Isle of Man in one week: the Senior, the lightweight 125cc and the lightweight 250cc. He only missed the quartet because of a broken gudgeon pin in his AJS, a mere fifteen miles from the finish. 1961 was also the year of his first World Championship when he won the 250cc class on a Honda.

The next seven years were phenomenal. He won the first of four successive 500cc world titles, all on an MV Agusta. He won five individual rounds in 1962, seven in 1963, seven in 1964 and eight out of ten in 1965.

In some ways 1966 was even more remarkable. Although he narrowly lost the 500cc title to Agostini, he did win three races. But he also won ten races in the 250cc class and six in the 350cc to win the world title in both classes. He repeated the double world titles again the next year with five 250cc wins and six at 350cc and had another titanic struggle with Agostini for the 500cc crown before finishing runner-up, despite winning five races. His successes over the two years in Grands Prix were unparalleled: nineteen wins in 1966 and sixteen in 1967.

During the same purple period in the world championships, Hailwood also continued to dominate on the Isle of Man. After his initial triple in 1961, he won the Junior in 1962 (the one that had eluded him in 1961) and followed it with five successive Senior titles from 1963 to 1967, added to which were the Lightweight 250cc in 1966 and the Junior and Lightweight 250cc in 1967.

He retired at his peak in 1968 to move into the cockpit of Formula One and did well enough to make the grade as a Formula One driver. But his best place was second, in 1971, at the Italian Grand Prix, in a Surtees-Ford. He scored twenty-nine points between 1971 and 1974 before retiring following a bad injury at the Nürburgring in the German Grand Prix. Whilst still in Formula One, in 1973 Hailwood won a rare distinction for a remarkable act of bravery. He was awarded the George Medal for pulling Clay Reggazoni from his blazing Ferrari at Kayalami, when others stood by and watched.

After briefly settling in New Zealand, restlessness got the better of him and he returned to the Isle of Man, the scene of his greatest days. He was thirty-eight years old. His victory in the Formula One TT, on a Ducati, brought him his tenth world title, and

Mike Hailwood's Career

MOTOR-CYCLING
World Championships

1961	250cc	(Honda)
1962	500cc	(MV)
1963	500cc	(MV)
1964	500cc	(MV)
1965	500cc	(MV)
1966	250cc, 350cc	(Honda)
1967	250cc, 350cc	(Honda)

Total Victories: (76)
125cc (2), 250cc (21), 350cc (16), 500cc (37)

Isle of Man TTs

1961	Senior, Lightweight, Ultra-lightweight
1962	Junior
1963	Senior
1964	Senior
1965	Senior
1966	Senior, Lightweight
1967	Senior, Junior, Lightweight
1978	Formula One
1979	Senior

Total Victories: (14)
Senior (7), Junior (2), Lightweight (3), Ultra-lightweight (1), Formula One (1)

MOTOR-RACING
Formula One: (48 races)
29 championship points, Best position – 2nd (1971 Italian Grand Prix)
Highest position in Drivers' championship – 8th (1972)

the following year he won his seventh Senior TT and his fourteenth title on the Island.

He retired for good after that and set up business in Birmingham. Sadly, it was a short and tragic respite from the rigours of over twenty years of life on a knife-edge. Mike Hailwood was killed in a car crash close to his home while going out to buy fish and chips with his two daughters. Michelle, one of his girls, also died in the crash.

• He never really enjoyed Formula One, saying, 'Formula One is too serious.'

'Mike Hailwood was at worst the 2nd greatest ever on a bike. At best he was one level higher. The fact that he is still talked of with reverence is testimony to his greatness. He raced in what could have been motor cycling's most exciting period. His skill and natural talent are shown by the fact he won in most classes.'

WALLY HAMMOND

WALTER REGINALD HAMMOND
CRICKET – BATSMAN
BORN: DOVER, 9 JUNE 1903
DIED: DURBAN, SOUTH AFRICA, 1 JULY 1995

Wally Hammond's Career

Tests	85
Test Match runs	7249
Average	58.45
Centuries	22
First-class runs	50,551
Average	56.10
Centuries	167

Facts about
Wally Hammond

- He in one of only three cricketers to score 1000 runs in the month of May.

- He scored two separate centuries in a match seven times.

- He twice hit four consecutive centuries (in 1936–37 and 1945–46).

- In 1928, Hammond took ten catches for Gloucestershire against Surrey at Cheltenham, and also scored a century in each innings.

- He scored more than 200 for England seven times, a record

- In the two test series in New Zealand in 1932–33, Hammond batted twice, scoring 227 in the first Test in Christchurch, and an undefeated 336 in

Wally Hammond's achievements on the cricket field mark him out as one of the finest exponents of the game the world has ever seen. He was an imperious batsman who could flay any attack, and whose record compares favourably with almost any player save possibly Bradman, a more than useful fast-medium bowler, and a truly great fieldsman. Yet, perhaps because his career was played out largely away from the cameras, and perhaps because his county was unfashionable and not terribly successful, his exploits are often overlooked today.

Hammond was born in Dover in 1903, the son of a soldier whose career took his family to China and Malta. He went to school in Gloucestershire and, as a result, decided his cricketing future lay there. Unfortunately, in those days his place of birth meant that he could only play for Kent until a two-year residential qualification period had been served, and the spurned Kent captain, Lord Harris, ensured that it was served in full. He was only able to start playing for Gloucestershire in 1920, but swiftly earned a call-up to the England team. However, once again his progress was interrupted. He was selected to tour the West Indies with the MCC in 1925–26 as in these days the West Indians were considered inadequate as Test opponents. He did well, scoring 733 at an average of over forty-five, but he contracted an illness which proved to be near fatal, and he lost the entire 1926 season.

On his return to active play, he had no equal in England. Perhaps his finest innings was one of 187 in three hours against Lancashire. He began with

five consecutive fours taken off McDonald, probably the fastest bowler in England at that time. He passed 1000 runs in May (as opposed to before the end of May) and finished that season with 2969 runs to his credit. As well as dominating county attacks around the country, he contributed hugely to an English Test renaissance culminating in the 1928–29 tour of Australia. Hammond scored 905 runs in the five-match series, including four centuries, two in the same Test. No Englishman has ever exceeded that aggregate. But Hammond was more than an outstanding batsman. He even opened the bowling for England in South Africa the previous winter, taking 5–36 in the first Test, part of a career haul of eighty-three Test wickets. In 1928, he took ten catches in a county match against Surrey, still a record for an outfielder.

Of course, the 1930s turned into the era of Bradman and, the 'Bodyline' series excepted, England found themselves a distant second throughout much of the decade. Hammond, though, still found himself briefly the holder of the individual Test record when he scored 336 not out in New Zealand in 1933. It remains the fastest Test triple century, in only 287 minutes, and the ten sixes he hit has also never been equalled.

However, performances against New Zealand were one thing. The Australians were the opponents that counted. In the Lord's Test of 1938, England slumped to 31–3. Hammond then played England out of their crisis with an innings of great authority and awesome fire-power. In six hours, he hit thirty-two fours as he bludgeoned the

Australians for 240. It was the seventh time he had passed 200 for England.

Sadly, the Second World War took six years away from Hammond. After the war he returned to first-class play, and finished top of the averages in 1946 with 1783 runs at 84.90, and then took England to Australia that winter. However, he was now forty-three, and, having played little worthwhile cricket in six years, he was now past his best and England were heavily defeated. He played his last first-class match in 1951, closing a career

Hammond on his way to do battle with the Australians at Trent Bridge in the first Test in 1930.

that lasted thirty-one years. He scored 167 first-class centuries, the third highest total of all time, including twenty-two in eighty-five Tests. In an age of great achievements at the crease, Hammond stands alongside the best, a large and powerful man whose speed, athleticism and grace destroyed the finest attacks of the day.

'Wally was the greatest English batsman of his generation, second to Bradman in the world. However, this does him an injustice because he was a magnificent all-rounder, being a good bowler and great slip fielder. His record stands the test of time.'

Auckland. His average for the series was therefore 563.00.

- He moved to South Africa after his career where he lost all his savings in the motor business. He ended his days as a groundsman-coach at Natal University.

ELLERY HANLEY

**ELLERY HANLEY
RUGBY LEAGUE – FORWARD OR BACK
BORN: LEEDS, 27 MARCH 1961**

Facts about Ellery Hanley

- A survey in 1994 suggested that Hanley was the 56th in a table of Britain's wealthiest athletes, with assets of £1.8 million. Nigel Mansell was listed at the top, with assets of £45 million.

- Maurice Lindsay, Chief Executive of the Rugby League and Hanley's former employer at Wigan, is fullsome in his praise: 'At his peak he was the greatest player I ever saw in forty years of watching rugby ... He was born with a rare spirit, a will. He's been as important to Rugby League as Bradman to cricket or Ali to boxing.'

- Hanley is a fastidious trainer, a teetotaller and a non-smoker.

Ellery Hanley is an intriguing and enigmatic character outside the game of rugby league. His refusal to have anything to do with the press, after they upset him by delving into his past several years ago, has made it difficult for scribes to offer the usual sporting deifications or, for that matter, the more frequent character assassinations.

Within the game, he is far from obscure and there is very little intrigue. He is universally regarded as the most complete rugby league footballer of modern times and by many as the greatest all-round player of any era. Much evidence is cited for his place at the pinnacle of the game: his ability to play almost anywhere – centre, stand-off, wing or lock forward; his phenomenal record as a try-scorer; his inspirational qualities and his power of leadership; and, most of all, his sheer professionalism and will to win.

The son of parents who came from the beautiful Caribbean island of St Kitts (to which they later returned), Hanley grew up in one of the toughest parts of Leeds. As a boy, it was association football that caught his imagination, not rugby league. His heroes were Pele and Cruyff, not Murphy and Fox. But he played any sport available and got better offers to play rugby league and was signed by Bradford Northern in June 1978 from the Corpus Christi amateur club in Leeds. He made two appearances that season, as a sixteen year-old, but didn't play again until 1981.

He made a huge impact and scored 127 points in his first season. In total, he scored nearly 500 points for them in four seasons, including 52 tries in 1984–85, the first time that feat had been achieved since Billy Boston scored the same number in 1961–62.

He was transferred to Wigan in September

Ellery Hanley's Career (to the end of the 1994–95 season)	
Challenge Cup Winner:	1988, 1989, 1990, 1991
Championship:	1986–87, 1989–90, 1990–91
Regal Trophy:	1986, 1987, 1989, 1990
Premiership:	1987
World Club Championship:	1987
Club appearances:	437
Club tries:	384
Test appearances:	36 (19 as captain)
Test tries:	20

1985 and became part of an astonishing era of success at Central Park. He scored thirty-five tries in his first season and fifty-nine in his second and, over the six seasons he played for them, a total of 189, at an average of over thirty per season. The silverware had to be brought in by barge at Wigan Pier: three Championships, four Challenge Cups, four Regal Trophies, three Lancashire Cups and one Premiership. Wigan also won the World Club Championship in 1987.

Hanley was also an outstanding player for Great Britain. On the 1984 tour of Australia, he played on the wing and scored twelve tries. Then, in 1988, when he became the first black player to captain Great Britain, he scored eight more and led

Britain to an historic third Test victory over Australia, its first Test win in ten years.

He went through a period of serious injury problems in the late eighties but came through them and transferred to Leeds, his home town, in September 1991. By the end of his fourth season, he had already scored over 100 tries for the Yorkshire team, including forty-five in 1994–95.

As the number of playing years available to Hanley began to diminish it did not suggest a diminishing of his role within rugby league. He was always a players' player, greatly respected as a motivator. He possessed a First Grade coaching qualification, one of the few leading players to have one, and was made coach to the Great Britain team. He may offer as much to the game in the future as he has in the past.

'Ellery has it all and can play just about anywhere. When he's playing anything is possible. Not just a natural talent, his professionalism and hard work are legendary. If he doesn't want to talk to the press, so what? Why can't we just enjoy those magical moments he has given us, for these are the best adverts rugby league has to offer.'

- Denis Betts, his former colleague at Wigan, said of Hanley: 'He's a great professional and he speaks for all the professionals on the pitch. He doesn't need to say another word to anybody.'

- Hanley was awarded the MBE in 1990.

- Both his transfer fees, £85,000, from Bradford to Wigan in 1985 and £250,000, from Wigan to Leeds in 1991, were world records.

- He captained Great Britain nineteen times, more than any other player.

- The last word on Hanley should go to Hanley himself. The normally silent rugby legend did give an interview to the highly respected interviewer (and fellow Yorkshireman), Michael Parkinson. These were Hanley's final words: 'In the end there's not much of a mystery. All I ever wanted to do was play rugby, enjoy it and hope the spectators enjoyed watching me. Then, one day, they might remember. That way, you're part of history, aren't you?

Hanley being a handful against Wigan.

DAVID HEMERY

DAVID PETER HEMERY
ATHLETICS – HURDLER
BORN: CIRENCESTER, 18 JULY 1944

Facts about David Hemery

- His British record was finally beaten after 23 years at the 1991 Tokyo World Championships by Kriss Akabusi.

- Hemery's opinion on the event: 'The secret of the 400 metres hurdles is keeping your rhythm in spite of the heaviness growing in your legs as the race progresses.'

The 400 metres hurdles is one of the toughest of all Olympic events. Not only must the athlete possess the speed of the 400 metre runner, it must be combined with the discipline and technical ability to maintain the same stride pattern around the whole lap. Hemery's performance in the 1968 Olympics was as complete a run as had been seen, and revolutionised his event.

Although born in Britain, Hemery spent ten years of his early life at the Thayer School in Massachusetts. He did not return to England until 1962 but, after only a couple of years as a promising junior high hurdler, he returned across the Atlantic to enrol in Boston College. He represented them at collegiate meetings in the USA, although he regularly returned to Britain for international matches. However, his times at both high hurdles and 440 yards hurdles were relatively modest, until suddenly he burst onto the international scene in 1966 with a string of world-class performances. He broke the British record for the high hurdles with a time of 13.9 seconds, and then won the Commonwealth title in Kingston,

Jamaica. Although 1967 was largely spoilt by injury, Hemery was considered a definite medal prospect for the 400 metres hurdles in Mexico City.

Standing in his way, though, were three very talented Americans: Geoff Vanderstock, Ron Whitney and Boyd Gittins, all with times superior to his own. However, Hemery gave Gittins and Vanderstock a nasty surprise by beating them at the NCAA Championships, in a British record time of 49.8 seconds. He took two-tenths of a second off that time shortly before leaving for Mexico, and was clearly reaching the peak of his form.

The 400 metres programme consisted of three rounds over three days. Hemery coasted through the opening section and then, after watching his team-mate John Sherwood set a British record time of 49.3 seconds in the semi-final, calmly matched it in his own race. The final, though, was special. Hemery did not take complete command of the race until the sixth of the ten hurdles, but he went through 200 metres in 23 seconds exactly, the fastest time ever. Remarkably, he maintained the pace, and was yards clear as he flew over the final hurdle. He crossed the line in 48.12 seconds. It was 1.2 seconds faster than he had run before, and it shattered the world record.

Hemery then went on to St Catherine's College, Oxford and, having achieved all he had set out to do as a hurdler, decided to try the decathlon. By the end of the season, he had reached seventh place on the British all-time list but decided his lack of power in the throwing events would count against

David Hemery's Career

Olympic Games

1968	(Mexico City)	400 metres hurdles	1st
1972	(Munich)	400 metres hurdles	3rd
		4 x 400 metres relay	2nd

European Championships

1969	(Athens)	110 metres hurdles	2nd

Commonwealth Games

1966	(Kingston)	110 metres hurdles	1st
1970	(Edinburgh)	110 metres hurdles	1st

World Record 48.12 Mexico City 1968

Hemery in the middle of a famous line-up, including Britain's Stuart Storey (left) and Alan Pascoe (right) and France's Guy Drut (no 1)

him. He reverted to the high hurdles instead, winning a silver medal in the European Champonships and, the next year, successfully defending his Commonwealth title.

Hemery decided to take a break from competition in 1971 but returned in time for the Munich Olympics. This time, though, Hemery was himself the victim of a phenomenal performance. He was still going well on the final bend when suddenly the Ugandan John Akii-Bua, in lane one, tore past him on the inside. Hemery's Olympic gold and world record were gone. He had to be content with bronze, although he did get a silver as part of the 4 x 400 metres relay squad, but his era had drawn to a close.

'Dave tried to recruit me when I was a young man, and he was head coach at Boston University – I decided not to go but he never held it against me. Dave is also one of the few members of the 'nice guy to finish first' club. There is a great chapter in his autobiography about the final in the Mexico Olympics. It draws such a complete picture that when I had finished reading it, I was breathless.'

- Hemery competed briefly on the American professional athletics circuit after the Munich Games.

- After retiring from competition, Hemery went back to Boston as head coach.

STEPHEN HENDRY

STEPHEN GORDON HENDRY
SNOOKER PLAYER
BORN: EDINBURGH, 13 JANUARY 1969

Many snooker observers consider Stephen Hendry to be the greatest snooker player there has ever been. Perhaps Joe Davis may have gone on for longer, perhaps Steve Davis may have won more championships, but no one, they believe, when he plays at the peak of his form could have been better than the young Scotsman.

Hendry was introduced to snooker when he received a quarter-sized table for a Christmas present and, within a fortnight had notched up a fifty break. He soon moved up to a full-sized table and, as a youngster in the junior tournaments in Scotland, was winning more often than not.

He turned professional in 1985, at the age of sixteen, and debuted at the Crucible in his very first season. He was the youngest player ever to make the final stages of the tournament, and he didn't disgrace himself, losing a close battle with Willie Thorne. It was invaluable experience, and the next year he was starting to be cast as Steve Davis's future threat. His manager arranged for the teenager to play a series of challenge matches against the World Number One in Scotland and,

---

'The only problem I can see for Stephen is that he is in danger of making it look just too easy and that makes it boring for people to watch. They don't care how much talent you have or how hard you work, they want the thrill of close contests. Come to think of it, Stephen would probably like more challenge himself so that he doesn't get bored over the next decade or two. With all that said, when marking, you can only mark for what he has achieved so far and not for his potential.'

---

although Davis won all six encounters, Hendry had learned a lot. 'I know how to beat him now', he told his manager, Doyle.

Davis was still some distance off, but Hendry moved closer to his Holy Grail. He took defending champion Joe Johnson to the last frame in the 1987 World Championship quarter-final after losing 7–1 at one stage. Later that season, he became the youngest winner of a world-ranking event when he took the Rothmans Grand Prix, beating Dennis Taylor 10–7 in the final. The kid had arrived.

His inexorable progression paid off when he became the first world champion of the 1990s. He had been the best all season, winning three major tournaments, and faced Jimmy White in a final of startling brilliance. The thirty frames took slightly more than six hours playing time, an average of twelve minutes apiece. Hendry took the lead on the first day, a 108 break seeing him 9–7 ahead, and then he took only forty-five minutes to convert that into a six-frame lead on the second afternoon. The final result was 18–12 and Hendry, the youngest-ever world champion, had reached his pinnacle.

With the exception of a hiccough in 1991, Hendry has been world champion ever since, and has got better and better. Perhaps his finest victory was in 1992. He trailed 14–8 to Jimmy White before a wonderful sixty-four clearance in the last frame of the afternoon session pulled him back to four behind. With White having been fifty-two ahead, it was the break that turned the tide.

**Facts about
Stephen Hendry**

● He was drawn against
Lee Doyle in a junior
tournament at Stirling.
After the match, Lee
said, 'I think I've just
played the future world
champion.' Lee's father
Ian agreed and
became Hendry's
manager.

● His cue was once
stolen. On its recovery
he was overwhelmed,
saying, 'Oh my baby,
it's sleeping next to me
tonight. I'll never leave
it alone again.'
Snooker players can
have special
relationships with the
tools of their trade.

● Stephen Hendry has
been the world number
one every year since
1990.

● He was awarded the
MBE in 1993.

**The perfect player. On his
way to a fifth world title in
1995 at the age of 26.**

Hendry won eight straight frames in the evening, finishing with breaks of 134 and 112. 'I can't feel gutted,' said White, 'Stephen played like God.' The two met again in the 1994 final. This time White nearly beat the Scotsman, but a cool 58 break in the deciding frame gave Hendry a memorable win.

In 1995, he made a 147 break on his way to another world title, and then hit another maximum in the UK Open. Despite the arrival of a lot of talented young players, Hendry, still only in his mid-twenties, has perhaps still not reached the peak of his form. Who knows what records he might eventually set.

GRAHAM HILL

NORMAN GRAHAM HILL
MOTOR-RACING DRIVER
BORN: HAMPSTEAD, 15 FEBRUARY 1929
DIED: ARKLEY, 29 NOVEMBER 1975

Facts about Graham Hill
• As a young man he was in an accident which left him with a badly twisted left leg which was an inch shorter than the right.

Graham Hill was the charismatic extrovert in one of motor-racing's most exciting eras, the 1960s. He was the perfect foil for the more introverted Scot, Jim Clark, as they swapped Formula One Drivers' Championships throughout the decade.

Hill has often been described as 'the worker' to Clark's 'instinctive talent'. It is also true that in the lists of the all-time greats – Fangio, Senna, Stewart, Clark, Prost – Hill's name is rarely included. His supporters find the former, 'damning with faint praise', irritating and the latter omission inexplicable. His record of achievements is certainly impressive.

Graham Hill's Career

World Drivers' Championship:	**1962, 1968**
Winner Indianapolis:	**1966**
Grands Prix Victories: (14)	
1962	Dutch, German, Italian, South African
1963	Monaco, United States
1964	Monaco, United States
1965	Monaco, United States
1968	Spanish, Monaco, Mexican
1969	Monaco
Grands Prix Summary:	
14 wins from 176 races	
Total points:	270
Pole positions:	13
Fastest laps:	10
Winner Le Mans:	**1972**

For example, his Formula One Drivers' Championship statistics from 1961 to 1969 read as follows: 1961, thirteenth; 1962, first; 1963, second; 1964, second; 1965, second; 1966, fifth; 1967, sixth; 1968, first; 1969, seventh. During this time he won fourteen races and accumulated 252 championship points – not bad for one of the workers!

Hill also achieved a unique triple in motor racing, in having won the Formula One Drivers' Championship in 1962 and 1968, the Indianapolis 500 in 1966, and the Le Mans twenty-four-hour race in 1972. In fact, he won the Indy 500 at his

first attempt — a feat that was thought to be impossible in modern times.

It would also be quite difficult to convince the passionate and knowledgeable racing fans of the principality of Monaco that Hill was merely a 'determined worker'. He won on the tortuous streets of Monte Carlo five times in seven years, in 1963, 1964 and 1965 and again in 1968 and 1969. As the Monagasques would be at pains to point out, their princely paradise is much more a haven for the world's stylishly flamboyant than for the workers of the world.

However, even Hill's most fervent supporters would accept two truisms about him: he was very very determined and he did start his life-long involvement in motor-sport as one of the workers. His rakish good looks, the pencil moustache, the gentlemanly demeanour and the cutting wit were not the product of public school and a life of ease and comfort. He served as an artificer engineer in ships' engine-rooms in the navy, didn't drive a car until he was twenty-four because he couldn't afford one, and started on the Lotus racing team as a mechanic. It was a hard apprenticeship, but at least, throughout his career in the driver's seat, he knew what was going on around him better than most.

Damon, the two-year-old heir apparent, pointing the way for his father in 1962.

• He took up rowing, because he was looking for a sport he could sit down in, and then stroked London Rowing Club's eight to victory at Henley in the Grand Challenge Cup.

Graham Hill sporting his distinctive 'rowers' helmet in his final year of competition, 1975.

- He hadn't fully recovered from his two broken legs when he raced in South Africa in 1970. He had to be lowered into his seat. In great pain, he managed to finish sixth.

- He always drove wearing a blue helmet with eight vertical white strips – the symbol of the eights' blades from his days at London Rowing Club.

Hill began his Formula One career with Colin Chapman at Lotus and drove for him in 1958 and 1959 but with little success. He then switched to BRM (British racing Motors) and again, for a couple of years, got nowhere. Then in 1962 BRM finally got the new 1.5 litre formula right, Hill won the Dutch, German, Italian and South African Grands Prix and the title was his. The next three years were all second-place finishes for Hill and his BRM, including a titanic struggle, in 1964, when Surtees joined Clark and Hill in a three-way British battle which went all the way to the final race in Mexico, before Surtees eventually took the title.

The formula for Formula One changed again in 1966, this time from 1.5 litres to 3 litres, and Hill eventually surprised everyone in the sport by giving up his number-one position at BRM to join Clark's Lotus team. 1967 was a fallow year for Hill as his new team-mate won four races, but with Clark's tragic death at the beginning of 1968 it fell to Hill to carry the team through the season. He did so magnificently, winning in Spain, Monaco and Mexico and taking his second World Championship. Graham Hill continued to race for another six years, even after breaking both legs at Watkins Glen in 1969, but with little success. He finally retired in 1975 and formed Embassy-Hill, his own team.

He was flying his own light aircraft into Elstree airport with five members of his team after a successful pre-1976 season test session at the Paul Ricard circuit in France, when he hit some trees in freezing fog and crashed onto Arkley golf course. Everyone on board was killed. Graham Hill was forty-six years old.

'He may or may not be mentioned in the same breath as the all-time greats, but he has done more than enough to be in the top half of our list. Very popular with the public due to the fact that he was so out-going and always seemed to be having a good time.'

JACK HOBBS

SIR JOHN BERRY HOBBS
CRICKET – BATSMAN
BORN: CAMBRIDGE, 16 DECEMBER 1882
DIED: HOVE, 21 DECEMBER 1963

'Summer-time means Oval-time, and Oval-time means Hobbs.' 'The Master' really did have no equal. His name is still liberally sprinkled throughout the record book and, given the preponderance of one-day cricket, most of those marks are probably untouchable. He scored more runs than anyone else (61,237) and hit more centuries (197), despite losing four years to the First World War.

Hobbs did not begin his first-class career until the age of twenty-two. He was a great admirer of Tom Hayward and, on the great man's recommendation, he qualified by residence for Surrey. On his debut, against a Gentlemen of England XI captained by WG Grace, he scored eighty-eight. Within a fortnight, he had scored 155 against Essex and was instantly rewarded with his county cap. This was swift progress indeed from a man who was to say that he didn't think of playing for England, cricket just seemed the best way of making a living.

Hobbs had a superb eye, which enabled him to move to the pitch of the ball very early. He was a completely natural player, and the only coaching he

ever received came from his father, a groundsman at Jesus College, Cambridge, who told him 'Never back away from the ball' after the young Hobbs took evasive action against an off-break.

In 1907, Hobbs was touring for England against the Australians and, two winters later, in South Africa, he scored 187 in Cape Town. From that point on, he was marked as England's premier batsman. In 1911–12, England beat Australia 4–1 'Down Under' and Hobbs scored three centuries in the series, and in 1914 Surrey became County Champions. Then, of course, the Great War interrupted everything.

When play resumed in 1919, Hobbs was thirty-six, an age when most careers are coming to a close. Hobbs, meanwhile, went from strength to strength. He made 132 centuries after the war, ninety-eight of them were scored after he reached the age of forty. He was a formidable attacking batsman. One of his favourite memories was sharing a stand of over ninety in thirty-five minutes to win a game against Kent, and he scored 100 before lunch twenty times. In 1923 he scored his 100th century and then, amidst immense public interest, overhauled WG Grace's career total of 126 centuries two seasons later. The occasion was a match at Taunton against Somerset. He started the match one century behind Grace, and had moved to ninety-one by the close of the first day. The second, a Monday, saw huge public and media interest. Journalists, even newsreel cameramen, had come down from London overnight and when Hobbs scored the nine runs needed to complete a century there was pandemonium. The game was held up as the crowd rose to him, and every Somerset player shook his hand. Grace's total

Jack Hobbs's Career

Tests	61
Test Match runs	5410
Average	56.94
Centuries	15
First-class runs	61,237
Average	50.65
Centuries	197
County Championship	1914

Facts about Jack Hobbs

- In 1925 he hit sixteen centuries and broke WG Grace's record for centuries. He was forty-two years old.

- His innings of 316 not out for Surrey against Middlesex at Lord's in 1926 was the highest score at Lord's until 1990.

- In 1926, he became the first professional to lead his team onto the field, when captain AW Carr was sidelined by tonsilitis during the fourth Test against Australia at Old Trafford.

- John Arlott wrote of Hobbs, 'No one ever batted with more consummate skill than his, which was based on an infallible sympathy with the bowled ball.'

'The Master craftsman'; testing the tools of his trade in 1922.

- He was the first cricketer to be knighted, in 1953, for services to the game.

- He scored 1000 runs in a season twenty-six times, and a century in each innings on six occasions.

- The Hobbs Gates at The Oval were named after Surrey's most famous player.

- Hobbs was only ever run out once, by a direct hit from Don Bradman in the first Test of the 1928-29 series with Australia. Bradman was making his Test debut.

equalled, the media packed up and went home. The next day, Hobbs hit another century in a run chase to complete a ten-wicket win. The landmark was still greater, but this time largely unrecorded.

What Hobbs enjoyed most was the challenge of a difficult wicket. On the 1928–29 tour of Australia Melbourne served up a frightful 'sticky' on which it was confidently predicted England could score no more than seventy. Hobbs and Sutcliffe put on 105, and England won the Test by three wickets to clinch the series.

Hobbs was also an occasional bowler, but was of more use in the field. He was an excellent cover, and ran out fifteen batsmen on the 1911–12 tour of Australia, lulling them into a false sense of security with his apparent lethargy.

He was, of course, still a valued member of the England team. His record of 12 centuries against Australia still stands, and in 1924–25 he once more scored three centuries. In 1926, he scored 100 at the Oval as England won the Test to regain the Ashes for the first time since the War. His Test career finally came to an end at the end of the Oval test of 1930. He was then forty-seven years old.

Hobbs finally retired in 1934. He had made 197 centuries, and there was regret that he did not stay on to complete 200. Hobbs was certain he had made the

right decision, though. By then, he was fifty-one, and felt he had nothing to offer the Surrey team. Also, he did not wish to be seen as an object of sympathy.

Hobbs's play was remembered as much for the dignity of his personality. He was popular with team-mates and opponents alike and, according to Wilfred Rhodes, he could have scored many more centuries had he not given his wicket away when Surrey were in an impregnable position to let a colleague have a bat.

He could play all shots equally well but had no particular favourite. As he once said, 'You like them all when you can hit them hard.'

'A lot of sportspeople have nicknames. Most mean nothing, and are just to catch your eye, but some of these really are deserved. In Sir Jack's case, 'The Master', really meant what it said. As a British batsman Hobbs was supreme. It was the quality of his run scoring, his dependability at wicket and his length of career that set the man apart. Some in the game will tell you how much harder it is now to reach the top, but Hobbs, or anyone else for that matter, can only play the balls bowled to them. He still had to stay around for 28 years to score those 61,237 runs!'

LEN HUTTON

SIR LEONARD HUTTON
CRICKET – BATSMAN
BORN: PUDSEY, 23 JUNE 1916
DIED: KINGSTON-UPON-THAMES 6 SEPTEMBER 1990

Len Hutton's Career

Tests	79
Test Match runs	6971
Average	56.67
Centuries	19
First-class runs	40,140
Average	55.51
Centuries	129
County Championship	1935, 1937, 1938, 1939, 1946, 1949 (shared)

Sir Leonard Hutton was one of the greatest batsmen of all time. That much is clear from a cursory glance at his statistics; yet he could have been even greater. He lost six of his very best years to the war. He went on to become the first professional to be appointed captain of England and, in 1956, was only the second cricketer to be knighted for his services to the game.

Hailing from Pudsey, near Leeds, Hutton was, by a kind accident of birth, qualified to play for the finest county of his day. Yorkshire were champions seven times in the 1930s, but Hutton still managed to force his way into the first XI in 1934 at the age of only eighteen. By 1937, he had forced his way into the England team, and scored nought and one on his debut against New Zealand. The selectors kept faith with him, and he scored a century the next time he batted. The next year the tourists were the Australians, led by the incomparable Bradman.

A stroke of genius, 'Sir Len' Yorkshire cricket's most famous son.

Facts about Len Hutton

- During the war he broke his left arm so badly in an accident during commando training that it required three bone grafts and an eight-month stay in hospital to mend. It ended up two inches shorter than his right.

- He scored 1294 runs in June 1949, and 1050 in August of the same year, the only man to score 1000 runs in two months in the same season since the War.

- He was out 'Obstructing the Field' for England against South Africa at The Oval in 1951. A ball from Rowan ballooned off the top-edge and, in protecting his wicket with his bat, he prevented wicket-keeper Endean from taking a catch.

- Hutton twice carried his bat for England, in 1950 against the West Indies at The Oval (scoring 202) and in 1950–51 against Australia at Adelaide (156).

The visitors retained the Ashes with a win at Leeds in the Fourth Test; however, the Fifth Test belonged to Hutton.

On a perfect batting wicket against, it must be said a moderate Australian attack, Hutton batted for thirteen hours. As a boy of fourteen, he had been present at the 1930 Headingley Test to see Bradman plunder 334. His innings of 364 upstaged that and was the highest ever seen in a Test match. Hutton batted with impeccable concentration, being especially harsh on Australia's unlucky spinner Fleetwood-Smith. His figure of 1–298 have a special place in cricket history. By the end of the second day, Hutton had reached exactly 300, and the next morning 30,000 people packed the Oval to witness more history being made. In the middle of the morning session, a perfect cut off Fleetwood-Smith raced to the boundary. The ground rose in acclamation, and every Australian congratulated Hutton. England's score of 903–7 declared remains the highest in Test cricket. The winning margin, an innings and 579 runs, also remains unsurpassed.

Sadly, the war deprived Hutton of what might have been the greatest years of his career. However, when cricket resumed Hutton and Yorkshire were once more County Champions. In 1949 Yorkshire shared the championship with Middlesex, and in June of that year Hutton was truly invincible. He scored 1294 runs, a record for any single month, and finished the season with a total of 3429, the second-highest ever. He was sometimes accused of being a negative batsman, but he was very often required, especially for England, to shore up an unreliable batting side. Compton called him, 'The greatest opening batsman I have ever seen ... His powers of concentration were remarkable, but, when he wanted to be, he was one of the best stroke-makers in the game.'

England toured Australia in 1950–51, and, although it was not a great success (England lost 4–1), Hutton's batting kept the team together. His average for the series was 88.83, over fifty better than any of his colleagues, and forty-five better than any Australian. Hutton was clearly England's most important player and in 1952, for the home series with India, he became their captain.

His appointment was controversial. For the first time, a professional was trusted with the most

important job in English cricket. It was not unprecedented. Hobbs and Compton had taken over the role because of incapacitation on previous tours, but the job had been seen as the preserve of the amateur, one who might play the game in the correct spirit. Hutton proved to be an unqualified success. India were easily seen off, by three Tests to nil, and the next year Hutton steered England to the Ashes for the first time in twenty years. In 1954–55, he expertly handled the young fast bowler Frank Tyson as England won a series Down

A huge ovation from the crowd at the Oval in 1938 after his world record 364 against Australia.

- His appointment was controversial. For the first time, a professional was trusted with the most important job in English cricket. It was not unprecedented. Hobbs and Compton had taken over the role for short spells in the field because of the incapacitation of the captain, but the job had always been seen as the preserve of the amateur, one who might play the game in the correct spirit. Hutton proved to be an unqualified success. India were easily seen off, by three Tests to nil, and the next year he steered England to the Ashes for the first time in 20 years. In 1954-55, he expertly handled the young fast bowler Frank Tyson as England won a series Down Under by 3-1.

- On his retirement, Hutton remained involved in cricket, acting as a selector in the mid-seventies.

Under by 3–1. He was never the most robust of men, and he retired shortly after being stricken with lumbago during a match against the South Africans in 1955.

On his retirement, Hutton remained involved in cricket, acting as a selector in the mid-1970s. Hutton was a great natural talent. He could play any shot, and his cover drive was especially attractive. He put efficiency above all else though, and never gave up his wicket lightly. That, after all, is the first rule of batting.

'It is intriguing to think how much closer to Hobbs he could have been had the War not taken away those six years. Not a big man, he relied more on the positioning of feet and the balance of a gymnast to supply him with the timing that his strokes demanded. By all accounts he was a quiet, shy man who conquered both to lead his country. The game of cricket was always his first love and he was a real gentleman.'

TONY JACKLIN

ANTHONY JACKLIN
GOLFER
BORN: SCUNTHORPE, 7 JULY 1944

Facts about Tony Jacklin

- He was awarded the OBE in 1972 and the CBE in 1990.

- Jacklin was the son of a Scunthorpe train driver and learned the game by caddying for him at Scunthorpe Golf Club.

- At sixteen he went to work in the Appleby Frodingham Steelworks.

- He turned pro a year later and in his first year was sixtieth in the Order of Merit, earned £344, and became Rookie of the year.

- In 1967 he won the Dunlop Masters at St Georges, Sandwich, but more importantly, he scored the first televised hole-in-one on British television at the 165-yard sixteenth.

- Jacklin's prize money when he won the Open in 1969 was £4250.

Tony Jacklin was to British golf what a brilliant comet was to the ancient civilisations: lighting up the sky for a brief but tumultuous few months and being a portent for things to come.

In 1969 Jacklin won the Open Championship at Lytham. At that moment British and European golf changed. It took a few years to materialise, but Europe in general, and Britain in particular, ceased to be the game's poor relations. He had already won in the US, at the Greater Jacksonville Open – the first British golfer to do so since Ted Ray in 1920 – and when he beat Bob Charles at Lytham in 1969 he became the first British winner of the Open since Max Faulkner, in 1951. In the year of Neil Armstrong's giant step, Jacklin made one for European and British golf.

He opened with an excellent sixty-eight, two shots behind Charles, the left-handed New Zealander, who broke the course record with a sixty-six. Jacklin then hit two seventies to go into the final round with a two-shot lead. By the eighteenth, on

Tony Jacklin's Career

Major Championships

British Open	1969
US Open	1970

Ryder Cup appearances:
1967, 1969, 1971, 1973, 1975, 1977, 1979

Summary:
(35 matches) 13 wins, 14 losses, 8 halves

European Tour victories:	13
US Tour victories:	3

the final day, he needed a bogey, or better, on the par-four to win. Henry Longhurst described one of the most famous drives in British golf, 'I saw the shot from just behind him and I shall remember it to the end of my days. His swing never left him and this might have been the practice ground. It might also have been fired from a rifle instead of a golf club – miles down the dead centre, veering neither to right nor left. He tossed the second up to within ten feet and won with the shortest putt that ever won a championship – call it three-eighths of an inch.'

In many ways, what Jacklin went on to achieve at Hazeltine in the US Open in 1970, was even more remarkable. The course at Chaska, Minnesota, was the second longest in US Open history. There were blind shots to eleven greens and a host of invisible bunkers. Dave Hill, who came second, commented, 'All the course lacks is eighty acres of corn and four cows.' It blew a gale on the first day; Palmer, Player and Nicklaus shot seventy-nine, eighty and eighty-one respectively. Jacklin was undaunted and full of confidence. He went two-up with an opening round of seventy-one, three-up with a second round of seventy, four-up after another seventy on the third day and eventually won by an amazing seven shots, after a third consecutive seventy. He became only the second man to win with all four rounds under par.

Jacklin stayed in contention for a while after the wonderful exploits of his year of two major championships. He was fifth in the 1970 Open and third in 1971 and won occasional tournaments as late as 1982. But the major titles eluded him, until, of course, his marvellous record as captain of the European Ryder Cup Team in recent years.

Much has been written about the impact on

Proudly raising the claret jug, and the fortunes of British and European golf.

Jacklin's future career of an incident while playing against Lee Trevino in 1972. It happened in the Open, at Muirfield, on the seventeenth green, in the final round. Trevino holed from an apparently hopeless position off the back of the green and Jacklin, already safely on, inexplicably three-putted for a six.

It was suggested that he never really recovered from the disappointment of that day. But that kind of simplistic explanation works better for golfers who have never won anything, and 'choke' on the big occasion, than for Jacklin who was a proven

winner. A far more plausible interpretation lies with the demanding nature of the game. Few players win consistently at the highest level over a long period. Jacklin's peak was shorter then most but more brilliant than all but a rare few.

'One of our most influential golfers, he helped to restore the image of British golf. In this company his time spent at the top was fleeting, but it still had impact.'

COLIN JACKSON

**COLIN RAY JACKSON
ATHLETICS – HURDLER
BORN: CARDIFF, 18 FEBRUARY 1967**

Facts about Colin Jackson

- He first tried the hurdles in his school sports hall aged twelve. He enjoyed them so much he tried to push in the queue for another go and was sent out.

- His personal best in the long jump is a wind-assisted 7.96 metres, not far off the British record.

- He shared, with long jumper Mike Powell, the prize of twenty gold bars for winning the 'Golden Four' Grand Prixs in 1994.

- In 1994, he had eleven sub 13.20 times and won all eighteen finals in which he competed.

- Jackson and close friend Linford Christie have founded a management agency called 'Nuff Respect'.

Opposite: Jackson pointing the way forward to the European Championship in Helsinki in 1994.

Colin Jackson is a combination of master technician and master sprinter. To go 110 metres over ten high hurdles in thirteen seconds requires more than just speed. Jackson, with an earlier reputation as a 'choker' now firmly behind him, can take his place as one of the all-time greats of this event.

Born in Cardiff to Jamaican parents, Jackson was discovered by Malcolm Arnold at a school sports day. By the time he was eighteen, he had run 13.69 seconds for the hurdles, and he'd excelled at high jump, long jump and javelin. His path may have taken him towards the decathlon, but when he became World Junior champion in 1986 in a time of 13.44 seconds his path was set. Arnold realised Jackson only needed to master one

Colin Jackson's Career

Olympic Games

1988 (Seoul)	2nd
1992 (Barcelona)	7th

World Championships

1987 (Rome)	3rd
1993 (Stuttgart)	1st

European Championships

1990	1st
1994 (Helsinki)	1st

IAAF (International Amateur Athletic Federation) Male Athlete of the Year 1993

World Record: 12.91 seconds, Stuttgart, August 1993

discipline to get to the top. When he went to Rome and pulled off a bronze medal, Britain clearly had a future champion in their ranks.

He had a marvellous Olympics in Seoul. Inspired by the performance of close friend Linford Christie, he chased Roger Kingdom home to pick up a silver medal. He had Kingdom firmly in his sights the next year when the American came across for the Grand Prix season in Europe, and beat him on four occasions. By the end of that season, he had recorded the fastest twenty-one times by a British athlete over the 110 metres hurdles. Becoming European champion in 1990 was simply a natural progression.

However, the bane of any sportsman's life is injury. Jackson had an operation on his right knee in 1990, and his left in 1991. Despite this, he was still installed as favourite for the Barcelona Olympics. In his first heat, he was superb. He ran 13.10 seconds and was slowing down as he went over the line. Behind him Canadian sprinter Mark McKoy saw that performance and decided to set his sights on the silver medal. Instead the Canadian was to end up with gold. Jackson failed horribly, barely scraping into the final and then trailing in seventh. He was devastated. It transpired later that he had a rib injury which, given the highly tuned mechanics of hurdling, affected the position of his trailing leg. Others, like silver medallist Tony Dees, suggested the problem was psychological.

Jackson had the chance to prove them all wrong the next year, at the Stuttgart World Championships. He had a lot of doubters, but with only a slight following wind he stopped the clock at 12.91 seconds. The world champion had broken the world record, shaving a hundredth

Hurdling to the top of the world. Jackson in Stuttgart in 1993.

of a second off Roger Kingdom's time. After the Championships, he embarked on a run of success that, between August 1993 and February 1995, brought him forty-four successive victories at sprint hurdles both indoors and out. He also completed the unprecedented double of 60 metres flat and hurdles at the 1994 European Indoor Championships.

Injury meant that Jackson could not defend his world title in 1995, but Jackson has other priorities. He wants the 1996 Olympics in Atlanta

to make up for the disappointment of Barcelona. No one could accuse him of lacking 'bottle' now.

'Colin has the chance in Atlanta to become only the second man to win Olympic-World Championships-European-Commonwealth and hold the World Record. This should tell you the pedigree of the man. On him being a choker? Sometimes you go out there and there just happens to be someone faster – just like being a gun fighter in the old West.'

PAT JENNINGS

PATRICK ANTHONY JENNINGS
FOOTBALL – GOALKEEPER
BORN: NEWRY, 12 JUNE 1945

Pat Jennings's Career

FA Cup
Winner 1967   (Tottenham)
Winner 1979   (Arsenal)

League Cup
Winner 1971   (Tottenham)
Winner 1973   (Tottenham)

UEFA Cup
Winner 1972   (Tottenham)

Club appearances

Watford	57
Tottenham	596
Arsenal	327
Total	880

International appearances
119

Pat Jennings was one of British football's most respected players. He had an amazing aura of quiet confidence in the most demanding of the eleven roles in a football team. All goalkeepers make mistakes, but he somehow seemed to be the exception to the absolute truth of human fraility. He was at his best during a wonderful period in English football from the late 1960s and into the 1970s, and for several years was widely acknowledged as the best goalkeeper in the world.

Softly spoken, his deep resonant voice was delivered with a lyrical Irish brogue. Although he spoke softly, he carried big hands. He had an ideal physique for a goalkeeper. He was tall and athletic with a tremendously gymnastic leap. And he really did have big hands, big enough to catch the ball one-handed, a technique that brought gasps from the crowd whenever he tried it. He also had a prodigious kick with both feet and could drop-kick his clearances almost as far as his clearances on the full.

There were more spectacular goalkeepers than Pat Jennings, but none more reliable. He was a professional player for twenty-three years and an international for twenty-two. In total, he played over 1000 games of senior football and won 119 caps for Northern Ireland, a world record at the time.

His career began with his home team, Newry Town, but he joined Watford in 1963 at the age of eighteen for a fee of £6000. Within a year he was at White Hart Lane, where he would become a Tottenham legend. He was there for thirteen seasons and played in some of Spurs' greatest teams. He made 596 appearances and won an FA Cup-Winners medal in 1967 against Chelsea, and two League Cup-Winners medals against Aston Villa in 1971 and against Norwich in 1973. He also won a UEFA Cup medal in 1972 against Wolves, in an all-English clash, when Spurs won 3–2 on aggregate. There were many personal honours for Jennings during these years, including being voted Footballer of the Year in 1973, and the Professional Footballers Association (PFA) Player of the Year in 1976.

To many people's surprise, especially to Jennings himself, he was sold to North London rivals Arsenal, in August 1977, for £45,000. Spurs were convinced that the Irishman was past his best at thirty-two, and that they had an ideal replacement in Jennings' under-study, Barry Daines. Arsenal were convinced that they had got a bargain.

Arsenal's judgement proved to be the shrewder

Facts about Pat Jennings

- When Arsenal lost, on penalties, to Valencia in the European Cup-Winners Cup final in 1980 it was surrounded by more bitter moments. First of all, they played an unprecedented number of games that year: they were the first English Club to play seventy matches in a single season and were exhausted. Secondly, they had lost the FA Cup final only four days earlier to West Ham, by a single goal after a titanic three-replay semi-final against Liverpool. And thirdly, they had a chance to qualify for Europe in the following season's UEFA (Union of European Football Associations) Cup if they won their last two League games. They won the first one against Wolves two days after the Valencia game, but collapsed 5–0 against Middlesborough two days after that. Their season ended in ruin. In the final fifty days of the season they played eighteen matches – lucky old Arsenal?

- Jennings was awarded the MBE in 1976 and the OBE in 1987.

Jennings watching one of his many throws initiate another Arsenal attack.

- He once scored a goal directly from a clearance kicked out of his hands. It was against Alex Stepney in the Manchester United goal, in the Charity Shield game in 1967. The game ended in a draw, 3–3.

- His two-footed drop kicks, salmon-like leaps and one-handed catches, were all techniques developed during the years Jennings played Gaelic Football. During this time he didn't play football as the Gaelic governing body, the GAA didn't approve of foreign games.

- He left school at fifteen and became a 'bobbin boy' at a spinning mill.

- Keith Burkinshaw, the Tottenham manager, later admitted to the monumental blunder of letting Jennings go to Arsenal in 1977. Barry Daines, Jennings' replacement, never fulfilled the expectation Spurs had of him and Burkinshaw eventually had to pay £300,000 to prise Ray Clemence from Liverpool.

of the two, but probably by much more than even they had imagined.

Jennings played on for another eight seasons for Arsenal. He played in three consecutive FA Cup finals – in 1978, 1979 and 1980 – losing to Ipswich in 1978 and West Ham in 1980, but collecting a winners medal in 1979, 3–2 against Manchester United, in what became known as the 'last five-minute Cup final'. He also played in his second European final when, in the 1980 European Cup-Winners Cup final, he watched agonised as Graham Rix missed a penalty in the shoot-out against Valencia that meant the Spaniards went home with the trophy.

Jennings's world-record international career was also established while with Arsenal. He played in

the World Cup tournaments in Spain in 1982, where Northern Ireland made it to the second phase of the competition, and in Mexico in 1986. The 1986 campaign signalled the end of his professional career.

He returned to White Hart Lane in 1993 as goalkeeping coach and continued an active life in football, a game he graced as a player like few others in British football.

'Longevity and reliability are the watch words with Pat, more efficient than spectacular. I read somewhere that Pat had said that the one handed saves were made when he was out of position or in trouble!'

BARRY JOHN

BARRY JOHN
RUGBY UNION – FLY-HALF
BORN: CEFNEITHIN, 6 JANUARY 1945

'The King' leading his men against New Zealand in 1971.

If Max Boyce's famous Welsh fly-half 'factory' ever did exist, it wasn't underground in the valleys. It was probably in production somewhere amidst the green hills of West Wales. It could have been in Cefneithin, a mining village between Llanelli, Swansea and Carmarthen, or it could have been at the local school, Gwendraeth Grammar School.

Carwyn James lived in Cefneithin, so did Barry John. Gwendraeth was where John learned his rugby. Around Carwyn and Barry, and a few more brave men in scarlet, Max Boyce embroidered the stories that reflected the greatest era in Welsh rugby. Not that Boyce exaggerated anything (much), he simply put into words everyone's emotions as they witnessed the great deeds. Like every Welshman, he could describe what he saw and could say what he said, because 'I was there.' And he was there to witness the feats of the one man who came to symbolise that special era in Welsh and British rugby, the 'King' himself, Barry John.

John had qualities in rugby like those of George Best in football: natural, instinctive; almost

Facts about Barry John

- His attitude to school was as carefree as his attitude to rugby. 'No, not academic, me. If the pass-mark was fifty, I'd get fifty-one. I'd just clear the crossbar. Why not, still get your three points, eh?'

- John would communicate with his scrum-half, Gareth Edwards, in Welsh if they didn't want the opposition to understand their plans.

- One of the best lines ever written about him was in 'Fields of Praise'. He was described as the 'dragonfly on the anvil of destruction who ran in another dimension of time and space'.

- When the Welsh team walked into the post-match dinner, in Paris, after their famous Grand Slam victory in 1971, the entire French team stood and applauded.

- He did such an outstanding job of embarassing Fergie McCormick, the Kiwis' full-back, with his kicks into space, during the first Test of the 1971 Lions Tour, that McCormick was never picked again. The Lions' tactic was quite deliberate because they

Barry John's Career

International appearances: 25

International points:
5 tries
6 conversions
13 penalties
8 drop goals
Total 90 points

British Championships:
1969, 1970, 1971, 1972

Triple Crown:
1969, 1972

British Lions Tours:
1968 South Africa
1971 New Zealand (a record 180 points on the NZ Tour)

transcendent. He was similarly ghost-like; a 'will-o'-the-wisp', who drifted past defenders as if they weren't there. Strangely enough, he always had an affection for soccer and thought it an ideal companion for a rugby half-back: 'The best game to develop skills for rugby. In a way, I think all fly-halves are frustrated soccer inside-forwards, fantasising about being at Old Trafford or Anfield or the Maracana – because, in both positions, you have to be born with the balance, the touch, the decisiveness, the boldness.'

Barry John was the son of a miner, one of six children. He played in the U-15s at Gwendraeth at the age of twelve. He started playing for the 'green and golds' of Cefneithin at the age of sixteen. His rugby mecca was Stradey Park where he would go and watch the scarlets of Llanelli on the 'tanner bank' with all the other boys from the village. Carwyn James was his idol; the man who would become his coach during his greatest days. It wasn't long before John was wearing the scarlet jersey himself. Later, he made the move to Cardiff where he would begin the famous partnership with scrum-half, Gareth Edwards.

John and Edwards didn't play together in their first few internationals and neither they nor Wales did particularly well. Their partnership began in

1967, against New Zealand – it was another defeat and another unsuccessful season. However, the new duo was impressive enough to be selected for the Lions party to tour South Africa, in 1968. Unfortunately, John was flung to the ground by the Springboks' centre, Jan Ellis, in the first test, breaking his collar-bone. He took no further part in the series.

John's influence on Wales began to take effect from the next home season onwards. The Welsh won the Five Nations Championship and the Triple Crown, in 1969, but they did less well on the subsequent tour to Australia and New Zealand, where they won only one test.

His greatest days followed immediately afterwards. Wales shared the Championship in 1970, won the Championship and the Triple Crown in 1971, and again shared the Championship in 1972. In between, he was the brightest star in the British Lions firmanent in New Zealand, in 1971. His performances in this short period were nothing short of miraculous.

On tour in New Zealand, he scored a record-breaking 180 points in sixteen matches as the Lions humbled Colin Meads' All-Blacks on home turf. Of the many examples of John's brilliance on that tour, a try he scored against New Zealand Universities, is remembered with special fondness. It seemed to typify everything about him. John Reason, the *Sunday Telegraph* rugby correspondent, wrote: 'The try left the crowd at Athletic Park absolutely dumbfounded. John had touched the ball down between the posts and was trotting back to take the conversion himself, before the realisation of what had happened sent the applause crashing round the ground.'

An equivalent moment of magic occurred in the 1971 Grand Slam decider at the Stade Colombes, in Paris. John scored a sensational try to clinch the game after Jeff Young won a scrum against the head. His pace, a dummy pass, a shimmy here and a shimmy there and he was in the clear. He called it the most important try of his life.

Barry John retired at the end of the 1972 season, at the age of twenty-seven. He was at his peak, but no amount of pleading would persuade him to change his mind. His reason was simple and a lesson to all who become too fond of the trappings that are associated with modern sport: he was losing touch with his own identity, the real Barry John. He left us to our memories of Barry John, the rugby 'god', and returned to being Barry John, the boy from Cefneithin; but not before he expressed his reasons better than anyone else could. He was opening a new bank in North Wales:

'There were a lot of people there, nice people. But I felt totally alienated. They clapped me, but such well-meaning warmth had become a barrier. When I was introduced to the head cashier she was shaking with excitement and actually curtsied. Curtsied! Everyone thought it was funny, but I was very, very upset. It was confirmation of my total alienation from real life. I drove home thinking, "I

'"The king" was the most revered player in what was probably the most exciting era in rugby history. A born natural if ever there was one. Many of us could learn from his reasons for retirement: he didn't like being the person people thought he was. How much self control does it take to quit when you still have so much more to give? As a boy growing up in the late '60s, early '70s, I knew of Barry John, but knew nothing of rugby so I guess he must have crossed a few barriers to reach the likes of me.'

may as well be their puppet, their mascot, their rag-doll". I said to myself, "That's it, finish. In future I am going to be me again, the real me with all my faults and weaknesses and a few plusses ..." and, I got home and I said to Jan, "That's it Love, the end".'

knew McCormick was the Kiwis' best choice and would rather play against anybody else.

- Barry John earned all his fame and adulation from an amazingly small number of major appearances. He played only twenty-five times for Wales and five times for the British Isles, while his international career lasted only six years.

- In the famous piece of dialogue between John and Edwards when they first met to discuss tactics, it was Barry who said, 'Look Gareth, you throw them — I'll catch them.' John later revealed Edwards' reply: 'Don't worry about my passes. I can get them to you from anywhere. Just make sure you catch them, that's all.' Barry John always did.

Poetry in motion. Perfectly balanced and perfectly poised; the complete footballer.

ANN JONES

ADRIANNE SHIRLEY JONES (NÉE HAYDON)
TABLE TENNIS PLAYER, TENNIS PLAYER
BORN: BIRMINGHAM, 7 OCTOBER 1938

Facts about Ann Jones

- The late Ted Tinling, who designed dresses for all the great women champions, wrote the foreword for Jones' autobiography. He described her with great affection and said she was the only player he ever saw who had genuinely golden hair.

- She had a severe virus at the age of eleven and the doctors told her parents that she had little chance of surviving. But, after a very long illness, she recovered with no ill-effects.

- One of her first press reports, when she was fifteen, by Frank Rostron in the *Daily Express*, said that she should smile more and called her the 'grim-faced champion'. She didn't seem to have too many problems with this later in her career.

Ann Jones's Career

Table Tennis

Singles	Runner-up	1956
Womens Doubles	Runner-up	1953, 1956
Mixed Doubles	Runner-up	1955, 1956

Tennis

FrenchSingles	Winner	1961, 1966
Womens Doubles	Winner	1968, 1969

Wimbledon

Singles	Winner	1969
Mixed Doubles	Winner	1969

In addition Jones was also a finalist in thirteen Grand Slam finals, six Singles and seven Doubles

Ann Jones made the transition from an era when tennis was a genteel game for 'nice girls' to an age when it became a tough competitive sport like any other. What's more, she did it without losing any of the honest values which typified the 'niceness' of the traditional game, while being able to 'whip' her groundstrokes and 'punch' her volleys on a par with the most determined and aggressive of her modern opponents.

Her quest to win tennis' greatest honours, a goal she largely achieved, was a reflection of her immense courage and dedication. She was universally respected in the game and taken to their hearts by British tennis fans who lived with her disappointments and shared her successes from the mid-1950s to the early 1970s.

For many years Ann Hayden (as she was then) blossomed with a small, hard bat rather than a highly strung racket. She was born into a table-tennis family who lived in the countryside to the south of Birmingham. Her father was a famous table tennis player and captain of the English team for many years, while her mother had also represented her country at the game.

She travelled abroad with her parents while they played and she developed a love for the competitive sporting environment, foreign travel and languages. In 1952, she became the youngest player to represent her country in a junior table tennis match against Wales at Henley. She was fourteen.

But, by then she was also playing the version of tennis where the balls have hair. In 1953 she played the Junior Wimbledon tournament for the first time and won it in 1954 and 1955. However, she was still winning major table tennis tournaments, including the French Championships in December

1956. At the World Championships in Tokyo the following year, Jones and her partner, Ivan Andreadis, lost in the final of the mixed doubles to the American pair, Erwin Klein and Leah Neuberger. Then in Stockholm in 1956 she suffered the huge disappointment of losing the finals of the singles and both the doubles in the World Championships. It was her fifth defeat in a world final. The growing influence of lawn tennis and various disputes about the style and design of bats in table tennis, meant that Jones slowly lost interest in the latter and the former began to take over her life.

She was one of an outstanding generation of young British tennis players which emerged in the 1950s and formed a powerful Wightman Cup team, including Christine Truman and Angela Mortimer. She made it to the Wimbledon semi-final in 1958, a stage she would reach on many more occasions, and played twelve times in the Wightman Cup, where she had an outstanding record.

At first she performed much better on clay and was a committed base-liner. She won the French title in 1961 and 1966 and was runner-up in 1963,

A deceptively good athlete, volleying at full stretch in 1970 as the reigning Wimbledon Champion.

1968 and 1969, and won the doubles in 1968 and 1969.

After turning professional in 1968, her game took a turn for the better. She had a winning position against Billie-Jean King in the Wimbledon final of that year, at 6–4 and 5–3, before eventually losing in three sets. But 1969 was the finest year of her career. She was a semi-finalist in both the singles and the doubles in Australia and won the doubles in Paris before laying aside all the ghosts of her Wimbledon disappointments by winning the singles title. It was a great occasion in front of a home crowd praying for her to win. She had to beat the two best players in the world to do so, Margaret Court (10–12, 6–3, 6–2 in the semi-final) and Billie Jean King (3–6, 6–3, 6–2 in the final). She rose to the occasion brilliantly to earn the respect of everyone in the game. To add to the excitement, she also won the mixed doubles with Fred Stolle.

Jones didn't defend her title in 1970 and made only one more appearance at Wimbledon, in the doubles of the Centennial Championships in 1977. She continued to be actively involved in tennis after her retirement from competition, turning to administration and television work as well as devoting herself to Pip Jones, whom she had married in 1962, and their family.

'Ann Jones was at her best during the start of the new era of professionalism. The old guard always resist no matter what the sport. The only thing that really has to change is the administration's attitudes and the workers make a few quid above board. By the time Ann finished, the British tennis fans had seen her go from 'also ran' to champion.'

- Jones' many post-competition jobs included: WITA (Women's International Tennis Association) Director of Operations 1980–87; ITF (International Tennis Federation) representative on the Women's Professional Tennis Council; and captain of all the British Women's team events in the 1980s.

- She became an international referee in 1985.

- Her record in the Wightman Cup was: twelve appearances, 1957–67, 1971 and 1975, winning sixteen of thirty-two rubbers (ten singles, six doubles). In the Federation Cup it was: eighteen Ties, winning twenty-one of thirty-four rubbers (ten singles, eleven doubles).

- Jones was English Junior Champion three times as a table tennis player, as well as winning Junior Wimbledon twice.

- She was the first left-hander ever to win the women's singles at Wimbledon.

- For a time, the British press called her a 'perennial loser' – great bunch of guys!

KEVIN KEEGAN

JOSEPH KEVIN KEEGAN
FOOTBALL – FORWARD
BORN: ARMTHORPE, 14 FEBRUARY 1951

Facts about Kevin Keegan

- His grandfather was a miner, and was involved in the Stanley Pit Disaster of 1911.

- After joining Hamburg, Keegan found himself back in front of the Anfield Kop a few months later when Hamburg met Liverpool in the Super Cup. It was an embarassing occasion for him. Liverpool won 6–0.

- He was once described by Duncan McKenzie as 'the Julie Andrews of Football'.

- Like a number of famous sportsmen, Keegan has been tempted by the record industry. His contribution, *Head Over Heels in Love* was recorded while he was at Liverpool. Sadly, his sporting ability was not enough to carry it to the top of the charts.

Kevin Keegan is the ultimate self-made player. He was never the most gifted player, but hard work turned him into a two-time European Footballer of the Year, England captain, and a truly successful player and manager.

Keegan was born in a small mining town near Doncaster, and, although he showed promise as a schoolboy, his small stature (only five feet eight inches), put off many scouts. He was eventually discovered playing for a Sunday League team, and signed up as an apprentice by Scunthorpe United. He broke into the first team as a right winger, and it was obvious Scunthorpe had a prize on their hands because the big clubs soon started to pay attention. In the summer of 1971, Keegan chose Liverpool and for £33,000 the Mersey giants had a bargain.

Keegan settled into a very profitable striking partnership with John Toshack and, under the guidance of Bill Shankly, a dynasty was created. In 1973, Liverpool were champions, and overcame Borussia Moenchengladbach to take the UEFA Cup. This trophy, Liverpool's first in Europe, was especially satisfying for Keegan, who scored twice as Liverpool tore the Germans apart for a 3–0 first-leg win. It was only just enough, as Borussia came back to win the second match 2–0, but that season set the standard for almost two decades of virtually uninterrupted success at Anfield.

The next year Keegan was once again the hero, as he scored twice in a 3–0 FA Cup final rout of Newcastle. Keegan was as much a creator as scorer, but he was a man for the big occasion. He had also now forced his way into the England team. He had been picked against Wales in a 1972 World Cup qualifier, but had not played to his full potential. He was selected again for the 1974 Home Internationals and from then on was a regular until 1982.

Kevin Keegan's Career

Football League appearances	500
Goals	171
Bundesliga appearances	90
Goals	32
International appearances	63
Goals	21
European Cup	1977
UEFA Cup	1973
	1976
Football League Championship	1973
	1976
	1977
FA Cup	1974
Bundesliga Championship	1979

In 1976, Liverpool once more completed the double of League Championship and UEFA Cup. In the latter competition, Keegan once more rose to the occasion, scoring a vital goal in the second leg of the final at Bruges to give his team a slender 4–3 aggregate win. The next season, Liverpool were at their best. They were in the running for a unique treble in May. After confirming their second consecutive title, they faced Manchester United in the FA Cup final. Unexpectedly, they lost 2–1, which was not the best preparation to go forward to Rome four days later to face Borussia Moenchengladbach for the European Champions' Cup.

Although England had had much success in the other European competitions, only Manchester United had ever won the Champions' Cup. Keegan gave one of the performances of his career, running the tough German centre-back, Berti Vogts, ragged. Eventually, Vogts ran out of

- A lot of Laker's wickets were catches taken in a 'leg-trap', a close ring of fielders on the leg-side. This fielding formation would be illegal today, as now only one man is allowed behind the bat on the leg-side.

On his way to another haul of wickets for Surrey against Sussex in 1957 and yet another County Championship, their seventh in eight years.

options ar
which, co
club a
for the
of £50
and SV
Hama
giants
won spinning finger. He used to soak his right forefinger in surgical spirit before the start of each season to harden the skin, but even then it would cut and, towards the end of his career, develop arthritis. He left Surrey and became registered for Essex in 1962, appearing occasionally for the next three years. After his retirement he became a noted cricket writer and commentator until his relatively early death, aged sixty-four.

'Jim Laker's incredible 19-wicket achievement against Australia should not cloud us to the other highlights in an outstanding career that befits a man rated as the world's best spinner.'

HAROLD LARWOOD

HAROLD LARWOOD
CRICKET – BOWLER
BORN: NUNCARGATE, 14 NOVEMBER 1904
DIED: SYDNEY, AUSTRALIA, 21 JULY 1995

Harold Larwood's Career

Tests	21
Test wickets	78
Average	28.35
First-class wickets	1427
Average	17.51
County Championship	1929

Facts about Harold Larwood

- He emigrated to Australia in 1949, and became close friends with Bert Oldfield, the wicketkeeper he had felled in Adelaide.

- He was awarded an OBE in 1995, shortly before his death.

- Larwood was a fair batsman, and hit three centuries in first-class cricket. His final Test innings of 98 was his highest in international cricket.

- Before joining Nottinghamshire, Larwood's job in the mines had been as a pit-pony boy. At slightly under five feet eight, he was not too tall for the role.

When the term 'Bodyline' is included in a cricketing conversation, the name Larwood is probably not far behind. Yet Larwood was a far better cricketer than is often realised, and certainly many who saw him consider that there could never have been a faster bowler.

Larwood was a Nottinghamshire miner who appeared for his county in 1924, at the age of nineteen. He was fair-haired, not particularly tall and of medium build, but he generated tremendous pace with an outstanding, almost textbook action. He ran about eighteen yards in to bowl, gradually accelerating, and opened his shoulders fully on the delivery stride, putting so much into the delivery that, when bowling at full pace, his knuckles would touch the pitch on his follow-through. Here, indeed, was a bowler of rare talent, and in only his third full season he was selected against the 1926 Australians. In the decisive fifth Test at the Oval, with Australia needing 415 to win, Larwood made the ball fly off the pitch. He quickly dismissed Woodfull and McCartney as the Australians were dismissed for 125 to give England the Ashes. He was taken on the tour of Australia in 1928–29, and started promisingly, but fell away as the series progressed. Back in England, though, he regained his form, and Nottinghamshire won their first County Championship in twenty-two years (and their last until 1981).

When the Australians arrived in 1930, Larwood was faced not only with Bradman in full cry but also a succession of featherbed pitches. He was

hammered mercilessly by the Don as the Ashes were prised from English hands. He did not play for England again until the next summer when, under new captain Douglas Jardine, he was selected for one Test against New Zealand. Jardine was still captain during the winter of 1932–33 as England prepared to travel to Australia, and had devised a new plan to win back the Ashes, or at least counter the batting of Bradman. 'Leg Theory' was a pace attack directed at the leg stump, for all intents and purposes the batsman's body. It would be supported by a packed legside field ready to snap up any chance offered, either by a mishook or a defensive shot. It required fast bowlers to make it work, and England selected Bowes, Voce and Larwood for the purpose.

In the first Test at Sydney, Larwood and Voce swiftly made inroads into the Australian batting which was devoid of Bradman, although McCabe scored 187, and demonstrated how leg theory might best be combated. Larwood took five wickets in the innings and then, with the Australians facing a first innings deficit of 164, removed Woodfull for a duck. He took five more scalps as England won by ten wickets. There were murmurings from the Australian camp about the fairness of Jardine's tactics. However, Australia squared the series on a lifeless pitch in Melbourne, and the scene was set for Adelaide.

A very lively pitch had been prepared and, after England had been bowled out for 341 on the second morning, Australia batted. In only his second over, bowling to a normal field, a short

Larwood unleashing another fearsome thunderbolt.

delivery from Larwood reared and struck Woodfull over the heart. The Australian captain recovered after lengthy treatment to be greeted by the sight of Jardine setting a leg field. The crowd, incensed, booed Larwood on every step of his run. In conversation with the MCC manager, Woodfull made his famous remark, 'There are two sides out there, and only one is trying to play cricket.' The next day, there was even more controversy when the Australian wicketkeeper Oldfield was felled by a Larwood bouncer while attempting to hook. Once again, Larwood was not using the leg theory at the time, but the sight of Oldfield prone in the middle of the pitch came close to causing a riot. The Australian Board of Control fired off a cable of protest to the MCC. It nearly caused a severing of cricket relations between the two countries as the MCC defended their team in the strongest terms. The Australians, while still aggrieved, agreed to let the tour take its course. That involved England winning the Ashes, with the 338-run victory being followed by another win in Brisbane.

Larwood once again troubled the Australians with his pace in the final Test in Sydney, taking his first three wickets for only fourteen, but it was with the bat that he caused most chaos, lashing ninety-eight after being sent in as nightwatchman. However, during the second innings, he was troubled by a foot injury, and was reduced to bowling in short bursts. An X-ray revealed a broken bone, and Larwood's Test career was over. Larwood was unrepentant about the controversy. 'I have no excuses for my bowling which I shall always hold needs no excuse. My conscience is absolutely clear that I have never bowled at a batsman, and I know I never shall,' he wrote.

On his return to England, he found that his injury curtailed his speed. He still bowled fast medium off a short run, but his best days were past. He finally retired in 1938. Larwood always sensed that he had been made something of a scapegoat for the Bodyline tour, and complained that he was not picked against the 1934 Australian tourists for political reasons. It was a shame that an honest cricketer should end his career feeling he was a scapegoat.

'Harold Larwood was the main reason we won the Ashes in 1932/33. He was made the scapegoat for the use of the 'Bodyline' tactic which was introduced by the captain of the day, Douglas Jardine. Things became so heated that questions were asked both in our own and the Australian parliament. As I see it, he was only doing his job within the rules.'

DENIS LAW

DENIS LAW
FOOTBALL – FORWARD
BORN: ABERDEEN, 24 FEBRUARY 1940

Denis Law's Career

League Championship:	1965, 1967
FA Cup Winner	1963
Total Club appearances	452
Total Club Goals	217
International appearances	55
International Goals	30

(a record, shared with Kenny Dalglish)

European Footballer of the Year	1964

Facts about Denis Law

- The clenched fist wasn't his only distinctive feature. He always wore his shirt outside his shorts and his spiky blond hair often hinted at a punk rocker ten years before his time.

- Law didn't have the best of disciplinary records. His fiery temperament and willingness to match the aggression of any of the defenders who tried to intimidate him got him into lots of disciplinary trouble. He was twice banned for twenty-eight days.

- He needed surgery to correct an eye defect which made him squint and even afterwards had good vision in only one eye. Prior to the surgery, which took place while already at Huddersfield, he played with one eye closed.

The late Sir Matt Busby was rumoured to be a shrewd judge of a footballer. He had this to say about Denis Law: 'He was the quickest thinking player I ever saw, seconds quicker than anyone else. He had the most tremendous acceleration, could leap to enormous heights, his passing was impeccable, and no other player scored as many miracle goals as Denis Law.' The Stretford End at Old Trafford, who have also cast their eyes over one or two good players over the years, have no doubts about their favourite, even in comparison to 'George' and 'Bobby' and the child-god, Duncan Edwards. Denis Law was the 'King' of Old Trafford – always was, always will be. Even those 'not worthy' to be in the presence of Eric, would 'ooh' and 'aah' much more about the legendary exploits of Denis the Menace, than those of Cantona, Giggs and Hughes.

Law was the first 'modern' player in British football, the first to communicate directly with the terraces, the first to salute the crowd. He paid homage to them, as much as they adored him. They knew that the tribal king's clenched fist, clutching the cuff of United's red shirt to celebrate a goal, was a battle cry. Law was the King of the first soccer bribe of the 1960s.

He was the youngest of seven children from a tenement block in Aberdeen which housed thirty families. His father worked on the fishing trawlers and his mother struggled to raise a family, largely on her own. Law's upbringing was particularly harsh because he was born during the Second World War and its economic impact was still felt until the early 1950s.

Law was determined to be a footballer from as far back as he could remember and played well enough as a schoolboy to be enticed away to Huddersfield at the age of fifteen. He played his first game for Huddersfield while still only sixteen and played for Scotland as an eighteen year-old in 1958, becoming the youngest Scottish cap since 1899.

He left Huddersfield to go to Manchester City in 1960 for a British record fee of £55,000, but stayed for only a year before joining several other British exports in Italy. Torino paid £100,000 for him in the hope that he could emulate the feats of John Charles at neighbouring Juventus. Charles and Italy fell in love; Law – like so many other British players – never came close to a bit of passion, let alone love.

Law was back in Manchester the following year, but wearing the blood red of Manchester United rather than the sky blue of Manchester City. He made his debut for Manchester United in 1962 against West Bromwich Albion and scored in a 2–2 draw. A year later Matt Busby, the United manager, introduced George Best to the Old Trafford faithful. The great Busby team of the 1960s, the third outstanding team he was to create during his reign at Old Trafford, was about to take shape around the famous trio: Bobby Charlton, George Best and Denis Law.

The first honour came at the end of the 1962–63 season when Law scored in the FA Cup final as United beat Leicester City, 3–1. He was voted European Footballer of the Year in 1964, and in 1965 and in 1967 won League Championship Winners medals.

Unfortunately, as the decade wore on, Law became increasingly troubled by a knee injury and it caused him to miss United's greatest night of celebration, when Matt Busby's journey of faith came to an end at Wembley in 1968. When United finally won the European Cup against Benfica, Law was lying in a Manchester Hospital recovering from surgery.

Injury continued to inhibit Law's career until he was given a free transfer to Manchester City in 1973. But there was a final ironic twist to that tale. By the end of the 1973–74 season, United stared relegation in the face. Busby had retired and many of his great team had either retired or were past their best. In the penultimate game of the season, United had to win against, of all teams, Manchester City, to have any hope of survival. With eight minutes to go, and the score 0–0, a city player found the ball at his feet with

The Law salute to the faithful at Reading in 1970.

his back to goal, only two yards from the line. He calmly back-heeled it into the net, condemning United to the Second Division. He didn't give his customary salute to the crowd, but simply walked away, head bowed, back to the centre circle. It was the only time Denis Law never acknowledged the faithful in either a blue shirt or a red.

He finally retired from football after the 1974 World Cup in Germany where he made his final appearance against Zaire. He had played fifty-five times for his country and scored thirty goals, a record shared with Kenny Dalglish.

Law pursued a successful career as a broadcaster and commentator after his retirement from football and brought the same passion, enjoyment and forcefulness to the microphone that he displayed for his tribe of football fanatics.

'Denis was the fans' 'man', because he shared their passion, showed them he cared, and enjoyed the game they loved.'

- Bill Shankly was the reserve team coach at Huddersfield when he first saw the young Law. 'He looked like a skinned rabbit,' was his caustic assessment.

- Having missed the European Cup final in 1968, Law's fondest memory was his opening goal in the 1963 FA Cup final against Leicester City at Wembley, when United won 3–1.

- Law's goalscoring feats at Old Trafford were remarkable: 171 goals in 305 League appearances, thirty-four goals in forty-four FA Cup games and twenty-eight goals in thirty-three European games.

- He refused to go to Grammar School despite having passed the tests to do so, because they didn't play football — only the alien rituals of cricket and rugby.

- Matt Busby first saw Law in a youth cup game when Huddersfield played Manchester United years before he eventually went to Old Trafford. Busby offered the Huddersfield manager, Andy Beattie, £10,000 on the spot for Law's services, but was refused.

LENNOX LEWIS

LENNOX CLAUDIUS LEWIS
BOXING – HEAVYWEIGHT
BORN: FOREST GATE, 2 SEPTEMBER 1965

Facts about Lennox Lewis

- Lewis was taken to Kitchener, Ontario by his mother at the age of nine after his parents divorced.

- He started boxing at the age of thirteen at the Kitchener Police Club.

Arguably the most talented heavyweight to be born in Britain this century, Lennox Lewis became the first British World Champion at that weight this century. Like the previous British-born incumbent, Lewis also learnt his boxing abroad. Bob Fitzsimmons, who became world champion in 1897, was born in Cornwall but taken to New Zealand by his parents. Lewis left London as a boy for Canada, and it was there that his skills were honed.

At close to six feet five inches, Lewis was a feared amateur fighter. He represented Canada in the 1988 Olympics, defeating Riddick Bowe on points in the final of the Superheavyweight division. His next step was to turn professional but, rather than do that in his adopted home, Lewis chose to come back to London. It was a controversial thing to do. Some felt that Lewis wished to become a very big fish in the small pool of European heavyweights. However, Lewis confounded that judgement by setting up home in east London, and fighting as much as possible in front of the British public.

Lewis's first professional fight was a two-round knock-out of the unheralded Al Malcolm at the Albert Hall in June 1989. Indeed, his first thirteen fights were against opposition largely selected to give Lewis experience rather than problems. In October 1990 he stepped up a grade and beat Jean Chanet of France in six rounds to give himself the European Championship. In his next bout, he took on Gary Mason, the British champion and a game if rather limited fighter. Mason took him seven rounds before the referee intervened, to give Lewis his second championship belt.

In July 1991, Lewis met Mike Weaver at Lake Tahoe in America. Weaver had once been WBA Heavyweight champion, but was now a spent force. Lewis took six rounds to stop him. He had rarely been in any trouble in his fights, but had not always been exciting to watch. This had caused problems. Other contenders knew he was more than capable of beating them, but he was not the box-office draw that a former Olympic champion ought to be.

Eventually, one of the main boxing bodies sanctioned a Lewis fight as a title eliminator. In October 1992, he fought Razor Ruddock in London and, demolished the Canadian in two rounds. It was a display worthy of a champion and that was Lewis's reward. In December, Riddick Bowe, who held three versions of the title, and whom Lewis had beaten in Seoul, gave up the WBC belt rather than sign for a defence against

Lennox Lewis's Career

Fights 28, Wins 27, Losses 1

Olympic Games

1984 (Los Angeles)	Quarter-final
1988 (Seoul)	1st (Superheavyweight)

World Championship fights

1993 WBC v Tony Tucker	W	points	12 rds	Las Vegas
1993 WBC v Frank Bruno	W	RSC	7 rds	Cardiff
1994 WBC v Phil Jackson	W	RSC	8 rds	Atlantic City
1994 WBC v Oliver McCall	L	RSC	2 rds	Wembley

European Championship fights

1990 v Jean Chanet	W	RSC	6 rds	Crystal Palace
1991 v Gary Mason*	W	RSC	7 rds	Wembley
1991 v Glenn McCrory*	W	KO	2 rds	Kensington
1992 v Derek Williams**	W	RSC	3 rds	Kensington

*also for British title   **also for British and Commonwealth titles

Lewis. Britain had its first heavyweight champion since Bob Fitzsimmons, although the effect was rather spoiled when Bowe called a press conference and ostentatiously threw the WBC belt into the bin.

Lewis set about proving he was a real champion. He outpointed Tony Tucker in Las Vegas, and then clubbed Frank Bruno into submission by the seventh round in Cardiff. This was the first time two British boxers had ever met for a World Heavyweight title, and Lewis had proved himself the better of the two. His next defence against Phil Jackson in Atlantic City ended in another win, this time in eight rounds. It took his record to twenty-five wins in twenty-five contests. However, Lewis had not looked impressive against inferior opposition, and he was badly caught out in his next fight.

Oliver McCall was a tough but limited boxer when he came to London in October 1994 to meet Lewis. His chief claim to fame was to have been Mike Tyson's sparring partner. He did have a good right-hand punch, as Lewis discovered when he walked straight onto it in the second round. The way back for Lewis will be hard, but as the most proficient British Heavyweight of his time he has every chance of success.

'It must be easier now to win a boxing title than before – more titles, more chance. At the time of writing, a question I'd ask is, how come the second best heavyweight in Britain is World Champion and the best isn't? The only reason that Lennox is at a lower place in the ranking than Frank Bruno is the impact factor, because in the other categories he is equal or better in my reckoning.'

Preparing for his title elimination against 'Razor' Ruddock in 1992.

- He was an outstanding Gridiron fullback at high school and was offered college scholarships to take this talent further.

- At the age of seventeen, he sparred with a boy named Mike Tyson at Cus d'Amato's training camp in the Catskill Mountains.

ERIC LIDDELL

ERIC HENRY LIDDELL
ATHLETICS – SPRINTER, RUGBY – WINGER
BORN: TIANJIN, CHINA, 16 JANUARY 1902
DIED: WEIXION, CHINA, 21 FEBRUARY 1945

Eric Liddell's Career

ATHLETICS

Olympic Games

1924 (Paris)	200 metres	3rd
	400 metres	1st

AAA Championship Wins

1923	100yrds, 220yrds
1924	440yrds

RUGBY UNION

Appearances	7
Tries	4

Facts about Eric Liddell

- Liddell played in seven Rugby Union Tests for Scotland in 1922 and 1923. Only one was lost, his last against England, and he nearly won it by going close to a try in the very last minute.

- The site of his death, in a remote area of Shandong province in China, is now commemorated by a plaque in his honour.

- On the Sunday on which the 100 metres heats at the 1924 Olympics were being run, Liddell was preaching a sermon at the Scottish church in Paris.

Opposite: Could be a scene from *Chariots of Fire*. Raised boaters in the background, Liddell in famous head-back style, crossing the line in Paris in 1924.

Everyone who saw the Oscar-winning film *Chariots of Fire* knows something of the story of Eric Liddell, the 400 metres champion at the 1924 Olympics. The story was embellished for the big screen, but Liddell was fascinating enough in his own right.

Liddell was born in Tianjin, China where his Scottish parents were Protestant missionaries, and was then sent back to Britain for schooling. He was a brilliant all-round sportsman at Eltham College, and then went on to represent Edinburgh University at both rugby and athletics. Indeed, he initially came to prominence as a rugby player. He was a winger who won seven caps for Scotland before giving the game up in 1923 to concentrate on athletics.

As a teenager, he won the 100 yards, and the 220 yards, in the 1921 Scottish Championships, and in 1923 he ran a time of 9.7 seconds for the 100 yards, a record that stood for thirty-five years. Indeed, the short sprints were his best events, and when he went to America to begin his preparation for the 1924 Olympics, he concentrated on these. However, when the schedule for Paris was announced, the 100 metres qualifiers were to be held on a Sunday, and the deeply religious Liddell immediately refused to participate. As a result, he was entered for the 200 and 400 metres.

In order to prepare, he entered the Imperial equivalent to those events (the 220 yards and 440 yards), in the AAA Championships and won the longer event. He finished second behind Kinsman of South Africa in the 220 yards, and went to Paris as one of the favourites.

The 200 metres was run first, and Liddell finished with a bronze. That left him with the 400 metres, and in the semi-final he improved his personal best time by over a second. In the final, he was drawn in the least advantageous position, the outside lane. Liddell set a devastating early pace which burnt off most of the opposition, and he maintained it to the line to win in a new Olympic record of 47.6 seconds. Liddell had a seemingly ungainly style, doing almost everything wrong with his head flung back and his arms flailing in front of him, but it proved effective in the most important race of his life.

Just to prove it was no fluke, he completed the season by making up six yards on the Paris silver medallist Horatio Fitch in the relay at the British Empire v USA match at Stamford Bridge.

His Olympic medal won, Liddell turned more to his religious duties. After winning three events at the 1925 Scottish Championships, he returned to China to join his father as a missionary. He did not entirely turn his back on running. In 1929, he beat Otto Preltzer of Germany in 400 metre race in Tianjin. Preltzer encouraged Liddell to train for the 1932 Olympics, but Liddell refused. The 400 metres at the North China Championship in 1930 was his last race.

Liddell continued to work in North China but he was caught up in the Japanese invasion of China, and in 1943 was interned in a concentration camp in Weixian. He died almost two years later at the age of forty-three.

'The 100 metres that he didn't compete in may have been his best event as he had already beaten Abrahams in it. Not even America's Michael Johnson could lay claim to a 100/400 double!'

GARY LINEKER

GARY WINSTON LINEKER
FOOTBALL – FORWARD
BORN: LEICESTER, 30 NOVEMBER 1960

Facts about Gary Lineker

- He was a Leicester City season-ticket holder at the age of eight.

- He is a very good snooker player. He has hit several century breaks, and one of his best friends is the snooker pro Willie Thorne.

- A play was written concerning the 1990 World Cup semi-final with West Germany entitled *An Evening with Gary Lineker*.

- Lineker's final matches were played in Japan, for Nagoya Grampus Eight. A toe injury restricted his effectiveness and he retired after two seasons there.

- He became a BBC media pundit, and is now regularly seen on *Match of the Day*.

One performance altered Gary Lineker's career. After an appalling start to England's World Cup campaign in Mexico – defeat against Portugal and a poor goal-less draw with Morocco – Lineker had come under serious pressure, and as England went into their final group game against Poland the whole team was staring humiliation in the face. By half-time, they were winning 3–0, and Lineker had scored them all.

With three more goals, two against Paraguay and one versus Argentina, Lineker became the first England player to win the World Cup's Golden Boot, and he returned to England a hero. Not for long, though, because a multi-million pound deal clinched during the World Cup saw him off to one of Europe's biggest clubs, Barcelona. Not bad for the son of a fruitseller from Leicester.

Gary Lineker had been brought up a Leicester City fan, and joined them as an apprentice. Before long, he had forced his way into the first team, a young, eager forward with pace and an eye for goal. He prospered with one of football's perennial Yo-Yo teams. In 1980 Lineker made the breakthrough as an occasional forward into the team that won the Second Division Championship with a late burst, but neither he nor Leicester were ready for top-flight football and they were relegated the next season.

Lineker spent the next couple of years honing his craft as Leicester's first-choice centre-forward, and in 1983 they scraped into the final promotion spot on the last day of the season. With twenty-six goals, he was easily the Second Division's top scorer, and he continued that record the next season. Leicester lost their first six matches but, with twenty-two goals, Lineker steered them to mid-table respectability. He also won his first England cap, as a substitute in a

1–1 draw with Scotland.

It was clear that Leicester would not be able to hang on to their star talent, and in the summer of 1985 he moved to the champions, Everton, for £800,000. He did not disappoint. He scored thirty goals in the league, and eight more in cup matches. Sadly, though, his team finished runners-up behind arch-rivals Liverpool in both league and cup, although Lineker did have the consolation of scoring in the FA Cup final.

Now Lineker was now established as England's premier striker, a position confirmed by his heroics in Mexico. Barcelona, managed at the time by Terry Venables, bid a record for a British player, £2,750,000, for him, and Lineker was bound for Spain. However, his three years in Barcelona colours were not happy. The Catalans lost out to Real Madrid in the league, and Venables was replaced by Johan Cruyff who was not a fan of Lineker's talents. Despite this, in 1987, Lineker scored all of England's goals as they beat Spain 4–2 in Madrid and he did win at least one European title, the Cup-Winners' Cup, as Barcelona beat Sampdoria of Italy 2–0 in 1989. It was virtually his last act in Barcelona colours, as he returned to England, and Tottenham Hotspur a couple of

Linekar against Egypt in Cagliari in 'Italia '90'.

- Lineker is also a useful cricketer, and once guested for MCC in a match against the German cricket team. He was out for one but, as he said later, 'It's always nice to score one against the Germans.'

- He was awarded an honorary Master of Arts degree by Leicester University in 1991.

months later. He spent five seasons there, helping them to win the FA Cup in 1991.

At international level, Lineker was still the leader of the England line, and he scored four goals as the team reached the 1990 World Cup semi-finals. The most memorable, of course, was his equaliser in the semi-final against West Germany. It was a typical Lineker goal, an instant control and shot from close-in. His goals were not usually spectacular, but he was a ruthlessly efficient poacher in front of the net. In the end he scoi forty-eight goals in eighty appearances, failin equal Bobby Charlton's record when he missed a penalty against Brazil.

Lineker's legacy to English football is not so much his record, although that is impressive enough. He was a true sportsman, and did not receive a yellow card throughout his career. With the modern game played and controlled the way it is, that is a fine achievement.

'Gary has built a reputation as one of soccer's 'nice guys', nothing controversial – no bookings (Vinny Jones says it's because he never tackles). Like Bobby Charlton he is a great ambassador for the game and second to the same in the England scoring lists.'

ANITA LONSBROUGH

ANITA LONSBROUGH
SWIMMING – BREASTSTROKE
BORN: YORK, 10 AUGUST 1941

**Facts about
Anita Lonsbrough**

- She married Hugh Porter, a cyclist who won the World Pursuit Championship four times.

- She was voted 'Sportswoman of the Year' by two different polls in both 1960 and 1962.

- She was awarded the MBE in 1965.

- She always got up at the crack of dawn for training and, even on the days of championship finals, never varied her routine.

Luxuriating in a Roman bath. Olympic Gold and a new world record for Britain in Rome in 1960.

Anita Lonsbrough was a latecomer in a sport where champions tend to be formed almost from birth. She did not appear internationally until she was seventeen, and for the next seven years was one of the best swimmers in the world.

Although she was born in York, Lonsbrough learnt her swimming in India, where her father had been posted as a Regimental Sergeant-Major with the Coldstream Guards. The family returned to Huddersfield, where she joined the local Borough Club as a freestyle swimmer. She was distinctly average at that discipline, so in 1957 she turned to the breaststroke, and instantly excelled.

Nine months after the switch, she was selected to represent England at the 1958 Commonwealth Games, and dominated the field to take gold in the 220 yards, the first of seven golds she was to win in her career. The second arrived only a few days later, as England's 4 x 110 yards individual medley team stormed to victory in a new world record time of 4:54.0. However, there was still a gap between her and the best swimmers outside the Commonwealth. At the European Championships in Budapest, she could only get a silver in the 200 metres breaststroke, while the medley team finished third.

She broke the 200 metres world record in 1959 but, despite that, was not considered favourite two years later at the Rome Olympics. She reached the final easily enough, where the German Wiltrud Urselmann was most experts' pick for the gold. Urselmann was extremely nervous before the race, while Lonsbrough was so calm that she was able to varnish her fingernails. She had also considered her tactics for the race. Urselmann was a fast starter, who would try to burn away the rest of the field in the first 100 metres. Lonsbrough, however, stayed a couple of yards behind and then increased the pressure on the third length. She drew level in the last 50 metres, and went into the lead on the last few strokes, winning in a new world record time of 2:49.5, shaving half a second off her own time. It was the only world mark set in the women's individual events in Rome.

She now needed the European title for a hat-trick of major championships. She had her chance at Leipzig in 1962. It had been a difficult season for her, as she had been plagued by illness and injury in the early part of the year. To cap it all, the Leipzig pool was outdoors, and the night of the

Anita Lonsbrough's Career

Championship wins

Olympic Games

1960 (Rome)	200 metres breaststroke

European Championships

1962 (Leipzig)	200 metres breaststroke

Commonwealth Games

1958 (Cardiff)	220 yards breaststroke
	4 x 110 yards medley relay
1962 (Perth)	110 yards breaststroke
	220 yards breaststroke
	440 yards individual medley

final was cold and wet. However, a typically determined performance saw her home a second ahead of her Dutch rival Klenie Bimolt.

At the end of that year, she went to Perth for the Commonwealth Games, easily retaining her 220 yards title, breaking the world record and taking two more golds, in the newly instituted 110 yards breaststroke and in the 440 yards individual medley. This was the last time she swam breaststoke in a major championship. She had nothing more to prove as world number one, so she decided to return to freestyle and concentrate on the individual medley. Lonsbrough was Britain's leading medley swimmer in 1963 and 1964 and in the Tokyo Olympics she reached the final of that event. She could only manage a seventh place finish though, and retired from competition after the Games. It was perhaps her only disappointment that she was never selected to swim freestyle internationally, either individually or in the relay, but in 1963 she did win the 220 yards freestyle at the English Championships. It was her only title in the discipline. With a total haul of seven golds, three silvers and two bronzes from major championships, Lonsbrough could never be considered anything other than a major star in this physically demanding sport.

'Anita held the Olympic, European and Commonwealth championships at the same time, plus she set 4 world records and won the BBC Sports Personality of the Year — so she must have had quite an impact on the public.'

WILLIE JOHN McBRIDE

WILLIAM JOHN MCBRIDE
RUGBY UNION – FORWARD LOCK
BORN: TOOMEBRIDGE, 6 JUNE 1940

Facts about Willie John McBride

- He had some very profound words to say about sport and rugby: 'Rugby has taught me tolerance and, I hope, the ability to win and lose with dignity – but above all to respect the other fellow. In this respect alone sport has a vital role to play in man's relationship with man.'

- His courage was epitomised in his first season of international rugby when he finished a game against France despite having broken his left tibia!

'Bill' McBride, as he was known in his younger days, was one of those rare people in team sport known primarily for their inspirational leadership. All his contemporaries admired him. Gareth Edwards said of him, 'Willie John McBride was a true leader of men – a great leader of men.'

Rugby forward play is a contest for big men and hard men. Willie John McBride was bigger than most and hard enough to take on both the Kiwis and the Springboks at their own uncompromising game. Stories about the toughness of rugby forwards abound, but one of the best known concerns the origins of the enormous mutual respect between McBride and the legendary New Zealand lock, Colin Meads. Apparently, they did everything they could, during their first encounter, to try and intimidate one another and gain a measure of superiority, such that, at the end of the game, they decided to call it a day, and agree from then on to play by the rules.

To call McBride the 'Colin Meads of British rugby' would not be an injustice to either man.

McBride was raised very humbly on a smallholding in County Antrim and played all his club rugby for Ballymena. He played for Ulster against the touring South Africans in 1961, and had the unenviable task of marking the great Johann Claassen. Within a year McBride was playing for Ireland and was picked to go on tour to South Africa with the British Lions.

He played in two Tests, both of them defeats, and was on the losing side again in New Zealand when the Kiwis dismissed a party of very tame Lions 4–0. Two subsequent victories against Australia, not then the force they were to become later, was scant compensation. He returned to South Africa, again in 1968, and again the Lions were mauled 3–0 with one match drawn. McBride learned several things from these three tours, the most important of which was the realisation that the only way to beat the Kiwis and the Springboks in their own backyards was to take them on at their own game – in other words, be harder than they were.

These experiences led to the famous battle-cries used by McBride to marshall his men during the Lions' victories in the 1970s. He developed a Churchillian reputation as he cried: 'Take no prisoners', 'Get your retaliation in first', and '99' – the call for all his men to stand and fight together should the opposition decide to mix it. Those were the days!

McBride was pack-leader in New Zealand in 1971 when the finest Lions team ever to take on the Kiwis on home soil won the series 2–1, with one match drawn.

But 1974 was his and British rugby's finest hour. The omens were not good at the beginning, with several key players missing. However, McBride

Willie McBride's Career

International appearances:	83	Test appearances:	17

Irish Tours:

Australia	1967		

Lions Tours:

South Africa	1962	0–3	
Australia and New Zealand	1966	0–2	
South Africa	1968	0–3	
Australia and New Zealand	1971	2–1	
South Africa (captain)	1974	3–0	

A hard man in a hard game.

would not be denied. Despite the fact that the Springboks had never lost a major series on home soil, the Lions won the Test series 3–0, with one match drawn, and their tour record was amazing: played twenty-two, won twenty-one, drawn one, lost nought, points for 729, points against 207.

In 1975 McBride retired as captain of the Lions and captain of his country in their centenary year. It was also Ballymena's centenary, and to celebrate they won the Ulster Cup. To cap it all, it was also

the year of his only try for Ireland against France in his penultimate appearance. He later became manager of the Lions in 1983 and, briefly, coach to the Irish team in 1984 before retiring to continue his career in banking.

'Willie John played rugby at a time when it was all about physical domination and he was a match for anyone at that. But it was also his leadership qualities that made his team mates play to a higher level.'

- Con Houlihan of the *Dublin Evening Press* had some profound words about McBride and the 1974 Lions tour: 'For Willie John McBride it was the Everest of a Himalayan career. That he unhesitatingly set out on such an unpromising quest is a measure of the man. In every community there is someone to whom one looks in time of crisis. McBride is such a man.'

- On the 1968 Lions tour to South Africa, McBride was also captain of the 'Wreckers', a group of practical jokers who revelled in using the cigarette lighters given to them as gifts by their South African hosts. They proceeded to set alight anything that took their fancy, until one night they managed to make the front garden of the Union hotel in Pretoria burn like a bush-fire.

- It wasn't always rugby and pyrotechnics for the Tourists. Two planes were chartered to take the 1974 Lions for a few days R and R in Kruger National Park, one for the players and one (stacked to the ceiling) for the beer. A day later the second plane had to go back to Johannesburg for a refill!

BARRY McGUIGAN

FINBAR PATRICK MCGUIGAN
BOXING – FEATHERWEIGHT
BORN: CLONES, 28 FEBRUARY 1961

Facts about Barry McGuigan

- His manager, Barney Eastwood, was a Belfast bookmaker.

- McGuigan never fought Azumah Nelson of Ghana, the WBC World Champion at Featherweight. It was said by both that the other was frightened of him.

Barry McGuigan had the unusual distinction of being a popular hero on mainland Britain, Northern Ireland and the Republic of Ireland simultaneously. He is also regarded as one of the greatest boxers Britain has ever produced. The highlight of his career, at Queens Park Rangers Football Ground, in June 1985, when he won the WBA (World Boxing Association) World Featherweight title against Eusebio Pedroza, was one of the great nights of British boxing.

He is articulate, outgoing, passionately celtic and pugilistically charismatic. Like Henry Cooper, he became one of boxing's few: he not only survived the rigours of the ring intact, but went on to be successful after his career was over.

Barry McGuigan's Career

35 Professional fights
Wins 32
Defeats 3
Wins inside the distance 26

Key Victories

British and European Featherweight Champion 1983–85

World Featherweight Champion 1985–86 (WBA)

Year	Opponent	Title	Result	Rounds
1983	Vernon Penprase	British	stopped	2 rounds
1983	Valerio Nati	European	knock-out	6 rounds
1984	Estebon Eguia	European	knock-out	3 rounds
1984	Clyde Ruan	British and European	knock-out	4 rounds
1985	Farid Gallouz	European	retired	2 rounds
1985	Eusebio Pedroza	World	points	15 rounds
1985	Bernard Taylor	World	retired	8 rounds
1986	Danilo Cabrera	World	stopped	14 rounds

McGuigan took up boxing in 1973 when he was twelve years old. He was only seventeen when he became Ulster Champion in 1978, and then went on to win a gold medal at bantamweight at the Commonwealth Games in Edmonton in the same year. He then endeared himself to the people of the Republic by boxing for Ireland at the Moscow Olympics in 1980. Unfortunately, he could not repeat the success he had had for the North and lost in the quarter-finals to a Zambian, Winfred Kabunda, who in turn lost in the semi-finals.

McGuigan turned professional in 1981 and won his first fight in Dublin in two rounds. His rise to the top followed quickly. Within two years he was British Featherweight Champion after stopping Vernon Penprase in Belfast in two rounds in April 1983. In November of the same year, he became European Champion when he knocked out Valerio Nati, of Italy, in the sixth round, again in Belfast. In just over two years he had eighteen bouts and had won all but three of them inside the distance. His devastating two-handed punching was the talk of the boxing fraternity. His only blemish in this period, a points defeat against Peter Eubank in 1981, was put right within a few months.

He defended his European title against Esteban Eguia and his British and European titles against Clyde Ruan in 1984. Then, in 1985, after another successful European defence against Farid Gallouze, he was ready for the big one.

The World Featherweight Champion was Eusebio Pedroza, already a living legend. A poor kid from Panama who had fought his way to the top, he had been Champion for seven years and had defended his title an amazing nineteen times. He was regarded as, pound for pound, one of the best boxers in the world.

On a famous night in West London, cheered on by thousands of Irish-Irish and thousands of London-Irish, McGuigan wrote for himself a special place in British boxing history. He won a unanimous points decision and took the great Panamanian's world title for Britain and Ireland.

His first defence was only four months later in his beloved King's Hall, Belfast, in front of an ecstatic crowd, when he stopped Bernard Taylor in the eighth round. He then defended his title for

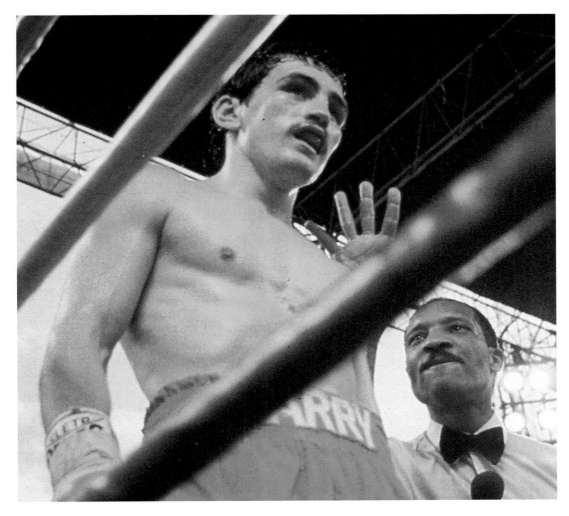

McGuigan's ordeal in the heat of Las Vegas against Steve Cruz.

the Dublin faithful and stopped Danilo Cabrera in the fourteenth.

However, everything went dramatically wrong in June of that year. McGuigan took his title to Las Vegas and fought Steve Cruz from Fort Worth, Texas, who was merely a late substitute. The temperature was 110°F and McGuigan almost literally melted away. He visibly weakened during the fight, lost on points and was so badly dehydrated at the end that, for a while, it was thought his life was in danger. There followed a long-term disagreement with his manager, Barney Eastwood, which eventually had to be settled through tortuous legal wrangling.

McGuigan didn't fight again for nearly two years but came back under the wing of London manager, Frank Warren, in 1988. He had three fights, all victories inside the distance. Then he came up against Jim McDonnell in Manchester in May 1989 – the referee stopped the fight in the fourth round when McGuigan sustained a bad cut, but not before it was obvious that the courageous Irishman was not the same boxer as he had been before that dreadful night in Las Vegas.

After taking on his former manager and by applying his charm and wits to a post-boxing career, McGuigan began a happy and successful retirement. His legacy was considerable: much-loved by the public and very highly regarded by boxing experts.

'Why is it that boxers find their way to the bosom of the nation? Why is it that boxers so frequently fall out with their managers? Barry did both, conquered the world and was successful after leaving boxing. What more can you ask?'

- McGuigan's nickname was the 'Clones Cyclone'.

- After Cruz took McGuigan's title in Las Vegas, in 1986, he immediately lost it again to Antonio Esparragoza of Venezuela, in his home town of Fort Worth.

- McGuigan's chirpy Irish voice and his effusive politeness led to his becoming the butt of many mimics and impressionists, especially his much caricatured line 'Thank you very much, Mr Eastwood.'

- In fact, he had much not to be thankful for as far as his manager was concerned. The dispute between them became a major legal battle until Eastwood paid McGuigan a huge sum out of court to settle their differences.

- McGuigan entered the ring for the Pedroza fight to the strains of 'Eye of the Tiger', the theme tune to Rocky. Then, with hardly a dry eye in the house, his father, Pat, sang 'Danny Boy'. After that, he couldn't lose!

BILLY McNEILL

WILLIAM MCNEILL
FOOTBALL – DEFENDER
BORN: BELLSHILL, 2 MARCH 1940

Billy McNeill's Career

International appearances	29
Goals	3
European Cup	1967

Scottish Championship
1966, 1967, 1968, 1969, 1970, 1971,
1972, 1973, 1974

Scottish FA Cup
1965, 1967, 1969, 1971, 1972, 1974, 1975

Scottish League Cup 1966, 1967, 1968,
1969, 1970, 1975

Facts about Billy McNeill

• Inter were kept behind closed doors before the 1967 European Cup final. Celtic went for a walk along the beach, and then took a short cut back. McNeill and some others got lost, and they had to clamber over rocks and fences to get back to the hotel.

• Apart from the 1967 European Cup final, Celtic's finest achievement was to beat Leeds home and away in the 1970 European Cup semi-final. The second leg, at Hampden, was watched by 135,826 people, Britain's largest post-war attendance, and McNeill led the team on a lap of honour after a 2–1 win.

• He was voted Scottish Footballer of the Year in 1965

'The Caesar' was the captain and mainstay of the most successful club team in British history. When the 'Lions of Lisbon' became the first British team to lift the European Cup, McNeill lifted the trophy that signified British clubs could now challenge the best in Europe. With a powerful physique, a surprising turn of pace and a dominating personality, he was the ideal captain for a great Celtic team.

McNeill was the son of a soldier and, while his father was based in Herefordshire, found himself only able to play rugby at school. Moving back to Scotland, he found himself playing for the noted junior club Blantyre Victoria, and Celtic, seeing his potential, signed him as a seventeen-year-old part-timer. The youth team coach, Jock Stein, was particularly interested in his progress and McNeill, in only his second season at the club, found himself moving into the first team. His progress was so swift that, by 1961, he was in the Scotland team. He could have chosen a more auspicious day for his debut. Scotland were torn apart 9–3 by a rampant England at Wembley.

When McNeill joined the club, times at Celtic Park were hard. They were deep in the shadow of eternal rivals' Rangers. By the start of 1965, McNeill was almost twenty-five and, in eight years, had won nothing of significance. He was ready to move clubs, until the Celtic board decided to appoint Jock Stein as manager. Stein had been allowed to move to Dunfermline, where he had brought a little club big success. Now he would use his talents for the benefit of Celtic. It was an instant success and Celtic, though already far behind in the League, reached the Cup final against Dunfermline. It was an enthralling contest, with Celtic twice falling behind and coming back to equalise. Then,

in the final minute, McNeill rose high above the defence to head home the winner. Celtic had their first trophy in nearly a decade, and it was vital for the supporters and the players' belief in themselves. Much later, Stein, in a moment of reflection, said, 'Maybe it wouldn't have gone so well for Celtic had they not won this game.'

It was the start of a period of unparalleled success. The next season Celtic swept the board, winning League, Cup and League Cup. In 1967, they did it again, except this time, there was an additional prize to aim for, the European Cup. Celtic were rank outsiders against Inter Milan. The Italians were two-time winners of Europe's biggest club prize and, under manager Helenio Herrera, had developed catenaccio, the ultradefensive system that served them well. The Scots approached the game in a carefree, light-hearted manner, in contrast to Inter's methodical attitude. When the game began, though, the Italians were first to strike. A penalty, converted by Mazzola in only the seventh minute, rocked Celtic back on their heels, but the game's pattern developed into incessant Scottish attacks, and desperate Inter defence. The equaliser had to come, and shortly after the hour it did, Gemmell lashing a shot in from the edge of the box.

The Celtic team were now buoyed up, and pressed for the winner. The Italian defence broke down a second time with just five minutes to go, as

Chalmers diverted a Murdoch shot into the net. Celtic were the first British side to win the European Cup, and the 'Lisbon Lions' went into history. McNeill, who had had an excellent game limiting the Italian threat, went up to lift the trophy.

McNeill continued in Celtic colours until 1975, and was chaired off by his colleagues after yet another Hampden triumph, a Cup final win over Airdrie. Three years later, he returned to the club he loved as manager, replacing his mentor Jock Stein. His first season climaxed with a Championship and, after spells in management in England, he returned north to find yet more success, including a Double in 1988, Celtic's Centenary Year. It was an achievement befitting a great club's greatest player.

'Billy was a great player in a great club during the greatest period in Scottish football history. His leadership style was to lead by example.'

- McNeill, as captain, was the player all other members of the great Celtic team of the 1960s and 1970s looked to. His team-mate Bobby Murdoch said in 1970, 'Billy McNeill sets a high standard of conduct for all of us, and this is the main reason why you do not see any long-haired wonders walking through the doors at Celtic Park ... Professional football is our business.'

- McNeill's managerial experience south of the Border was limited to spells at Manchester City and Aston Villa. He won promotion with Manchester City in 1985.

Escaping with the European trophy in the car park of the Estadio de Luz in Lisbon in 1967.

NIGEL MANSELL

**NIGEL ERNEST JAMES MANSELL
MOTOR-RACING DRIVER
BORN: UPTON-ON-SEVERN, 8 AUGUST 1953**

Facts about
Nigel Mansell

- He was the third driver to win the Formula One Drivers' Championship and the Indy Car title (following Emerson Fittipaldi and Mario Andretti).

Nigel Mansell retired in 1995 a rich man. His perseverence had finally secured his place in the sun. If ever hard work and determination in sport deserved a happy ending, it was the case with Mansell. There was never any doubt about three things that were central to the Mansell story: his courage in the face of adversity, his undying popularity with the public, and his unquestionable speed around the track.

Nigel Mansell's Career

Formula One

World Drivers' Championship

1992		Williams-Renault

Grands Prix Victories (31)

1985	British, South African	Williams-Honda
1986	Belgian, Canadian, French, British, Portuguese	Willams-Honda
1987	San Marino, French, British, Austrian, Spanish, Mexican	Williams-Honda
1989	Brazilian, Hungarian	Ferrari
1990	Portuguese	Ferrari
1991	French, British, German, Italian, Spanish	Williams-Renault
1992	South African, Mexican, Brazilian, Spanish, San Marino, French, British, German, Portuguese	Williams-Renault
1994	Australian	Williams-Renault

Grands Prix Summary

31 wins from 185 races	Pole positions 32
Total points: 480	Fastest laps 30

Indy Car

World Series Champion 1993	Newman-Haas

Indy Car Victories

1993 Surfers Paradise, Milwaukee, Michigan, New England, Nazareth (Newman-Haas)

Mansell started in the most modest of circumstances. His first step on the pedal of racing was in karting where he made it to the British Junior Team. However, progression beyond this wasn't supposed to happen. The boy from the Midlands, with the monotone drawl, was supposed to settle down with his wife and become an engineer with British Aerospace. But Mansell was determined not to have an 'ordinary' life.

At this point, the faith and support from his wife, Rosanne, which would continue to be the vital pillar of support throughout his career, was crucial. He worked long long hours, seven days a week, sold his personal possessions and eventually sold his house to pay his way through Formula Ford, Formula Three and Formula Two. Even when he had accidents which demanded inactivity to allow the bones to heal, he chose to ignore medical advice and lived with the pain.

By the time he made his debut into Formula One in Lotus' third car at the Austrian Grand Prix, Mansell was already twenty-seven years old and had been struggling to make his breakthrough for nearly ten years. He continued to drive for Lotus for the next four seasons, but the death of Colin Chapman at Lotus was a bitter blow for Mansell and he seemed to lose his way. Without Chapman as a mentor, he got into a series of feuds with the media and his fellow drivers.

Salvation came in the form of the Willams team in 1985 and Peter Collins, the Team Manager. He improved every year after his first Grand Prix win at Brands Hatch. He had five wins in 1986, but then became one of the country's most precious commodities – 'the Great British loser' when, in the final race in Adelaide, his rear tyre exploded on the main straight, ruining his chances of the Championship. There was more disappointment in 1987, when not even six victories could bring him the Championship. Senna was quicker, even though Mansell did try to strangle him after they collided at the Belgian Grand Prix!

1988 was never going to be a successful year after Williams lost the Honda Turbo and in 1989 'Our Nige' departed for Ferrari. To everyone's surprise, the Italian's loved him and he won his first race in Brazil. He regarded it as his preparatory year, finishing fourth in the Championship, before his assault on

- Mansell is an excellent golfer with a four handicap.

- He crashed in 1977 just after giving up his job to drive professionally. He broke his neck and crushed several vertebrae. He was told he needed to lie flat on his back for six months. He discharged himself from hospital, put on a neck brace and was back into a car within six weeks.

- In 1979 Mansell injured his back again, just before he was asked by Lotus to do a test drive at the Paul Ricard circuit in France. He simply didn't tell anyone about his injuries, climbed gingerly into the car and got himself the contract as a test driver.

- When he got his first Formula One drive in 1980 in Austria, the mechanics accidentally spilt petrol down his back at the start of the race. He didn't complain and raced until his engine failed. He finished with severe burns to his back and buttocks.

the ultimate prize in 1990. But, once more, there was to be disappointment. Alain Prost – full of charm and fluent in Italian – joined Ferrari and it all started to go wrong again. Mansell only had one win and was fifth in the Championship. In 1991, he came home to Williams, but not before an emotional retirement.

The 1991 season was a superb battle between Mansell's Williams Renault and Senna's McLaren Honda. Despite five victories for Mansell, Senna and his McLaren beat him to the Championship, Mansell's cause not helped by some early season technical problems.

However, at long, long last, it all came good in 1992. The Williams Honda was unbeatable, he drove superbly and with a massive total of 108 points from nine wins, Nigel Ernest James Mansell was World Champion. He was thirty-one years old.

But there would be several more twists yet. Instead of capitalising on his year of victory and a superb Williams car, with a second Championship, Mansell up and left! He was disconcerted at the prospect of the arrival of Prost and relations with the team were apparently far from perfect. In fact, Mansell left Formula One altogether, for the razzamattaz of the American Indy Car Circuit.

To say he was a smash hit would be a massive understatement. Driving for the Newman-Haas team, he was on pole for the first race in Australia, proceeded to win it, and then went on to win five more races and the Championship. Amusingly, he became Champion, Driver of the Year and Rookie of the Year all at once.

His second year in America was not as exciting for Mansell. Newman-Haas' Lola chassis couldn't compete, and the Penske Team won everything. He became restless and returned to Williams and Formula One in 1994 and even won a race – the Australian Grand Prix, at the end of the season.

By mid-1995 and a couple of races for McLaren (having moved on from Williams), Mansell was forty-two and seemed to think he had finally done enough to show the world what he could do, sufficient at least to bring a retirement and the opportunity to spend at least a part of his massive fortune.

'I think there are better drivers in this list but Nigel's in here because of perseverance and the motoring fans' love of him.'

STAN MATTHEWS

SIR STANLEY MATTHEWS
FOOTBALL – FORWARD
BORN: STOKE-ON-TRENT, 1 FEBRUARY 1915

Stan Matthew's Career	
Football League appearances	698
Goals	71
International appearances	54
Goals	11
FA Cup (with Blackpool)	1953

Facts about
Stan Matthews

- When Ghana became an independant nation in 1957, they invited Matthews to take part in the celebration and in a special ceremony crowned him 'King of Football'.

- He won two Second Division Championship medals, both with Stoke City. The first was in 1933, at the beginning of his career, and the second was three decades later, in 1963.

- At the age of fifty-five, he made a short comeback with Maltese First Division club Hibernians.

- John Carey, captain of Manchester United said of Matthews, 'Playing Stanley Matthews was like playing a ghost.'

Stan Matthews is possibly the most famous player England has ever produced. His career lasted for over thirty years, and, as 'The Wizard of the Dribble' he attracted huge crowds wherever he played.

Matthews was of sporting stock. His father was Jack Matthews, the 'Fighting Barber of Hanley', quite a well-known boxer in his day. He also had a obsession for physical fitness which was inherited by his son. Stan Matthews was well known for early nights, long walks and complete abstention from alcohol and tobacco. At the time it was considered extreme, but as Matthews was fifty when he finally retired from English football, the years of self-discipline clearly had their reward.

Matthews was an early developer. He once scored ten goals from centre-back in a schoolboy game, and he made his debut for Stoke City as a right winger at the age of seventeen in 1932, and in September 1934 he made his England debut against Wales. He then played two months later in the infamous 'Battle of Highbury' against world champions Italy. England won this violent game 3-2, but Matthews had singularly failed to impress in either game. One journalist accused him of 'slowness and hesitation'. It was indicative of his future England career. Although he spent over three decades at the top, he only played fifty-four official internationals, spending long periods out of favour. He was accused of being too individualistic, an accusation that his recursed many times with players of genius. However, when he was selected, he could easily turn a game around. He scored three goals in a 5–4 win over Czechoslovakia at

White Hart Lane in 1937, a game that England could easily have lost. The next year, he destroyed Ireland's defence, helping Willy Hall score five goals in a 7–0 win in Manchester.

Of course, the war interrupted his career when, at the age of twenty-four, he was starting to come into his prime. Matthews joined the RAF and played in many wartime and Victory internationals. When hostilities ceased, though, he found his England position under threat. Another right winger, Tom Finney, took his place in the team, but a compromise was found. Finney switched to the left, and with Matthews on the right, they destroyed Portugal 10–0 in Lisbon in 1947. The next year, against an excellent Italian team, England once again ran riot, winning 4–0 in Turin.

By this time, Matthews had changed club. Stoke, although never in the hunt for honours, had been able to let Matthews's artistry flourish. However, by 1947 the time had come for a move and Stoke sold him to Blackpool, where Matthews had a home and business interests, for £11,500. He was considered a veteran, aged thirty-two by this stage, but he gave Blackpool fifteen years of sterling service. He was also now at a club that could challenge for silverware. They reached the Cup final in his first season, losing 4–2 to Manchester United, and returned in 1951 when Newcastle beat them 2–0. When they arrived at Wembley again, in 1953, Matthews was thirty-eight. Many thought it would be his last chance to win an honour, and when Bolton took a 3–1 lead it looked like Blackpool would once again leave the capital empty-handed. Famously, though, the 'Matthews Cup final' had one of football's great finishes. Matthews didn't score, but he tore the Bolton defence apart on the right wing in the last twenty minutes. He helped Mortenson complete a hat-trick, and Blackpool to a 4–3 win.

The next year, he was recalled to England's World Cup team. He had gone to Brazil in 1950, but only played against Spain, selected after the defeat by the USA. Now, in 1954, he was thirty-nine years old. He was superb in the quarter-final against Uruguay, a wonderful match which England finally lost 4–2. His last England appearance was in May 1957, in a World Cup qualifier against Denmark in Copenhagen. England won 4–1. The respect in which he was held by foreign observers could be judged when he was won the first European Footballer of the Year award in 1956

In 1961, he returned to Stoke for a nominal £2500, and the gates instantly doubled. The new interest inspired the team, and the next season, the last in which Matthews played a major role, they won promotion back to the First Division. He finally retired in 1965. He was knighted, the first footballer so honoured, and a special benefit match was organised in Stoke. Players came from all over the world and over £25,000 was raised.

After retirement, he moved to Malta and then Canada, but he was still an instantly recognisable name in wherever he went. Few could match his skill, and none his longevity and dedication.

'33 years at anything is special but at football it's unbelievable. As a role model Stanley had few peers. He is one of the few footballers with the magnetism that persuades punters that win, lose or draw, it was worth the entrance fee just to see them!!'

- Matthews was never booked.

- He was voted Footballer of the Year in 1948 and 1963 and European Footballer of the Year in 1956.

The 'wizard of dribble' playing for Stoke, his home-town team.

PETER MAY

PETER BARKER HOWARD MAY
CRICKET – BATSMAN
BORN: READING, 31 DECEMBER 1929
DIED: LIPHOOK, 27 DECEMBER 1994

Facts about Peter May

- He was a Cambridge Blue in football and rugby fives as well as cricket.

- He finished top of the national averages three times (1951, 1957 and 1958).

- He captained England in a record forty-one Tests, winning twenty and losing only ten.

- He sued, and won, for libel against a journalist who accused him of letting his outside interests interfere with his captaincy of Surrey.

- He selected his godson Christopher Cowdrey as England captain for the 1988 Headingley Test against the West Indies. Unfortunately, it did not pay off, and May resigned at the end of the season.

Peter May grew to represent the ideal of English cricket. He was tall and handsome, and his batting technique, very straight and very powerful, was close to perfection. Many consider him England's finest post-war batsman.

He was born in Berkshire, to a family with no cricketing background. However, such was his instinctive ability that he had already been marked for greatness while still a schoolboy at Charterhouse. When he was thirteen, the headmaster banned him from the first XI for his own good, and when he finally let him play he scored a century against Harrow and broke all the school records.

His progression continued after school, starring for the Combined Services during his two-year National Service. Indeed, in 1949, he finished third in the national averages behind Hutton and Hardstaff. The next year, he went up to Cambridge, where he scored 227 against Hampshire, and then, during the holidays, won his county cap with Surrey.

Peter May's Career

Tests	66
Test Match runs	4537
Average	46.77
Centuries	13
First-class runs	27,592
Average	51.00
Centuries	85

County Championship 1952, 1953, 1954, 1955, 1956, 1957, 1958

There was only one final rung to climb and in 1951 he made his first Test appearance, against the South Africans at Headingley scoring 138. He was paid the ultimate compliment by the Australians two years later when they deliberately set out to play him out of England contention. It worked too, for three Tests, but May was back in the team for the last, when two solid contributions helped his team win back the Ashes for the first time in thirty years. He was selected to tour the West Indies that winter, and a determined innings of 135 in a drawn Test in Port-of-Spain finally secured his place in the England team.

He became England captain in 1955 and, for an amateur, developed an extremely professional attitude toward winning Tests. That did not stifle his natural talent though, and in 1957 came probably his finest performance for his country, a flawless and unbeaten 285 that nearly turned defeat into victory against the West Indians. It was then the highest score by an England captain and the stand of 411 he shared with Colin Cowdrey remains the highest in English Test history. It was a remarkable innings not least because it finally dispelled the aura of invincibility surrounding the West Indian spin bowlers. His chief victim was Sonny Ramadhin, who had to bowl ninety-eight overs in the second innings.

Domestically, he was also an outstanding success, taking part in each of Surrey's record seven successive championships, between 1952 and 1958, and as captain the last two years. In that last Championship season, an unusually wet summer, May averaged sixty-four, seventeen more than any other batsman.

However, that was the height of his career. That

England against Australia at the Oval in 1956. May was the backbone of the England batting.

winter, he captained England in Australia, where the hot favourites slumped to a 4–0 defeat to lose the Ashes. Much was made of the fact that May's fiancée, Victoria Gilligan, accompanied him on tour, and he was deeply hurt by press criticism of this. They were married the next April, and May interest in cricket seemed to slowly fade, a situation not helped by health problems. An abscess forced him to miss much of the 1959 season, and he was forced home early from that winter's tour to the West Indies. He did not return to cricket until 1961, when he was unable to help England recover the Ashes, and he played his last first-class match in 1963 at the age of thirty-three.

May went to work for Lloyd's of London and his involvement in cricket became increasingly peripheral, a Test selector between 1965 and 1968, and president of the MCC in 1980–81. In 1982, though, he agreed to become chairman of selectors. Initially, he met with a certain amount of success; although 1984 saw the first West Indian 'Blackwash', England wrested the Ashes from Australia in an exciting series the next year. From then on, however, trouble stalked May's stewardship. His captain, Mike Gatting, became involved in the infamous incident with Pakistani umpire Shakoor Rana in 1987, and the next year, no less than four captains saw service in a horrible 4–0 defeat to the West Indies. May seemed unable to relate to a new generation of cricketers and, unfortunately, the debacle did somewhat tarnish his reputation.

May died shortly before his sixty-fifth birthday after a short illness. Richie Benaud considered him possibly the only truly great batsman England produced since the war, and any who saw his trademark off-drive, and the ease with which he dismantled any attack, would surely agree.

'Peter May had it all, and he could play a fair bit too. For most of the '50s he was England's most outstanding batsman. He followed Hutton as captain and was highly successful.'

RICHARD MEADE

RICHARD JOHN HANNAY MEADE
RIDING – THREE-DAY EVENTER
BORN: CHEPSTOW, 4 DECEMBER 1938

Richard Meade was one of Britain's most successful Olympic and World Championship competitors and one of Britain's greatest riders.

His background and upbringing were more suited to an English country squire than an Olympic athlete. He went to Lancing College, was commissioned into the 11th Regiment, Hussars,

and read engineering at Magdalen College, Cambridge. His parents were joint masters of the Curre Hounds, in Monmouthshire, and bred Connemara ponies. It was not surprising that he was a good rider; what was a revelation was how good he was. What's more, Meade's chosen sport, the Three-day Event, is the complete test of horse and rider: dressage, endurance and show-jumping.

Meade had his first success in 1961 at the International Students Rally in Amsterdam. By 1964 he had risen to international prominence. He won Burghley on Barberry, in 1964, and competed in the Tokyo Olympics on the same horse, where he came eighth. Barberry was his mount for the next three years as he won a Team bronze in the European Championships in Moscow, an Individual silver in the World Championships (held at Burghley) and his first gold medal, a European Team, at Punchestown in Ireland.

At the Mexico Olympics in 1968, Meade got together with his mount Cornishman V only two weeks before the Games, but he managed fourth place in the Team event and, thanks to the Individual silver medal performances of team-mate Derek Allhusen, won a Team gold medal with the third member of the team, Reuben Jones.

After Mexico, Meade found a new mount which would bring him great success, The Poacher. An Individual silver and Team gold in the Worlds in 1970, first place at Badminton in the same year and a Team gold in the Europeans in 1971 was a marvellously rich haul of medals and trophies.

However, the Munich Olympics were the highlight of Meade's career. He had a new horse, Laurieston and the pair were never seriously threatened and took the gold medal. Mary Gordon-Watson's fourth place and Bridget

Richard Meade's Career

Olympic Games

1964	Individual	8th	Barberry
1968	Individual	4th	Cornishman V
	Team	Gold	Cornishman V
1972	Individual	Gold	Laurieston
	Team	Gold	Laurieston
1976	Individual	4th	Jacob Jones

World Championships

1966	Individual	Silver	Barberry
1970	Individual	Silver	The Poacher
	Team	Gold	The Poacher
1974	Team	Silver	Wayfarer II
1978	Individual	5th	Bleak Hills
1982	Team	Gold	Kilcashel
	Individual	5th	Kilcashel

European Championships

1965	Team	Bronze	Barberry
1967	Team	Gold	Barberry
1971	Team	Gold	The Poacher
1973	Individual	4th	Wayfarer II
	Team	Bronze	Wayfarer II
1981	Team	Gold	Kilcashel

Burghley

1964		1st	Barberry

Badminton

1970		1st	The Poacher
1982		1st	Speculator III

found himself facing Vito Antuofermo in Las Vegas for the prize.

The middleweight division was the only one at the time to have an undisputed champion, and Antuofermo was a very brave fighter. In boxing parlance, he 'fought with his face'. He had great courage and an iron jaw, and had retained the title after a controversial draw with Marvin Hagler. Antuofermo's method was to wade through everything his opponent could throw at him. It was a style that suited Minter well. The fight went the full fifteen rounds, with Minter scoring constantly, as Antuofermo presented an easy target. However, Antuofermo kept coming forward, and knocked Minter down in the fourteenth, for the first time in his career. The verdict was close and controversial, a split decision in favour of Minter, but with the English judge giving Minter the verdict by twelve points.

There had to be a return fight, and at Wembley minter dispelled the doubts. He stopped Antuofermo in eight rounds. He had watched footage of the first fight, and knew that the way to beat the American was to stand his ground and start fast. He followed the plan and won easily, with Antuofermo cut badly by the end.

Three months later, his title was gone. Marvin Hagler later became one of history's great fighters, and he won the title in three rounds of complete mayhem at Wembley. Minter was left with a broken nose and a face full of stitches. He was now thirty years old, and he had achieved his dreams. It was time to leave the stage.

Minter bang on target against Don McMillan in 1973.

'Alan and I used to live in the same town, Crawley, and like a lot of world class British boxers of the time, he was a true fighter. He didn't mind getting hit, as long as he gave back a better one. The fight he had in Las Vegas with Vito Antuofermo was the first big fight I had been to. It was really exciting, especially when the bloke you're supporting wins!'

BOBBY MOORE

ROBERT FREDERICK MOORE
FOOTBALL – DEFENDER
BORN: BARKING, 12 APRIL 1941
DIED: PUTNEY, 24 FEBRUARY 1993

TOP 20

Facts about Bobby Moore

- He idolised Malcolm Allison and Noel Cartwell when he arrived at Upton Park as a boy. He used to follow them around like a lap-dog and sit with them for hours drinking coffee and analysing the game. By sheer coincidence they arrived at the same resort as Moore and his new wife during their honeymoon, whereupon he left his bride to spend the evening with them talking football.

- He played eight times as an Under-23 international and eighteen times as a Youth international, the latter being an English record.

- Moore was voted Footballer of the Year in 1964, Player of the Tournament in the 1966 World Cup and the Best Defender in the World by

Bobby Moore was an heroic figure in British sport. It wasn't simply that he was the captain when England finally won the World Cup, it was his bearing, his manner and the symbolism he brought to England's finest hour that made him so special.

His qualities of leadership were obvious enough for him to be made captain of his country at the age of twenty-two, the youngest captain there had ever been. He was calm and dignified on the field of play and equally so in life. He commanded respect wherever he went. Most significantly, he looked the part: he walked upright, barrel chest to the fore, with a footballer's athletic gait; he was blonde and handsome; he was 'Bobby Moore, captain of England'. He made everyone feel proud. He always seemed to know how to behave. At the moment of his greatest achievement, after all the drama of extra time and the emotion of victory, as he was about to collect the Jules Rimet trophy, he

Bobby Moore's Career

World Cup Winner	1966
European Cup-Winners Cup Winner	1965
FA Cup Winner	1964
FA Cup Runner-up	1975
International appearances (90 as captain)	108
Goals	2
Club appearances	792
Goals	24

paused, and wiped his hands on the velvet cloth that adorned the wall of the Royal Box, before he shook hands with the Queen. He even remembered to bow.

Moore was a 'properly brought up' East London boy. A child of Barking, an area that has produced so many players, such as Martin Peters and Tony Adams, and England managers, Terry Venables and Sir Alf Ramsey.

West Ham United were the only team a young man from Barking would have considered if he had any local loyalty, and Moore duly signed for them in 1958 at the age of seventeen. He became a youth international almost immediately and actually became an Under-23 international before he made it into the West Ham first team. He was fortunate to find Malcolm Allison and Noel Contwell at Upton Park when he arrived, and within a few years, Ron Greenwood – who all became significant influences on his career. West Ham's Academy of Football was in the making.

Moore was only just twenty-one when he made his full international debut against Peru in May 1962. The game was played as England were en-route to the World Cup in Chile. Moore had an excellent game, as England won 4–0, and he kept his place in the team for the World Cup finals. England came second in Group IV and were then outplayed by Brazil – and Garrincha in particular – in the quarter-final and lost 3–1. Brazil went on to win the tournament and England went home to prepare for the best chance they would ever get to win the World Cup in four years time – home advantage.

Alf Ramsey was appointed manager of England in 1963. Almost his first decision was to make

journalists at the 1970 World Cup.

- He was awarded an OBE in 1967.

- Moore always acknowledged that he lacked pace, was poor in the air and wasn't a particularly strong tackler — not much of a recommendatioin for one of the world's greatest defenders.

- All the England World Cup players received a bonus of £1000 for their achievement in 1966.

- He got into trouble twice in his playing career. Once when he was dropped by Ron Greenwood for breaking a team curfew with Jimmy Greaves, before a cup-tie at Blackpool. The second time was when he was accused of shoplifting in an hotel jewellery shop, in Bogota, just before the 1970 World Cup. He was arrested and went through four days of investigations and allegations until it became clear that the whole thing had been a fabrication.

Bobby, the English hero, as he will always be remembered.

- British football gathered for a Thanksgiving Service for Bobby Moore at Westminster Abbey in July 1993. It was only the second time the Abbey had been used for an athlete – the first was for Sir Frank Worrell.

- Among the huge number of tributes paid to Moore, after his death, were the following:

- 'The boy from Barking became the golden icon of the sixties'. Michael Parkinson

- 'He was one of the immortals ... he enhanced sport by his behaviour and skill'. John Major

- 'He was a great person in every sense. A footballer of intelligence and vision, a man of dignity and stature. I admired him and respected him immensely'. David Platt

- 'He was one of the great captains and a great man'. Sir Alf Ramsey

One of the beautiful game's most famous private moments. Pele and Moore in Mexico in 1970.

Moore his captain. He was only twenty-two and had only played eleven games for England, but Ramsey knew his mind. Moore would be the rock around which he would build his team to win the World Cup.

And so it came to pass. Ramsey added the sword of Charlton to the rock of Moore. Then came the workhorses, Stiles and Ball, and finally all the rest, to play in front of the world's greatest goalkeeper, Gordon Banks.

Moore had an outstanding tournament and played especially well in the final. His free-kick, quickly taken as he saw Hurst unmarked, brought England's second goal. While his incisive pass at the end of extra time was the largely forgotten, but nevertheless brilliant, beginning of the sequence that moved on with commentator, Ken Wolstenholme's immortal line: 'There are some people on the pitch, they think it's all over …', continued with Geoff Hurst's thundering shot into the German net to make the score 4–2, and finished with Wolstenholme, as he delivered the most famous words of commentary ever uttered: '… It is, now!'

When Moore held aloft the tiny World Cup trophy in 1966, he was in fact repeating a ritual he had performed in both of the previous two years. The West Ham 'academy' was by now fully operational. Moore's two England colleagues, Geoff Hurst and Martin Peters, were part of West Ham's finest era. In 1964, they had beaten second division team, Preston North End, 3–2 in a thrilling Cup Final at Wembley. The following season, in the European Cup Winners Cup Final, they returned to Wembley. In another excellent game, West Ham beat TSV Munich 1860, 2–0 through two goals from Alan Sealey. Manager Ron Greenwood was unstinting in his praise of Moore: 'This was Bobby Moore's greatest game. Technical perfection.'

It is ironic that the England team that Alf Ramsey took to Mexico was probably better than the one that had won the World Cup in 1966. The key players were older and wiser and some of the new players brought added strength. England came close to winning it, or at least to giving Brazil a run for their money in the final. But circumstances conspired against them and they lost in a dramatic quarter-final to West Germany.

However, Moore shone like a brilliant beacon.

His performance against Pele in England's Group III match against Brazil will be remembered by everyone who saw it. On that day, playing against the world's greatest player, Moore exhibited the qualities of one of the world's greatest defenders. At the end there was a swapping of shirts and an embrace that was simply an exchange of admiration from one great player to another.

Bobby Moore retired from international football before the next World Cup in 1974, but not before he had collected 108 caps, ninety of them as captain. England had failed to qualify for the 1974 World Cup anyway. It was the end of an era.

But he had a swansong at Wembley at club level. He finally left West Ham in 1974 and joined Fulham. The following season, despite being a Second Division team, they made it to Wembley with Moore as captain, only to meet West Ham in the final. Unfortunately, the fairy story didn't quite come true as Fulham lost 2–0.

Moore retired in 1977 and went to play in America for a while. He later moved into management, principally with Oxford City and Southend United but didn't meet with much success. His various business ventures were not particularly successful either and he eventually settled into a role as a journalist and a commentator. Regrettably, he was never offered a role within the game that many felt would have been appropriate to his talent and his status.

Although there were many disappointments in his life after his retirement from competitive football, he remained the calmly dignified man he was on the field of play. This was particularly true when he discovered he had cancer and yet more true when he was told it would kill him. The world of football was heart-broken when he died in 1993. The more so, because it took his death to remind us of how great he was.

'Moore was said to have so many weaknesses that it's a wonder he played for his school more than once. However, what he did have was a quickness of mind and the ability to read the situation. He never stopped trying to learn the game, always picking people's brains and asking questions. He enriched sport by the example he set, both on and off the field.'

- 'Bobby's type of Englishness drew on the better side of our national character, on our sense of fair play and of dignity. People of all ages feel we have lost a link to a better, more decent time'. Reg Burr

- 'Words cannot sum up the grief I feel for my great friend. He was one of the world's finest defenders and a great sportsman'. Pele

ADRIAN MOORHOUSE

ADRIAN DAVID MOORHOUSE
SWIMMING – BREASTSTROKE
BORN: BRADFORD, 24 MAY 1964

Facts about Adrian Moorhouse

- His first national title came in 1981 when he won both the 100 and 200 metres breaststroke.

- He was so disgusted by his performance in Los Angeles, that he almost split with longtime coach Terry Denison.

- In early 1985, Moorhouse set a short-course world best of 1:0.58.

- Moorhouse took up swimming when a specialist told him it would help him overcome his asthma by widening his diaphragm and increasing his lung capacity. His lung capacity is now 7.7 litres, more than double an average person's.

Adrian Moorhouse's Career

Championship wins

Olympic Games

1988 (Seoul)	100 metres

European Championships

1983 (Rome)	200 metres
1985 (Sofia)	100 metres
1987 (Strasbourg)	100 metres
1989 (Bonn)	100 metres

Commonwealth Games

1982 (Brisbane)	100 metres
1986 (Edinburgh)	200 metres
1990 (Auckland)	100 metres

Britain's best breaststroke swimmer since David Wilkie achieved his proper reward in the swimming pool at Seoul, winning a gold medal by the narrowest possible margin over Karoly Guttler of Hungary. He triumphantly punched the air as his win erased the memory of his failures in 1984.

Moorhouse was a dazzling prospect, a swimmer with the City of Leeds club who won the 200 metres breaststroke in style at the 1983 European Championships. With that success behind him he was favoured to win gold at both 100 and 200 metres in Los Angeles. Yet he fell far short of expectations. In April, after performing poorly in training, he took a blood test which revealed he was suffering from German Measles. It meant a break from training at entirely the wrong time, and on his return to the pool he overtrained, trying to make up for lost time. His performances in the Games reflected that. He finished fourth in the 100 metres, and failed even to make the final in the 200 metres. He was accused by the media of overconfidence, and of swimming 'a foolish race' in his heat. Winning the B final was no consolation, and he returned to Britain low in confidence and angry with the media.

He re-evaluated his goals, and set about preparing for the next European Championships, showing he was back on form with a world best short course time of 1:00.58. He performances could still vary wildly though, an immaculate swim to land the 100 metres European title was followed once more by a poor 200 metres heat, and the B final. This pattern was repeated the next year, when he lost to Victor Davis in the Commonwealth 100 metres, and then turned on the style to beat the Canadian in the 200 metres. Davis turned slightly ahead going into the final length, but a devastating late turn of speed by Moorhouse gained him a thrilling revenge. Moorhouse swam with even more authority at the World Championships in Madrid, and touched the wall nearly a second ahead of Davis in the 100 metres final. Then, for the first and only time in his career, he was disqualified, the judges accusing him of an illegal 'frog' kick going into the final 50 metres. Moorhouse was less deflated. He knew that but for a dubious technicality, he would have been crowned the best swimmer in the world. By Seoul, he was even more certain.

Early in 1988, he broke the European 100 metres record with a 1:1.78 time and, this time, kept his build-up low-key. He arrived in Seoul, swam the fastest time in the heats, and began the final as favourite. It was a far more thrilling race than Moorhouse would have hoped. Dmitri Volkov of Russia swam an impossibly fast first 50 metres. Moorhouse looked at him and thought, 'I hope he dies soon, because otherwise I won't be able to catch him, but whatever happens, I'll race him to the wall, because that's what I came here for.'

Moorhouse gradually closed the gap as the Russian tired and touched the wall first. The Hungarian, Gutter, came alongside and almost

pipped Moorhouse at the last, but the gold belonged to the Yorkshireman.

Moorhouse then set his sights on Barcelona, but to no avail. Although he was still the best 100 metres swimmer in 1989 and 1990, setting a world record of 1:1.49 in Bonn and equalling it twice, he was overhauled by a new Hungarian Norbert Rozsa, at the Perth World Championships who took the gold and his world record. Swimming is a young man's sport and, as Moorhouse observed after the race, 'I did feel my age, especially when I sit next to an eighteen-year-old who's just beaten me.' Britain has yet to find an eighteen-year-old to equal Moorhouse.

'Obviously very talented and with a pretty good record over ten years. His weakness is perhaps a certain amount of inconsistency which, if he'd been able to deal with it, might have meant a bigger reward. Deserves credit for winning in Seoul despite a major setback in LA, and for hard work – swimmers do amazing hours in training with little support, and I hate swimming!'

The moment of triumph. 100 metres breaststroke Gold medal, Seoul 1988.

CLIFF MORGAN

CLIFFORD ISAAC MORGAN
RUGBY UNION – FLY-HALF
BORN: TREBANOG, 7 APRIL 1930

Cliff Morgan's Career

International appearances:	29
International tries:	3
British Championships:	1956
British Triple Crown:	1952
British Lions Tour: (4 tests) (1 try)	1956

Facts about Cliff Morgan

- He was awarded the OBE in 1977 and became a Commander of the Victorian Order in 1986.

- It was Morgan's voice on the commentary for 'the try' on that famous day in Cardiff in 1973 when Gareth Edwards' score began the most breath-taking of matches. The transcript reads: Kirkpatrick ... to Bryan Williams ... This is great stuff ... Phil Bennett covering ... chased by Alistair Scown ... Brilliant ... oh, that's brilliant ... John Williams ... Pullin ... Jonn Davies, great dummy ... David, Tom David, the halfway line ... Brilliant by Quinnell ... This is Gareth Edwards ... a dramatic start ... WHAT A SCORE!

Cliff Morgan exudes pride and joy. It was there in his play, there in his full-time profession and is still there in his long-running radio programme *Sport on Four*. He is an archetypal Welshman, articulate, passionate and nostalgic, and he was the quintessential Welsh outside-half, inventive, dynamic and tough.

He was a child of the Rhondda and played for his local Grammar School, Tonyrefail, under the guidance of his mentor, 'Ned' Gribble. Mr ER Gribble taught woodwork, metalwork and rugby. He used to call Morgan, 'soccer-mad Joe', soccer being young Cliff's first passion, but soon demanded that rugby become his first love because, 'it will sweat the vice out of you'. Morgan later described Ned with great affection: 'He was a gale of humanity and displayed total and utter availability. He had massive judgement and cared for his flock and for standards of performance, skill, behaviour, discipline and fair play.'

Despite being a tiny five feet seven inches, Morgan quickly advanced in the game and made his international debut against Ireland in March 1951. His opposite number that day was the great Jack Kyle. He proceeded to do Morgan two massive favours: first of all he was extremely generous before the match, saying, 'I hope you have a wonderful, wonderful cap today, Cliffie'; secondly, he taught the young man a huge lesson by skipping past him effortlessly for a try, just when Morgan was beginning to relax.

It was a lesson in concentration he never forgot and always regarded Kyle as the best fly-half he ever played against, 'The loveliest of players, the loveliest of men.'

Morgan then had to accept another salutary lesson, against the visiting Springboks, later that year. He was put under pressure, especially by the big flanker, Basie Van Wyk, and kicked instead of playing himself out of trouble. Unfortunately, he kicked badly and admitted that his inexperience had cost Wales the game.

He learned from his mistakes and soon became established as one of Wales' greatest fly-halves. Perhaps his finest moment was as the star of one of the greatest games ever played. It was also the occasion for Morgan's revenge against Van Wyk. It was his first test for the British Lions at Ellis Park, Johannesburg, in 1955. The crowd was 95,000, the biggest throng ever seen at a rugby match. The Lions won 23–22 and Morgan scored a brilliant try early in the second half, leaving Van Wyk trailing in his wake. The great Welsh rugby journalist, JBG Thomas, was one of only two British journalists to witness the match and called it British rugby's greatest victory. The series eventually ended 2–2 and Morgan was made captain for the third test. In total, he played fourteen times on the tour, his only trip for the British Lions.

He went on to play twenty-nine matches for Wales which became a Welsh record for a fly-half. He was the architect of Wales' Triple Crown in 1952 and was captain for their British Championship victory in 1956.

After his retirement he became a broadcaster, writer and television executive and later became Head of Sport and Outside Broadcasts at the BBC.

'Cliff is everything you expect in a Welshman – great with the lads, charming to the ladies and likes nothing better than to sit and reminisce with both. I really enjoy our meetings, as they are always full of sporting tales and inspirational deeds.'

- It is claimed that one of Morgan's skills in resisting challenges was immediately to go limp when held, lulling his opponents into a false sense of security and thus persuading them to loosen their grip, whereupon the diminutive Welshman would spring to life and break away.

- Morgan was awarded an honorary MA from the University of Wales, and an honorary doctorate from Keele University.

- In his time at the BBC he was editor of *Sportsview* and of *Grandstand*.

- Morgan worked hard for various charities, including the Welsh Sport Association for the Mentally Handicapped and the National Children's Home.

- The Lions Tour to South Africa, in 1955, when Morgan played so inspirationally, is still referred to by Springbok rugby fans as the 'Cliff Morgan Tour'.

'Morgan's tour'. His finest hour against the Springboks in 1955.

STIRLING MOSS

**STIRLING CRAWFORD MOSS
MOTOR-RACING DRIVER
BORN: WEST KENSINGTON, 17 SEPTEMBER 1929**

Facts about Stirling Moss

- Moss and Denis Jenkinson had prepared meticulously for the 1995 Mille Miglia. Jenkinson had a note for every bend, hill, etc. and fifteen rehearsed hand-signals to tell Moss what to do. Moss did as he was told, including cresting blind bridges at 170mph.

- His victory in the British Grand Prix at Aintree in 1965 was the first time an English driver had won it.

- He was awarded the OBE in 1959.

- Moss's sportsmanship was legendary. In 1958. Moss had won the Portuguese Grand Prix with Hawthorn second. But Hawthorn faced disqualification after being accused of travelling the wrong way on the track after he had stalled on the last lap. Moss came to his defence and said that Hawthorn had been on the footpath,

Stirling Moss has become so synonymous with fast driving that people are still admonished for their too-rapid exploits behind the wheel with the words, 'Who do you think you are, Stirling Moss?' And this despite the fact that he retired from driving over thirty years ago.

Moss would, and did, drive anything. He was obsessed by the excitement of speed. He is still regarded within the motorsport fraternity as the best all-round driver Britain has ever produced ... and the unluckiest. His bad luck is apparent in having finished second three times in the World Drivers' Championship behind the greatest driver of them all, Juan Manuel Fangio, and once behind Mike Hawthorn, by a single point, when by any logic Moss should have been champion.

He was born into a family immersed in motorsport. His father had raced internationally in the 1920s and his mother had been a trials driver in the 1930s.

As a teenager he made a name in hill-climbing events and started racing Formula Three in 1949. He was talent-spotted to drive for the HWM Formula Two car in 1950 and continued to drive sports cars and in rallies. He even finished second in his first start in the Monte Carlo Rally, in 1952.

When he did make the breakthrough to Formula One, he won little at first because of his determination to drive British cars. But in 1954 he was persuaded to join Maserati. He had an excellent year, including holding the lead in the Italian Grand Prix for nineteen laps before his oil tank split. Without Moss knowing, his father and his manager Ken Gregory had already asked Alfred Neubauer, the team manager of Mercedes, at the start of the season if he was interested in the young Stirling. Neubauer had been watching and at the

Stirling Moss's Career

World Drivers' Championship

2nd	1955, 1956, 1957, 1958
3rd	1959, 1960, 1961

World Championship Grands Prix wins: (16)

1955	British (Mercedes)
1956	Italian, Monaco (Maserati)
1957	British, Italian, Pescara (Vanwall)
1958	*Argentinian, Dutch, Moroccan, Portuguese (Vanwall; *Cooper)
1959	Italian, Portuguese (Cooper)
1960	Monaco, United States (Lotus)
1961	German, Monaco (Lotus)

**Summary:
66 Grands Prix; 16 poles; 20 fastest laps; 16 wins; 185.5 points
Winner Mille Miglia: 1955**

end of the season Moss signed for Mercedes.

1955 became a magical year. The stunning silver Mercedes, with Fangio as number one and Moss as number two, dominated Formula One. Moss won his first Grand Prix – the British, at Aintree (although Fangio probably let him win!) and came second in the Drivers' Championship as Fangio won by a country mile.

Moss was also in a Mercedes when he won with a brilliant performance in the Mille Miglia that year. In a hair-raising chase against the clock, over a thousand miles of public roads, Moss shattered every record, with his navigator Denis Jenkinson, to win by more than thirty minutes.

Mercedes pulled out of racing soon afterwards following an awful accident at Le Mans which killed eighty people. Fangio and Moss went their separate ways; Fangio to Ferrari and Moss to Maserati. Despite two epic victories in 1956, he was second again behind Fangio. In 1957 he drove for Vanwall and this time had three wins, but still

Right: Exhausted and in need of support, from team owner Tony Vandervell, after winning the Pescara Grands Prix in a Vanwall in 1957.

Moss in a Maserati at Brands Hatch in 1977.

not the track, when the offence took place. Moss was adamant he did the right thing. 'It was absolutely the right thing to do. To me, that's what sport is all about. Or at least, that's what it should be about.'

• For years Moss refused to drive for Ferrari after Enzo Ferrari had snubbed him years before. The old man of Ferrari eventually came cap-in-hand, in 1962, and pleaded with him. Moss agreed. Sadly, he never got the drive because of his Aintree accident.

came second to the great Argentinian.

Moss later took great comfort from those three years chasing Fangio: first because the maestro paid him the compliment of calling Moss his most talented rival; and second from the forging of a life-long friendship between the two of them.

After Fangio's retirement in 1958, Moss's rival, became Mike Hawthorn in the Ferrari. Moss stayed with Vanwall. It was Moss's most frustrating year. He won four times to Hawthorn's one, but still didn't win the championship. Hawthorn's five second places were crucial. The scoring system did much to thwart him. At that time a single championship point was awarded for a driver with the fastest lap. Moss may well have lost the title in the Portuguese Grand Prix in August when he misinterpreted a pit signal and failed to set the fastest lap, which Hawthorn went on to do. Hawthorn's subsequent point made the difference in the end.

Moss continued to drive well for the next three seasons in a Cooper and, eventually, a Lotus. Remarkably, after all that had happened, he had three years of coming third in the championship

despite winning two races each year, and despite a bad accident at Spa in 1960 which cost him two broken legs.

His career came to a sudden and almost fatal end at Goodwood in 1962. In an accident that he still finds difficult to explain, he came off the outside of a bend when trying to pass Graham Hill, and hit a bank head-on. He wrapped the car around himself and was trapped for forty minutes. He eventually recovered but never raced again at the highest level.

Moss' popularity never diminished and he remains one of Britain's favourite sports personalities.

'Stirling had some bad luck in that he had to face Fangio, but this also worked in his favour because the British have passion for the man they see as theirs, and who is a trier. His talent is evident in his record, which shows he could win when not even driving the best machine.'

ALEX MURPHY

ALEXANDER JOHN MURPHY
RUGBY LEAGUE – HALF-BACK
BORN: ST HELENS, 22 APRIL 1939

Ray French, the Rugby League commentator, doesn't pull any punches in his assessment of Alex Murphy: 'The most complete footballer I have ever seen in either code of rugby.' That kind of accolade doesn't come often in any sport.

Alex Murphy was always precocious. He played for the junior and senior XIIIs simultaneously at school whilst still only ten years old. On the eve of his sixteenth birthday, the club scouts were camped outside his house waiting for midnight to strike to be the first to get his signature. He eventually signed for his home-town club, St Helens. By the age of nineteen he was acknowledged as the finest scrum-half in the world.

He was coached by the legendary Jim Sullivan at St Helens, but most of Murphy's gifts were natural. His ebullience was boundless, his speed phenomenal. Often his approach to the game – his arrogance, his swaggering bare-faced cheek – had a game won before a pass was thrown. He had scant regard for authority from the beginning; he even challenged the awesome Jim Sullivan. Murphy apparently asked for a transfer from St Helens when he was refused a game in the first team, despite only being a member of the 'A' team at the time. He got short shrift.

Murphy went to Australia at the age of nineteen in 1958 and beat Billy Boston's record as the youngest player to tour 'Down Under'. He was an outstanding success, scoring twenty-one tries in only twenty matches. Great Britain won the series 2–1.

He went on to play twenty-seven times for Great Britain, including a memorable match against France in 1959, when he scored four tries from scrum-half in a 50–16 annihilation. That particular feat was not bettered until 1991 when Martin Offiah scored five against France from the wing. In all, Murphy scored seventeen tries for his country.

1959 also brought the first of a series of honours in his club career that would fill a large trophy room. St Helens won the championship in 1959 and 1960 and added the Challenge Cup with Murphy's first trip to Wembley, in 1961. The great Lancashire team won two more championships, in 1965 and 1966, and, with Murphy as captain, won the double by beating Wigan 21–2, at Wembley.

But Murphy's career at St Helens came to an end in 1967 as his fiery temperament and a series of incidents took him to Leigh who were not then at the forefront of the game. Murphy transformed them. He became player-coach at twenty-seven and in 1971 took them to Wembley. He gave a brilliantly shrewd display as the little Lancashire

Alex Murphy's Career

League championships (6)

1959	St Helens
1960	St Helens
1965	St Helens
1966	St Helens
1973	Warrington

Challenge Cups (4)

1961	St Helens
1966	St Helens
1971	Leigh
1974	Warrington

Club Tries:	275
Great Britain	
International appearances:	27
International Tries:	17

Facts about Alex Murphy

- Murphy was never afraid to voice his opinions, nor was he in awe of ferocious forwards. When once challenged by Hull Kingston Rovers forward, Frank Foster, about a disputed last-minute try, Murphy responded, 'Read the Liverpool Echo tomorrow night Frank, then you'll see it was a try.'

- His signing-on fee at St Helens was £80.00.

- 'Murphy the Mouth' was the title of his weekly newspaper column.

- Like many league players of his generation, the rules allowed him to play rugby union while doing his National Service. However, he wasn't always keen to play the amateur game for King and Country and had, on one occasion, to be threatened with a posting to the Pacific Island of Guam to persuade him to play.

- Murphy's presence in the RAF team, in the fifteen-man code, was largely responsible for their success in matching the soldiers and the sailors in the inter-services competitions of 1958–60.

- His best performance for the RAF at rugby union won him rare praise. It came against Cambridge University when he played at stand-off. His opposite number was Richard Sharp, the current England rugby union fly-half. He outplayed Sharp and scored three tries. Pat Marshall, rugby union correspondent of the Daily Express, described him as 'One of the truly great players of our time.'

team beat Leeds, the odds-on favourites, 24–7. Murphy was named 'Man of the Match'.

He then pulled off the same trick again, at Warrington, as player-coach. They won the league in 1973 and, in 1974, won the Challenge Cup, at Wembley. Murphy had won four times at Wembley with three different clubs, having been captain of all three; had played in three different positions – centre, stand-off and scrum-half; and scored in all four finals.

After retiring at the end of that season, Murphy continued to be a successful coach and was much sought after to revive flagging fortunes. He later became as forceful a TV pundit as he had been on the field.

'Alex was a brilliant player with extraordinary speed. Going to small teams and making them big shows the true stature of the man.'

Murphy crowning St Helens' great double year in 1966 with the Challenge Cup trophy at Wembley.

MARTIN OFFIAH

**MARTIN OFFIAH
RUGBY LEAGUE – WINGER
BORN: HACKNEY, 29 DECEMBER 1966**

Martin Offiah has taken to the game of rugby league like a duck to the waters of Hackney marshes. In turn, the world of rugby league will be forever grateful that a boy from Hackney, in East London, should have ventured north to forbidding sounding places like Batley, Dewsbury and Hunslet to earn his living.

When Offiah's father returned to Nigeria in the late 1970s, his mother heard of Wolverston Hall, a boarding school run by the Inner London Education Authority. It had been called 'the working class Eton' and seemed ideal for young Martin who, as a teenager, needed the extra guidance and tuition Wolverston could provide. It

must have worked because he left with a long list of 'O' levels and a place at the University of Bath to study Physical Education.

Unfortunately, for players and supporters at the Recreation Ground, Offiah didn't go to Bath but, after playing for Ipswich Rugby Club for a while, he went to play for Rosslyn Park. This was rugby in the fifteen-man formation of course – he was still a long way from the gritty northern pastures of Mount Pleasant, Crown Flatt and McLaren Field.

He made a dramatic impression, and it is of course 'union's' loss and 'league's' gain that that impression was made before the fifteen-man code could offer Offiah the kind of rewards that 'league'

**Facts about
Martin Offiah**

- Northern quick-wittedness soon had him nicknamed 'Chariots ...'. Aussies being Aussies, this was adapted to 'Great balls ...'

- Offiah has also won the World Club Championship with Wigan against the Brisbane Broncos, in 1994.

- The new situation in rugby union opens up all sorts of possibilities for Offiah to rediscover his talent at the fifteen-man game. There is already talk of a Wigan versus Bath two code confrontation.

- Offiah's best time for 100 metres is 10.8 seconds.

- He has beaten Ade Mafe in a sprint and Jonathan Edwards in a broad jump.

'Chariots' in full flight!

- He is proud of his single entry in Wisden, in 1986, as a cricketer for Essex second II. 'Played in one match, M Offiah 0 and 1–1 – 66–0.' But is even more proud of once having bowled one, G Gooch in the nets at Essex. The great cricketer's response is etched in Offiah's memory: 'Jolly well bowled Martin.'

- Offiah was very sorry to hear of the closure of Wolverston Hall, the boarding school which had helped him such a lot as a youngster. It didn't survive the government's education 'reorganisation.'

- He is an avid Manchester United fan and often can be seen in the Old Trafford VIP's box. He is great friends with Paul Ince. In rugby league, his closest associates are Ellery Hanley and Shaun Edwards.

- Offiah can sing, has worked as a model and done extensive television work, and all these activities are part of his plan for a future after rugby league.

Martin Offiah's Career
(up to end of 1994-95 season)

Challenge Cup finals (4)

1992* (2 tries)	Wigan
1993	Wigan
1994* (2 tries)	Wigan
1995	Wigan
* Lance Todd Trophy	

League Championship (6)

1987–88	Widnes
1988–89	Widnes
1991–92	Wigan
1992–93	Wigan
1993–94	Wigan
1994–95	Wigan

Premiership Trophy (6)

1987–88	Widnes
1988–89	Widnes
1989–90	Widnes
1991–92	Wigan
1993–94	Wigan
1994–95	Wigan

Regal Trophy (2)

1992–93	Wigan
1994–95	Wigan

**Man of Steel Award
(Player of the Year award): 1988**

Club tries: 378

International appearances: 33

International tries: 26 (including a record five in one game against France in 1991)

could lay at his door. He was chosen for the Barbarians' tour of Wales and then had an outstanding tournament in the Middlesex Sevens, at Twickenham, when he was still only twenty.

But the Widnes coach, Doug Laughton, had already spotted him and he signed up to join the 'Chemics' of Naughton Park, in 1987.

He was an immediate sensation. In 1987-88, his first season, he was leading try-scorer in the league with forty-four tries. In 1988–89 he scored an amazing sixty tries, nearly twice the number of anybody else, and he was leading try scorer for the next two seasons with forty-five and forty-nine respectively.

During the remarkable four-year period Widnes won two league Championships, in 1987–88 and 1988–89, and three consecutive Premiership trophies, in 1988, 1989 and 1990.

Offiah refused to play for Widnes from the beginning of the 1991–92 season because of contractual disputes and was placed on the transfer list at an asking price of £700,000. He eventually signed for Wigan for £440,000 on 3 January 1992, nearly doubling the record transfer fee. The trophies then started to arrive at Central Park like confetti at a wedding.

Even though he missed half the season, Offiah still managed thirty tries. The next season brought thirty-two, followed by thirty-seven and eventually fifty-three for the season 1994–95.

Vivaldi must have had a vision of Offiah's future at Wigan when he wrote his glorious Four Seasons in 1725: they won the Challenge Cup in all four years and Offiah scored two tries and won the Lance Todd trophy for Man of the Match in both 1992 and 1994; they won the Championship in all four years and in doing so won ninety-three games and lost only eighteen; they won three Premiership trophies, missing out only in 1993; and they won two Regal trophies in 1993 and 1995. The best season of the four was 1994–95 when they became the first team in rugby league history to win the modern Grand Slam of all the game's domestic honours.

The 1995–96 season saw Offiah sign a new three-year contract with Wigan and pass the 400 tries landmark in his career. He has already done enough to rank with Billy Boston as the game's most exciting winger and prolific try scorer, and was only thirty in December 1996. It is hard to imagine what assessments will be made of him ten years from now.

'Martin is a sensation wherever he plays. This man is no shy wallflower, he works and plays hard, and why not? He's one of those players you watch and sometimes think, what's all the fuss about, then comes that magic moment and you understand.'

STEVE OVETT

STEVEN MICHAEL JAMES OVETT
ATHLETICS – MIDDLE-DISTANCE RUNNER
BORN: BRIGHTON, 9 OCTOBER 1955

The gesture that became synonymous with Ovett's greatest days, this time saluting his 800m gold medal in Moscow.

Facts about Steve Ovett

- Ovett's worst injury was suffered on a training run in November 1981. He ran into some railings, smashing his knee ligaments and requiring surgery.

- Ovett once said, of himself, 'I enjoy being myself 90 percent of the time, and Steve Ovett, the runner, 10 percent of the time.

- Mel Watman, a coach and athletics writer said of Ovett, 'One can state with some authority that Steve Ovett is the greatest big-time competitor ever to wear a British vest.'

The late 1970s and early 1980s was a golden era for British middle-distance running. Coe, Ovett and Cram broke world records and won championships galore. The first of these three to rise to prominence was Steve Ovett.

Ovett was born in Brighton and, encouraged by his parents, turned into an excellent junior runner. In 1970, he was English Schools champion over 400 metres, but soon moved up to middle-distance, achieving his first world ranking at 800 metres by 1974. Already, he was seen as a tactically astute runner, and, from 200 metres out, had a devastating final sprint that could see off any opponents.

Ovett's progression over 800 metres was steady, gold in the European Junior Championships in 1973, silver at senior level the next year and gold in the 1975 European Cup, his first major victory. He went to the Olympics in Montreal but he could do nothing against the great Alberto Juantorena, and finished fifth as the Cuban streaked to a world record.

Ovett now started to move beyond 800 metres, and started performing well at the 1500 metres and the mile. In 1977, he set a new UK mile record of 3:54.69 at Crystal Palace, and took the UK Championship at 1500 metres. He embarked on a run of success that would see him win forty-five consecutive races at the two distances between 1977 and 1980.

In 1978, at the European Championships, Ovett won the 1500 metres and then over 800 metres faced Seb Coe, who was starting to challenge his dominance over that distance. Ovett finished ahead of Coe, but both of them trailed in behind Olaf Beyer of East Germany. From that point on, the two runners avoided each other.

Coe's performances in 1979, breaking three world records in forty-one days, seemed to give him the crown of Britain's best middle-distance runner, but in 1980, Ovett started setting records himself. On 1 July, three weeks before the Moscow Games, he broke Coe's world mile best with a time

of 3:48.8. He then equalled Coe's world mark at 1500 metres, 3:32.1, just nine days before he was due to be in action in Moscow.

The confrontation between the two runners was one of the most eagerly awaited events in Moscow. Although they had not met for two years, they were now clearly the best two athletes at both 800 and 1500 metres. Ovett was favoured in the longer distance, while Coe was tipped to beat him in the other. Unlike his rival, Ovett prepared very quietly, not talking to the press. His only statement was that the 800 metres was wide-open, and he was 90 percent sure of winning the 1500 metres.

The 800 metres final played right into Ovett's hands. After a very slow first lap, Ovett found himself boxed in, and forced his way through to second place; Coe was way behind. At 70 metres, when Ovett burst past the Russian Kirov into the lead, he suddenly found his rival was in no position to challenge. Ovett won by three metres in a time identical to his fifth-place finish in Montreal.

Ovett was now clear favourite to complete a golden double. Perhaps, though, with one medal already pocketed, he was not as hungry as his rival. Certainly, he coasted into the final without any great problem, but when he kicked on the final bend this time he found that Coe's finishing burst was even faster. He saw the race was lost, and eventually settled for third place, behind Straub of East Germany who managed to hold the Englishman off. Ovett, though, had no complaints. He informed waiting journalists that he was as pleased with his bronze as he had been with his gold. He finished the season in fine style. A month after the Games, he lowered the 1500 metre mark to 3:31.36 in Koblenz.

The next season belonged to Coe, who set four world records. Ovett chipped in with his own contribution. For two days he held the world mile record after a run of 3:48.40 in Koblenz. The media rivalry between the two great runners was still alive.

At the same time a new rival, Steve Cram, appeared on the scene. Cram won the gold at the first World Championships in Helsinki in 1983, while Ovett, now twenty-seven years old, could finish only fourth. His talent still appeared from time to time, and in September that year he set his

Steve Ovett's Career

Olympic Games

1976	(Montreal)	800 metres	5th
		1500 metres	did not qualify
1980	(Moscow)	800 metres	1st
		1500 metres	3rd
1984	(Los Angeles)	800 metres	8th
		1500 metres	did not finish

World Championships

1983	(Helsinki)	1500 metres	4th
1987	(Rome)	5000 metres	10th

European Championships

1974		800 metres	2nd
1978		800 metres	2nd
		1500 metres	1st

World Records

1500 metres	3:32.09	Oslo	July 1980
	3:31.36	Koblenz	July 1980
	3:30.77	Rieti	September 1983
Mile	3:48.8	Oslo	July 1980
	3:48.40	Koblenz	August 1981
2 Miles	8:13.51	Crystal Palace	September 1978

sixth and final world record at Rieti in Italy with a time of 3:30.77. At the Los Angeles Olympics the next year, Ovett was affected by a viral infection. He could only manage eighth in the 800 metres and then, as a British medal sweep looked a tantalising possibility, stepped off the track and out of the 1500 metres when the illness affected his breathing.

He decided to step up to the 5000 metres in 1986, and was rewarded with a gold at the Commonwealth Games in Edinburgh. However, he failed to finish in the European Cup final later that season, and Ovett's career at the very pinnacle was over. He continued to run for the next few seasons, although he was best remembered for his tearful falling-out with Britain's athletics supremo Andy Norman over payments at the 1989 AAA (Amateur Athletic Association) Championships. Ovett, always a great runner, was also a very private and complicated individual.

'Ovett, with the help of Coe and Cram, transformed athletics. He was the first of the famous trio to take on and beat the world. He was also one of the few talents who has been able to sustain form, from being a child star through all the levels, until becoming Olympic Champion and World Record Holder. In the media he was 'bad-guy' the opposite to the 'Mr Nice Guy' Coe. Most people had their favourite between the two, and a lot of them liked the one who played the villain. Due to earlier criticism he mostly refused interviews, but as the years went by he mellowed and, after 1980, he became much more media-friendly. I think that, had he done the double in Moscow, he would have made himself the greatest middle distance runner of all time, but he is still an all-time great which is not too shabby!'

ANN PACKER

ANN ELIZABETH PACKER (LATER BRIGHTWELL)
ATHLETICS – 400/800 METRE RUNNER
BORN: MOULSFORD, 2 MARCH 1942

Facts about Ann Packer

- Packer (and Brightwell) were awarded the MBE in 1969.

- Their sons made a name for themselves in sport: Gary was a useful 400 metres runner. Ian and David became professional footballers with Manchester City. In fact, Ian played for England Schools, Youths and Under-21s.

- The 800 metres for women had only been run twice before in the Olympics; in 1928 and 1960. 1928 was its inauguration in the Games and, understandably, at the end of one of the toughest races on the programme, several women were lying exhausted by the side of the track. The male authorities were horrified, as were the press: It was 'undignified' and 'dangerous for the fairer sex!' It took

Ann Packer had a remarkably brief career at the forefront of world sport, but such was its fairytale quality that she will always be remembered for a single supreme moment. Before the Tokyo Olympics in 1964, her only medal had been a silver in the sprint relay at the 1962 Commonwealth Games in Perth. In fact, Packer had only become a world-ranked athlete the year before, when she had moved from sprinting and jumping to 400 metres. The story of the next twelve months was one of those enchanting and inspiring tales that create the folklore of sport.

Packer was born into a peaceful rural environment in the Berkshire village of Moulsford. She was a naturally gifted athlete and had an idyllic outdoor upbringing. Because she was naturally athletic, she was seen as a 'tomboy', a patronising label readily pinned on girls of her generation who didn't conform to the pink and frills of convention.

She progressed through school athletics and teacher training at Dartford Training College, and began a career at Lady Edridge Grammar School in Croydon in the autumn of 1963. The Tokyo Olympics were less than a year away and Packer's lonely winter training would have to be done on top of the demands of a full-time teaching job. The life of a top-quality athlete is always difficult, but it is easy to forget the extra dedication and heartache it must have involved in the days when the amateur code predominated.

As Packer looked forward to Tokyo, in 1963, she could look back less than five years to the beginnings of a remarkably short but varied athletics career. She had won the 100 yards at the 1959 English Schools Championships; then, in 1960, had won the Women's Amateur Athletic Association (AAA) long jump title and had

Ann Packer's Career

Olympic Games
Gold	800 metres	1964
Silver	400 metres	1964

Commonwealth Games
Silver	4 x 100 metres relay	1962

World Record*
800 metres	1964	2:01.1

* Ann Packer's time in Tokyo of 2:01.1 knocked over a second off Australian, Dixie Willis's, previous record. However, a time of 1:59.1 had been set by Sin-Kim Dan of North Korea at the GANEFO Games in Jakarta in November 1963. The GANEFO games were not recognised by the IAAF (the governing body of Athletics) nor by the International Olympic Committee and the Korean's record was not ratified. However, many statisticians regard it as a perfectly good record. The GANEFO Games were the Games of the New Emerging Forces and were thought to be too politically inspired by Communist China. Sadly, Sin-Kim Dan was barred from competing against Packer in Tokyo because of her participation in the GANEFO Games. The Korean was clearly an outstanding athlete, because she had also a recorded time of 51.9 for the 400 metres, better than Cuthbert's and Packer's 400 metres times in Tokyo: 52.0 and 52.2 respectively.

competed in her first international in the same event. In 1962, she had surprised everyone in reaching the final of the 200 metres in the European Championships, in Belgrade, and later that year came sixth in the 80 metres hurdles and won a silver medal with the British team in the sprint relay at the Perth Commonwealth Games. It had been as recently as the summer of 1963 that she had moved up to 400 metres and in only four races had produced a world-class time of 53.4.

Packer travelled to Tokyo in 1964 to compete in both her new speciality, the 400 metres, and, out of curiosity, the 800 metres.

The 400 metres proved to be an outstanding race. Betty Cuthbert, the great Australian runner had a point to prove. She had won three gold medals in Melbourne in 1956, but in Rome four years later, had had to withdraw because of injury. Packer ran a personal best and set a European record, but it wasn't enough and Cuthbert beat her by a yard in a new Olympic record time of 52.0. Cuthbert said it was 'the only perfect race I have ever run'.

Packer was desperately disappointed and tired and considered withdrawing from the 800 metres altogether where it was thought she had little or no chance of even making the final. However, when Robbie Brightwell, who would later become her husband, finished fourth in the 400 metres, Packer found the motivation to run.

She had only just qualified in the heats, was the second slowest qualifier from the semi-final and had only run five races over two laps before departing for Tokyo.

With a little less than the finishing straight to go, the race seemed to be concluding as expected. Maryvonne Dupureur, from France, who had set a new Olympic record in the semi-final at 2:04.1, was leading and Packer was still bunched with the pack. But she'd been finding the race remarkably easy and suddenly burst from the group with about 70 metres to go, overhauled Dupureur and won by an amazing four metres. Her sprinting background had been crucial and she had smashed the world record in a time of 2:01.1.* Packer said afterwards, 'It was so easy, I could not believe I had won. I was thinking about Robbie and not about myself, and so I wasn't nervous.'

The fairy-tale ending; Packer on the winners' podium in Tokyo in 1964.

One of the most remarkable of all Olympic fairytales was made complete when Robbie Brightwell repaid Ann's gesture by winning a silver medal with the British 4 x 400 metres relay team. Packer and Brightwell were married after the games and Packer retired from competition to concentrate on her career and family. She was twenty-two years-old. The short but amazing flight of a beautiful butterfly of British sport was over.

'They say truth is stranger than fiction. Having read Ann's story, you wouldn't believe it if you didn't know it was true. I mean, to just be there at the Olympics to see how it goes, and to become Olympic champion and world record holder after eight races! There is no telling what Ann could have gone on to, had she carried on, but sometimes, once up the mountain is enough.'

thirty-two years to persuade the authorities to allow the race to be included again, four years prior to Tokyo, in Rome in 1960.

- Packer played hockey to a high standard at school and played for the South of England in 1969.

RODNEY PATTISON

RODNEY STUART PATTISON
YACHTING – HELMSMAN
BORN: CAMPBELTOWN, 15 AUGUST 1943

Rodney Pattison's Career

Olympic Games

1968	Gold	Flying Dutchman
1972	Gold	Flying Dutchman
1976	Silver	Flying Dutchman

World Championships

1960	Winner	Cadet
1968	Winner	Flying Dutchman
1969	Winner	¼ ton
1969	Winner	Flying Dutchman
1970	Winner	Soling
1970	Winner	Flying Dutchman
1971	Winner	Flying Dutchman
1985	Winner	1 ton

European Championships

1968	Winner	Flying Dutchman
1971	Winner	Flying Dutchman
1972	Winner	Flying Dutchman
1975	Winner	Flying Dutchman

Facts about Rodney Pattison

- The Flying Dutchman yachting class uses a centreboard dinghy and a crew of two, one of whom is attached to the boat by a rope and a trapeze, which allows him to lean far beyond the craft without falling overboard. In Olympic yachting, each class runs seven races over a course marked by buoys. Those first across the line get the lowest scores as follows: first place 0, second place 3, third place 5.7, fourth place 8, fifth place 10. At the conclusion of the seventh race, each crew is allowed to drop its worst score.

- Pattison was very proud of his Olympic achievement in Mexico. 'It's the ultimate in one's sport, and standing on the rostrum was special. It felt like being on top of the world.'

Rodney Pattison was a perfectionist in a sport where even the minutest technical detail, the slightest error of judgement, or the tiniest nuance of wind can make the difference between winning and losing. Pattison's record in yachting is unparalleled and he is respected throughout the world as one of the greatest sailors of all time.

Yachting, even at the Olympics, takes place away from the crowds, away from the television cameras and often miles away from the main Olympic venue itself. For that reason, although many people will know the name, few would recognise the man who has won two Olympic gold medals and a silver at consecutive Olympics, eight World Championships and four European Championships.

Pattison's speciality is the Flying Dutchman class, probably the most spectacular of all the Olympic classes. It has a massive area of sail which generates high speeds, but it also makes it a very difficult craft to handle for the two-man crew. All three of Pattison's Olympic medals were with different crew members.

He was born in Campbeltown in Argyllshire in 1943 and was a World Champion by the age of seventeen, when he won the International Cadet Championships in 1960, with his brother. Sailing then became his profession as well as his hobby and passion when he joined the Navy.

In 1968, he made a dramatic impact on the world of competitive sailing by winning both the European and World titles in the Flying Dutchman class, and then travelling to Acapulco for the Olympic regatta at the Mexico Olympics.

The conditions were hot and humid, but Pattison was immaculately prepared as always and won easily with Ian McDonald-Smith as his partner.

He resigned his commission in the navy, joined a boat-building company and set about challenging the record books. He won eight more World and European titles before travelling to Kiel for the 1972 Olympic competition. The Baltic Sea port of Kiel, was the traditional centre of German yachting and huge preparations were made for the Olympics. An entire new harbour and range of boat-house facilities were built, and during the competition itself, forty boats were put to sea for the press and officials. Pattison and his new partner, Christopher Davies, won by a wide margin. They won four of the first six races and didn't bother to race on the final day.

Pattison won the European Flying Dutchman class in 1975 before attempting to win his third successive gold medal, this time with Julian Brooke-Houghton as partner. The Olympic regatta was held at Kingston Ontario and the first signs were good for the British team.

Pattison won the first race, but fell away for the

final three, finishing eighteenth, twelfth and eleventh out of twenty starters. By the final race the German pair, Jorg and Eckart Diesch, were ten points clear when disaster almost struck. On the way to the start, they discovered they had a cracked centreboard. They rushed back to replace it and just made it to the start in time. They finished fifth in the race, good enough for gold, and the British pair had to settle for silver. Pattison took it as a personal failure.

Rodney Pattison concentrated on boat-building after Montreal, from his base at Poole in Dorset. But he was still good enough to come close to qualifying for the 1984 British team for the Los Angeles Olympics and to be co-skipper of 'Victory', Peter de Savary's British entry for the 1983 Americas Cup.

A fierce competitor and a great Olympian, Rodney Pattison is one of British sport's unsung heroes.

'Two Olympic golds and a silver will get you into most lists when you are looking for all-time greats, but I think it would be true to say that the only other well known sailor I know of is Nelson!'

- The Olympic Flying Dutchman class is classified as a team sport, so Pattison's three medals are recorded as having been won by Great Britain, although both members of the team get a medal. But, as skipper, Pattison takes all the glory.

- He was a submariner in the navy. Steering was a lot easier because he didn't have to contend with the wind. However, he did have to do it in the dark.

- He was awarded the MBE in 1968.

- He was not above using a trick or two to confuse his eagle-eyed opponents:

- In 1968, he appeared to fit a new radically-shaped centreboard to his dinghy just to get the opposition guessing. It worked and a debate ensued about what the Brit was up to. Pattison secretly discarded it before the race and went back to the conventional shape.

- He also sported an intriguing new electronic wind indicator, but it had no battery.

Pattison in a more mundane crewman's role; Britain's most famous sailor since Nelson!

FRED PERRY

FREDERICK JOHN PERRY
TABLE TENNIS PLAYER, TENNIS PLAYER
BORN: STOCKPORT, 18 MAY 1909
DIED: LONDON, 2 FEBRUARY 1995

Facts about Fred Perry

- His comments about the early days at Wimbledon were bitter: 'I was born the wrong side of the tram-lines for some at Wimbledon. I was too brash for their tastes. It was a class-ridden set-up. I can still get angry when I think of the shabby way I was treated.'

- In order to develop extra fitness, Perry trained with Arsenal Football Club in the 1930s.

- After he turned pro, in 1936, he was shunned by the LTA (Lawn Tennis Association). When he toured as a professional with Ellsworth Vines, in 1937, he had to play at the Empire Pool Wembley, Bournemouth Football Ground and Edinburgh Town Hall.

Fred Perry was Britain's greatest ever tennis player by a long way, and one of the best half-dozen players ever to play the game anywhere in the world. He was world number one for several years during the 1930s and had the unusual distinction of being world champion at another sport before he won any of his tennis titles.

His first love was table tennis and in 1929, at the age of twenty, he travelled to Budapest, where he beat Mihail Szabados of Hungary to win the world singles title. In the same year he qualified for Wimbledon, but lost in the first round.

Perry did not have the conventional upbringing of a tennis player of his day. He didn't go to public school or university and was the son of a Labour MP. That represented a much greater divide then than it would now. The 1920s were the era of the General Strike and great social upheaval. It is a testament to Perry's great talent that eventually he swept aside any opposition the establishment might have presented to him.

He soon played more and more lawn tennis and less table tennis. In 1931 he made his debut in the Davis Cup and reached his first Wimbledon final, losing in the men's doubles with his partner GP Hughes, to the French 'Musketeers', Borotra and Brugnon.

His first Grand Slam title came in 1933 when he beat Jack Crawford in the US Championships in five sets. He then beat Crawford twice in 1934, first to capture the Australian title and then to win

Perry at his magnificent best, playing at Wimbledon in 1936 during his third consecutive Championships victory.

- He once agreed with the organiser to play in a Los Angeles tournament on the condition that he could have a date with the screen goddess, Jean Harlow. Perry was joking, but the date was arranged. He is rumoured to have got home at eight the following morning.

- Perry once played in a celebrity match between the USA and Great Britain. The British team was Fred Perry and Charlie Chaplin, the USA was represented by Ellsworth Vines and Groucho Marx.

- He was made a member of the All-England Club after his victory in 1934. His beaten opponent, Jack Crawford, an Australian, was given much praise and a bottle of champagne. Perry's badge of membership – the club tie – was left draped over his chair without a word being said. As he lay in the bath after the victory, he heard a committee member say to his beaten opponent, 'Well, today the better man lost.' When Perry turned professional in 1936, his All-England membership was automatically rescinded.

- The Italian player, Umberto de Stefani, humiliated Perry in the 1934 French Championships when Perry had twisted an ankle. Not wanting to default, Perry offered the Italian an honourable victory as long as he didn't make him run around too much. De Stefani reneged and ran Perry ragged. Perry promised revenge 6–0, 6–0, 6–0. It took him two years to find his opportunity, but he got it in Melbourne and taught the Italian the lesson he deserved.

- Perry's father was MP for Kettering in 1923, lost the seat in 1924 and won it back in 1929.

- In 1932 Perry beat Borotra, then ranked world number one, in the Paris Tennis Tournament in the afternoon, and then in the evening beat the reigning world table tennis champion, Victor Barna, in the Paris Table Tennis Tournament.

- When Bjorn Borg won his fourth Wimbledon singles title against Roscoe Tanner in 1979, Perry was the first down on courtside to congratulate him, despite the fact that he was supposed to be finishing his commentary with Gerry Williams in the BBC Radio box.

Fred Perry's Career

Table Tennis

World Singles Champion	1929
English Doubles Champion	1928
	1929
	1930
English Mixed Doubles Champion	1929

Lawn Tennis

World ranking:

1931	4th
1932	7th
1933	2nd
1934	1st
1935	1st
1936	1st

Wimbledon Championship

Singles:	1934
	1935
	1936
Mixed Doubles:	1935
	1936

French Championships

Singles:	1935
Mens Doubles:	1933
Mixed Doubles:	1932

Australian Championships

Singles:	1934
Mens Doubles:	1934

United States Championships

Singles:	1933
	1934
	1936
Mixed Doubles:	1932

Summary: 8 Singles, 2 Doubles, 4 Mixed Doubles, Total 14 titles

Davis Cup Victories: (4)
1933, 1934, 1935, 1936

Summary: 20 matches, 52 rubbers, won 45, lost 7

his first Wimbledon. He then went on to beat Wilmer Allison to win his second US title.

When he beat Gottfried Von Cramm in the 1935 final of the French Championships, he became the first player to have won all four Grand Slam events. He was indisputably the world number one and would remain so until he turned professional in 1937. In total he won eight Grand Slam singles titles: one Australian, one French, three US and three Wimbledons. It is obviously for his Wimbledon exploits that he is best remembered in Britain. After his victory against Crawford, in 1934, he demolished Von Cramm twice, in 1935, 6–2, 6–4, 6–4 and in 1935, 6–1, 6–1, 6–0. It is hardly surprising that the gates at the All-England club are named after him and that his statue gazes out over the concourse.

However, two of Perry's best matches were played at Forest Hills in the US Open. In 1934 he won a five-set thriller against Allison and then beat the great Don Budge, the following year, in one of the greatest matches ever played, 2–6, 6–2, 8–6, 1–6, 10–8.

Perry turned professional at the end of the 1936 season and became United States professional champion in 1938 and 1941. He took American citizenship and served in the war as an American. He lived life to the full on the West coast and rubbed shoulders with stars and celebrities. He was the first modern tennis player but was rejected by the British establishment. He in turn rejected them and sought his fortune elsewhere. It was typical of him and no more than his British peers deserved.

Perhaps Perry's greatest achievement was in the Davis Cup, for his country, rather than in the Grand Slams, for himself. With Perry as number one, ably

'Fred was one of the all-time greats when it came to tennis. His playing record clearly states that. The odds must have been stacked against him because of his upbringing, which would have been insurmountable to all but the great. You only have to look at the last vestiges of the class system that are still entrenched in tennis 60 years later, to see what he was up against. The Fred I met at Wimbledon each year still had a real love of life, God only knows what he must have been like in the '30s and '40s when he had Charlie Chaplin, Douglas Fairbanks and Groucho Marks for friends!'

Being saluted by the great and the good at Wimbledon. He finally got all the accolades he deserved.

- In 1993 Perry had a special reunion at Wimbledon. Sixty years on, all the members of the British Davis Cup team of 1933 were still alive. They got together to remember the occasion when they beat the 'invincible' French. Pat Hughes was ninety, Bunny Austin and Harold Lee both eighty-seven, Perry eighty-four and Raymond Tuckey seventy-seven. Tennis had been good to them.

- Towards the end of his life he had heart surgery. He was typically flippant about it. 'They used part of a pig in the operation. Sometimes I grunt a lot.'

- He and the All-England Club eventually forgot their differences. He said, 'All the hatchets have been buried now. We've got the statue, the Fred Perry Gates. I've always loved Wimbledon, the place, the event. If someone said, "Fred, you've got one more set before you die," I'd choose the Centre Court at Wimbledon. That would be lovely.'

assisted by Bunny Austin, Britain achieved what was thought to be unattainable: four Davis Cups in a row from 1933 to 1936. Perry played in twenty Davis Cup ties. He won forty-five of his fifty-two rubbers.

Fred Perry's achievements were staggering. No one played big points like him until Borg and Becker came along. His legendary running forehand may have been the finest ever played, and he had a will to win not seen again until Jimmy Connors exhibited the same sense of purpose.

When he finished playing competitive tennis he became a renowned broadcaster and gave his name to one of the most famous brands in sports clothing. He died in 1995 at the age of eighty-six.

MARY PETERS

MARY ELIZABETH PETERS
ATHLETICS – PENTATHLETE
BORN: HALEWOOD, 6 JULY 1939

Facts about Mary Peters

- She was awarded the MBE for her sporting achievements in 1973, but perhaps her later activities brought even greater pleasure to many in Northern Ireland, and a CBE was forthcoming as recognition of her work in the community in 1990.

- She was an excellent shot-putter in her own right, and won the Commonwealth Games gold medal in 1970 with a put of 15.93 metres.

1972 was not a good year in Northern Ireland. The civil unrest had reached a height and it seemed that the only stories to come out of the province were depressing. All except one. Mary Peters, the veteran pentathlete, won the Olympic gold medal in Munich with a new world record points total.

Peters was thirty-three at the time of her victory, and had been taking part in pentathlons for no less than seventeen years. She was born in Lancashire, and moved to Northern Ireland while still young. It was clear very early that she was a talented all-round athlete, and she took part in her first pentathlon in Ballymena in 1955, and, in all, she won seven WAAA pentathlon titles.

She took part in her first Olympics in 1964 in Tokyo. Peters came a creditable fourth in an event new to the Games. Her only real disappointment was the long jump, 5.60 metres was a long way behind her rivals. Four years later, she was back, but her own standard had not risen sufficiently and she could only trail in ninth. Two years later, though, she did win the Commonwealth Games title in Edinburgh.

Mary Peters's Career

Olympic Games
1964 (Tokyo)	4th
1968 (Mexico City)	9th
1972 (Munich)	1st

Commonwealth Games
1966 (Kingston)	2nd
1970 (Edinburgh)	1st
1974 (Christchurch)	1st

After that event, she devoted the whole of 1971 to intense training under the watchful eye of her coach, Buster McShane. When the 1972 season started, it was obvious from her early performances that she would be a genuine contender for a medal at the Munich Olympics. She was not the favourite, though. That honour went to Heide Rosendahl, who had missed out on a medal four years earlier due to injury, and was now going to be competing in front of her home crowd. She had also won the long jump gold medal a mere two days earlier.

Peters gave the performance of her life on the first day. In the first event, the 100 metres hurdles, she recorded a personal best time of 13.29 seconds. The next discipline, the shot put, was her best, and although she had thrown better than 16.29 metres, it was still better than any of her rivals. The third and final event of the day was the high jump, and Peters excelled herself. She cleared 1.82 metres, easily a personal best, and the German crowd cheered her to the echo. She ended the first day ninety-seven points in front of Pollak of East Germany, and 301 clear of Rosendahl.

However, the second day was always going to be Rosendahl's strongest, featuring the long jump and 200 metres. Sure enough, Rosendahl leapt 6.83 metres, only a centimetre short of her world record, while Peters, in her worst event, failed to break six metres. It all depended on the 200 metres. The two runners were drawn in the same heat, and Rosendahl ran a personal best time of 22.96 seconds. Peters kept the German in her sights, and crossed the line 1.22 seconds later to take the title by just ten points. If she'd taken a tenth of a second longer, the gold would have been

Rosendahl's. To cap it all, her total of 4801 points was a new world record.

Peters didn't retire after the Games, and in 1974 retained her Commonwealth Games title in her last major event. She then devoted herself to sports-related civic activities in Belfast, and also kept in touch with athletics as a manager for women's international teams – an athlete who gave back to the sport that gave her so much.

'"Mary P" as she is known to those who love her, and there are a lot of us, is a warm, out-going woman whose enthusiasm for life is infectious. Through her sport, Mary has helped, in no small way, to bring a little sunshine to her province, and also with the "Mary Peters Track" bring a little normality to Northern Ireland.'

Out of the blocks to Olympic gold in Munich in 1972.

LESTER PIGGOTT

LESTER KEITH PIGGOTT
JOCKEY
BORN: WANTAGE, 5 NOVEMBER 1935

Piggott's 30th classic, the 2000 Guineas on Rodrigo.

When Sir Gordon Richards retired in 1954, few could imagine a jockey who could match his record. Yet the eighteen-year-old who guided Never Say Die to the Derby that year would perhaps find an enough greater place in the hearts and minds of punter and public alike. Lester Piggott finally retired at the end of the 1995 season, aged sixty, and after a career little short of miraculous.

Piggott was born into the racing world. His father, Keith, was a jump jockey before becoming a trainer, and young Lester was apprenticed to his father's stable. He was a shy and introverted twelve year-old, partially deaf and weighing only five stone, he won his first race at Haydock in August

Lester Piggott's Career

English Classic wins

2000 Guineas	1957, 1968, 1970, 1985, 1992
1000 Guineas	1970, 1981
Oaks	1957, 1959, 1966, 1975, 1981, 1984
Derby	1954, 1957, 1960, 1968, 1970, 1972, 1976, 1977, 1983
St Leger	1960, 1961, 1967, 1968, 1970, 1971, 1972, 1984
Champion Jockey:	1960, 1964-71, 1981–82
Rides	25,000
wins	5,300 (est)

1948. His riding had a bit of a reckless streak though, and he had already fallen foul of the stewards four times when he won his first apprentices' title aged fifteen. Eventually, the powers-that-be had enough. Two weeks after that first Derby win, his riding on Never Say Die at the King Edward VII Stakes at Royal Ascot was so careless that he was stood down and reported to the Jockey Club. They suspended him for the rest of 1954, and it was stipulated that before he could apply for renewal of his licence, he had to attached himself to a trainer other than his father.

Piggott moved to Jack Jarvis's stable at Newmarket, and never had to serve the full sentence, being back in the saddle by September. It was a salutary lesson. Although he still had the occasional brush with the stewards, he was a generally safer rider. One other problem he encountered was that, during his enforced idleness, he had allowed his weight to soar to nine stone seven pounds, and had to waste to get back to eight stone.

Piggott then moved to Noel Murless's stable. It was a fruitful partnership that was only broken in 1966. Piggott guided Crepello to the Derby and Carozza to the Oaks in 1957, a notable Epsom double. Between 1959 and 1961, he also piloted Petite Etoile, arguably the greatest filly of all time,

to many successes including the Oaks.

In 1968, Piggott went freelance, and was rewarded with a ride on a truly superb horse, Sir Ivor. The horse was bred in America and trained in Ireland. He won the 2000 Guineas in impressive style, and then beat Connaught going away in the Derby, for which he was odds-on favourite. Sir Ivor didn't stay to complete the Triple Crown, but Piggott did, winning the St Leger on Ribero. Piggott did pilot Sir Ivor one more time, in the last race of the horse's career that November, winning the Washington DC International, perhaps the world's first truly international horse race. The jockey came in for criticism after that ride, winning by less than a length after letting Sir Ivor ease up with the race won. He made a great horse look like a moderate one, was the accusation.

Two years later, Piggott won the Triple Crown again, this time on the same horse. That was the great Nijinsky. The horse had been outstanding as a two year-old, and started at 7–4 on favourite for the 2000 Guineas, winning without too much fuss. However, doubts were expressed about his ability to stay a mile and a half and, for the only time in his career, started odds against. Piggott kept Nijinsky with the field until they were well past Tattenham Corner, then asked him to quicken. The horse simply eased away to win by two and a half lengths. All doubts about his staying power were quelled, and Nijinsky won the St Leger as a 7–2 on favourite to become the first horse to win the Triple Crown for thirty-five years. None has managed it since.

The trainer of Sir Ivor and Nijinsky, Vincent O'Brien, also gave Piggott his Derby wins on Roberto and The Minstrel. Piggott was developing a reputation as the greatest Classic jockey of all time, and when he won the Derby again in 1983 on Teenoso it was his ninth win in the most famous English race, a record touched by no other. The next year when he guided Comanche Run to the St Leger, it was his twenty-eighth Classic win, a new, and probably unbeatable, record. Not only had Piggott conquered the English track but he had won big races in France, Germany, America, and almost anywhere top-class racing was staged. His total number of wins, including those abroad, therefore exceeded that of Gordon Richards.

In 1985, the 'Long Fella' decided enough was

Facts about Lester Piggott

- Piggott came from riding stock. His grandfather Ernest Piggott rode two Grand National winners, his father Keith was a jump jockey, and his great-grandfather was Tom Cannon, who rode thirteen Classic winners.

- Of all the great horses he rode, Piggott considered Sir Ivor the very best.

- Piggott has had twenty wins over hurdles.

- He has won many races abroad, including the Prix de l'Arc de Triomphe three times, and the Irish Sweeps Derby five times.

- He once said he wanted to be a millionaire and a racing driver, and he has received at least ten speeding tickets.

- His attitude was best summed up by himself. 'I still get a kick out of every ride, every winner. All horses, every race is different. The challenge is to get it right.'

- His best season was 1966, with 191 winners.

The most famous face in racing.

enough, and, a month before his fiftieth birthday decided to become a trainer. His Eve Lodge stables produced thirty winners in 1986, and thirty-one the next year, but there was a rather large cloud on the horizon. Piggott was accused of tax evasion and, in October 1987, was sentenced to three years behind bars. He served a year, but it was a sad time for all his fans and admirers.

While serving a final period of parole, he was refused a trainers' licence, and so he made a decision to return to the saddle. In December 1989, he came back in Peru, and India, Hong Kong, Italy and Spain all saw Piggott in action before he returned to England to ride at Leicester in October 1990. Two

years later, he won the 2000 Guineas on Rodrigo de Triano. It was his thirtieth Classic win, and the world of horse racing rejoiced. There can never have been, and will never be, anyone to compare with Lester.

'In terms of achievement Lester compares with the best in this list. His only failing (if it is one) is that he has never had that outgoing personality, but he has given his public what he thinks they deserve most – his best ride. What else can be said of him except that as a sporting superstar he is a giant and that his legend is built on substance and achievement, unlike some who are invented by their PR and management companies.'

MARY RAND

MARY DENISE RAND (NÉE BIGNALL, LATER TWOMEY)
ATHLETICS – LONG-JUMPER, PENTATHLETE
BORN: WELLS, 10 FEBRUARY 1940

Mary Rand was the 'Golden girl' of British sport throughout the 1960s. She exuded fitness and vitality, was good-looking and vivacious and adored by the sporting public. Her versatility and track record make her Britain's finest multi-event female athlete.

Rand came from a modest background in Somerset. Her mother was a nurse, her father cleaned windows and chimneys. Inclined to be a tomboy at school and happy to help her father in his work, she started to show her athletic talent at an early age. After she came second in the English Schools long jump in 1955, she was offered a scholarship to Millfield School which, conveniently, was located in her home town. Millfield's reputation in sport is second to none, and it was a great challenge, but she was concerned about accepting a place in a school, 'full of kids from big houses, when I just lived in a council house'.

But she accepted the offer and came under the influence of John 'Brom' Bromfield, who was to set her on her way to an athletics career. In 1957, she broke the English record in the pentathlon in her first attempt at the event, and later made her international debut as a high jumper. She was seventeen years old.

She left Millfield in 1958 and joined London Olympiades AC, went to her first Commonwealth Games, in Cardiff, and came back with a silver medal in the long jump, with a leap of seventeen feet seven inches. Although there wasn't to be a medal in the European Championships the following year, her seventh place in the pentathlon was a new British record at 4466 points. There

Gold medal, World and Olympic record - the supreme achievement. Rand in Tokyo in 1964.

Facts about Mary Rand

- The late Ron Pickering had no doubts about Rand's qualities. 'In attempting to define what makes her so distinctive, I keep coming back to the term, "Star Quality". It is almost impossible to avoid clichés. I can think of no other athlete who combines sheer athleticism, dedication to hard work, competitive temperament and such a magnetic personality.'

- Her best performances were as follows:
100 metres - 11.7
200 metres - 23.9
80 metres hurdles - 10.8
High jump - 5' 7¾"
Long jump - 22' 2¼"
Shot put - 40' 2¼"
Pentathlon - 5035 points

- She competed in nine different events in British international matches.

Mary Rand's Career

Commonwealth Games
1958	Silver	Long jump
1966	Gold	Long jump

European Championships
1962	Bronze	Long jump
	Bronze	4 x 100 metres relay

Olympic Games
1964	Gold	Long jump
	Silver	Pentathlon
	Bronze	4 x 100 metres relay

World Records
1964	Long jump	22' 2¼"

were more milestones in 1959, she became the first British woman to clear twenty feet, with a jump of twenty feet four inches and she set a new pentathlon record of 4679 points.

1960 was an Olympic year. Rome was the venue, and for the first time an Olympic Games would be televised. Rand (then Bignall) was the clear favourite for the long-jump. She had beaten her own British record in May and when she became the best qualifier for the final by a good margin, everything seemed on course.

Then disaster struck. Her first two jumps went hopelessly wrong and her third, a poor effort, more than a foot less than her qualifying mark, put her in a dismal ninth place. She was mortified. A fourth place in the 80m hurdles was little compensation for the biggest disappointment in her life. She said later, 'I'd come for the long jump and I'd failed. Nothing could take away the sick feeling. When the band played for the victory ceremony, I was in the stand. I said to the girl next to me, "I feel like taking a gun and shooting the three of them."'

Defeat was a test of her true character and she set about preparing for Tokyo in 1964, but not before marrying Olympic rower, Sidney Rand and producing a daughter, Allison. Only four months after the birth, Rand won two bronze medals at the

European Championships in Belgrade, in the long jump and in the sprint relay.

She agreed not to go to Perth for the Commonwealth Games in order to stay at home with Sid and look after Allison, and so the preparations began in earnest for Tokyo.

It became one of those rare, once in a lifetime experiences. This time her Soviet rival, Schelkanova, was the favourite. She had all five of the best all-time jumps, but none of them counted in the Olympic final. Rand broke her British record, and set a new Olympic record, with her first jump, and bettered it with her fourth. Then came the great moment. No one describes it better than herself in her autobiography.

'You're on your way. Picking up speed ... You can see the check mark, throwing the switch – gliding on, settling. Ready – three, four, five, bang in the middle of the board. Now the feet have a grip in the sand, holding you, holding your backside clear of the sand. You stand-up, skip out of the pit. A white flag. They're measuring. 6.76 flashes on the board. A roar goes up from the crowd. 'My god, what have I done?' You can't think in these centimetres. You're running back to get your programme from your bag to check the world record. There it is at the top of the page, '6.70'. Back on the board they've got 6.76. There must be some mistake, there must be'.

There was no mistake. With a phenomenal leap of 22 feet 2¼ inches, Mary Rand had won her Olympic gold medal, broken the world record and become the first British woman to win an Olympic title in athletics.

She then completed a full set of medals to take home. First, she won a silver in the pentathlon behind Irina Press, who set a new world record thanks to a huge throw in the shot put, her specialist event. Then Rand ran the second leg for the British sprint relay team with Janet Simpson, Daphne Arden and Dorothy Hyman, as the British team won the bronze medal behind the Poles and the Americans.

Rand continued to compete for another three years after Tokyo and added another gold medal to her collections. It was another long jump gold in the Commonwealth Games, in 1966, in Jamaica, with a leap of 20 feet 10½ inches.

Injury finally put an end to her attempt to compete in a third Olympic Games in Mexico in 1968 and she decided to retire. Her marriage to Sidney Rand ended in 1969 and she later married Bill Twomey, the American decathlete, who won the Olympic gold medal in 1968.

This marriage also ended some years later, but Rand stayed in the United States and lived quietly with her family.

'All the things said about Mary, being good looking, vivacious etc. are still true today. She had a natural talent, with that rare gift for hard work (I know it doesn't seem rare, because most people in this list have it, but that's why they are in this book). A full set of Olympic medals, and a world record are not bad for a week's work.'

- The Polish winners of the Tokyo 4 x 100 m relay race, in which Rand won a bronze medal, were initially given a world record time. However, the record was later removed when one of their team, Ewa Klobukowska, subsequently became the first athlete to fail a sex test. Their Olympic title was allowed to stand.

- Rand's amazing winning jump in Tokyo was achieved into a 1.69 metres per second wind.

- Four of her six jumps in the Tokyo final were her best ever. She was so consistant, even her worst jump would have won the silver medal.

- Her skills as an all-rounder meant that when the Tokyo Olympic Games qualification levels were set, she could have qualified for six different events.

- Rand had to turn down lots of lucrative contracts after Tokyo in order to maintain her amateur status. She was even sounded out about a Hollywood role as a female James Bond.

- She was awarded the MBE in 1965.

Four years from Tokyo and still Bignall, but the talent was obvious.

STEVE REDGRAVE

TOP 20

STEVEN GEOFFREY REDGRAVE
ROWER
BORN: MARLOW, 23 MARCH 1962

Facts about
Steve Redgrave

- Redgrave carried the flag for the British Olympic team at the opening ceremony in Barcelona in 1992.

- He doesn't take too well to coaches. One of the British coaches claimed that they had made him what he is today. He accepted the opinion in part. But only because he used to do the opposite to whatever they told him.

- Sadly, because of the unglamorous image of his sport, Redgrave has always found it difficult to attract sponsors, despite his amazing track record.

'The Marlow mint', more gold medals than an athlete should even dream about.

Steven Redgrave's Career

Olympic Games

1984	Coxed Four	Gold
1988	Coxless Pairs	Gold
1988	Coxed Pairs	Bronze
1992	Coxless Pairs	Gold

World Championships

1986	Coxed Pairs	Gold
1987	Coxless Pairs	Gold
1987	Coxed Pairs	Silver
1989	Coxless Pairs	Silver
1990	Coxless Pairs	Bronze
1991	Coxless Pairs	Gold
1993	Coxless Pairs	Gold
1994	Coxless Pairs	Gold
1995	Coxless Pairs	Gold

Commonwealth Games

1986	Single Sculls	Gold
1986	Coxless Pairs	Gold
1986	Coxed Four	Gold

Steve Redgrave must be the biggest unsung hero in British sport, and not just because he's six feet five inches tall!

His record is unparalleled in his sport, he is Britain's most successful Olympian and he's still only thirty-three. If, as seems likely, he wins his fourth consecutive gold medal in Atlanta in 1996, he will join a very rare club of Olympic champions. Currently there are only three members of that club: Al Oerter, the American discus thrower, Aladar Gerevich, the Hungarian fencer and Paul Elvstrom, the Danish yachtsman. Yet he's never in the headlines. In fact, he rarely gets into the sports pages at all. The sport of rowing doesn't sell newspapers and doesn't make prime-time television.

However, that should change briefly in Atlanta. For once, the British media will focus its attention on the man who has rewritten the record books. He will deserve his moment of fame because there can't have been many more dedicated athletes anywhere, at any time, in British sport.

Redgrave was introduced to rowing at school, Marlow Comprehensive – it is fortunate for British rowing that he was born and raised near the Thames! He left school at sixteen and seems to have been in a boat ever since. He was a physical dream for his chosen sport. His strength is one thing, but he also boasts a phenomenal aerobic capacity, supposedly as much as 10 percent better than even other top rowers.

He first represented Britain at the Junior World Championships in 1979, and joined the Senior team in 1981. A year earlier he had only just missed selection for the 1980 Moscow Olympic team. His main focus was always Single Sculls, and, indeed, he won the prestigious Diamond Sculls at Henley in 1983 and 1985. But his best place in the World Championships was twelfth in 1985.

Possibly too big and too strong for the single event, he was persuaded to stroke the British Coxed Four in the 1984 Los Angeles Olympics. It was a crucial switch. The British won the gold medal in a great race against the Americans, and Redgrave began his assault on the world's gold reserves in earnest.

He then formed the first of two brilliant pairs partnerships with Andy Holmes, who had also been in the winning Four in Los Angeles.

In 1986 they won the Coxed Pairs at the World Championships and the Coxless Pairs at the Commonwealth Games. Redgrave also won the Single Sculls at the Commonwealths and was in the winning Coxed Four boat, to become the first rower to achieve a triple at the Games.

He and Holmes then started to get really greedy. They decided to go for the double at the 1987 World Championships – the Coxless Pairs and the Coxed Pairs – and attempted to repeat the double in Seoul at the 1988 Olympics. The task was awesome, requiring as many as eight races in seven days on each occasion. In very difficult conditions at the World Championships they won gold in the Coxless Pairs and silver in the Coxed. In Seoul, they again won the gold in the Coxless event and bronze in the Coxed.

The partnership with Holmes dissolved after Seoul, and Redgrave sought the rush of adrenalin derived from the precarious thrills of top-quality bobsleigh. He was good enough to be a member of the four-man crew that won the British

- Redgrave is one of many people in Britain who suffer from dyslexia. Sometimes he can see words clearly, sometimes words and even single letters are a complete blank.

- Matthew Pinsent, his partner in the pairs since 1990, is the godfather of one of Redgrave's children.

- His wife Ann is a former international rower, and team doctor to the British Rowing team.

Redgrave saluting victory in 1988 with Andy Holmes in the coxless pairs.

Championship in 1989, and reached the final trials for the British team.

However, he returned to rowing and found a new rowing partner in Simon Berrisford, and with him won a silver and a bronze at the 1989 World Championships, before a back injury forced Berisford to withdraw from racing in 1990.

This led to Redgrave's pairing with his second significant partner with whom he was able to dominate the early 1990s just as he had dominated the mid-1980s with Holmes.

Matthew Pinsent, old Etonian and winner of the Boat Race, was the second perfect foil for the 'Monster from Marlow'. In 1991 they won the Coxless Pairs at the World Championships and repeated the feat in 1992, 1993 and 1994. In between they won at the 1992 Olympics, in Barcelona, bringing Redgrave his third consecutive gold medal. His haul by the end of 1995 was a staggering thirteen gold medals in major events.

The 'Monster from Marlow' is so-called only because of the awesomeness of his performances. As a personality he is disarmingly reserved and modest. He is totally single-minded and keeps his own counsel. He doesn't bang his own drum, his record makes a big enough noise.

'Steven ranks highly in nearly all the categories. The only medium mark is in the impact area. The fact is, that he's a quiet, reserved man, who goes about his business regardless of who's watching or writing about him. In one way it is easier to perform when the expectations of others are less and how expectations also keep you hungr because you want to show others what you can do. For every man or woman on this list, hunger is the first requirement.'

GORDON RICHARDS

SIR GORDON RICHARDS
JOCKEY
BORN: OAKENGATES, 5 MAY 1904
DIED: KINTBURY, 10 NOVEMBER 1986

In terms of number of wins, no British jockey can be compared to Gordon Richards. He won 4870 races, a British record, was Champion Jockey twenty-six times and became the only jockey ever to be knighted.

Richards was the son of a Shropshire miner, one of a family of twelve, who became involved in horse racing after answering an advertisement for stable-lads placed by the trainer Martin Hartigan. The next year, in October 1920, he had his first ride and, on 31 March 1921, came his first winner, a horse called Gay Lord, at Leicester. He was a hard worker and steadily improved. He had five winners each in 1921 and 1922, forty-nine in 1923, sixty-one in 1924, and in his first season as a fully fledged jockey became Champion Jockey with 118 wins. People were amazed by his riding style. Some laughed but others saw the mark of true genius.

Then came a hiatus. Richards contracted tuberculosis, and he missed almost all of the 1926 season and it looked for a time as if his career would be over. He made a full recovery though, and in 1927 regained his Champion Jockey title with 164 wins. From then on, with two exceptions, won that title every year until his retirement.

Richards was jockey to Tommy Hogg between 1925 and 1931, and Richards, who was equally at home on sprinters and stayers, won him the title every year except 1926, and 1930, when he lost to Freddie Fox by one win. In 1932, he moved to Fred Darling's stable at Beckhampton, and they began a sixteen-year partnership. Immediately, the combination of Richards's acumen and Darling's preparation of horses paid dividends. He won 190 races that first season, easily his personal best, and in 1933 rode 259 winners. It shattered the mark set by Fred Archer in 1885, and his closest contender for Champion Jockey had only seventy-two wins. In October that year, he rode twelve consecutive winners, still a world record.

Richards's record in the Classics was good, although not as outstanding as some of his later rivals. His first win was in the 1930 Oaks on Rose of England. He also took the last Classic that year, riding joint favourite Singapore to victory in the St Leger. However, he did not win his first classic for Fred Darling until 1937, when he piloted Chulmleigh in the St Leger. Despite this, he was without equal on the British racetrack. He rode a double century of winners every year between 1933 and 1938, with the exception of 1936 when 177 triumphs was still well clear of the rest.

British racing continued during the war, although there were fewer meetings, and Richards was champion in 1940 with only sixty-eight wins. In 1941, he broke his leg in a fall, but returned the

Gordon Richards's Career

Rides: 21,815
Wins: 4870

English Classic Wins

2000 Guineas	1938, 1942, 1947
1000 Guineas	1942, 1948, 1951
Oaks	1930, 1942
Derby	1953
St Leger	1930, 1937, 1940, 1942, 1944
Champion Jockey	**1925–29, 1931–40, 1942–53**

Facts about Gordon Richards

- When he joined Hartigan's stable as a youngster, he was known as 'Moppy' because of his hairstyle.

- He scored a century of wins twenty-three times, and a double century twelve times.

- His first win was on Gay Lord at Leicester on 31 March 1921, and his last was on Princely Gift at Sandown on 9 July 1954. He was thrown by Abergeldie later that day, and retired.

- He won a total of fourteen English Classics, including three 2000 Guineas, three 1000 Guineas, one Derby, two Oaks and five St Legers.

- Richards said of his honours, 'Mother always told me my day was coming, but I never realised I'd end up the shortest knight of the year.'

Richards on Pinza in 1953. His first Derby win at the 28th attempt.

- In 1970, he was elected an honorary member of the Jockey Club, the only professional jockey ever to be awarded this distinction.

moved to Noel Murless's Abernant stable. The change affected Richards not at all, still Champion Jockey every season, still with over 200 winners a season. In 1953, at the age of forty-nine, he became the oldest Champion Jockey; in the week of the Coronation of Queen Elizabeth he was knighted; and then, on his twenty-eighth attempt, he won the Derby on Pinza. Even though the Queen's colt, Aureole, trailed in behind, it was a very popular triumph.

The next year Richards intended to retire, but the decision was forced on him early when a horse reared up and fell on him at Sandown. He suffered a broken pelvis and his career as a jockey was over. He became a trainer, and although he did have some success with the likes of the champion miler Reform he never attained the heights he did as a jockey and retired in 1970. He then became racing manager for Sir Michael Sobell and Lady Beaverbrook. He died in 1986 at the age of eighty-two.

Richards had a somewhat unorthodox riding style, being very upright in the saddle, and controlling his mounts off a long rein. There was no more thrilling sight than Richards almost turning himself sideways, driving his horse to the finish. Richards also never needed to waste to keep his riding weight of less than eight stones. This was a useful aid to his success, as the privations endured to this end were believed to have contributed to the suicide of Fred Archer, Richards's great nineteenth-century predecessor. He himself believed his secret lay in his will to win, and his ability to concentrate at all times. His career's longevity and consistency set records that may well never be broken.

next season to take four out of the five Classics. He won the 2000 Guineas on Big Game, and then guided Sun Chariot to the fillies' Triple Crown (1000 Guineas, Oaks and St Leger). Once again, the Derby stayed out of his reach.

That looked set to change in 1947. Richards was partnered with Tudor Minstrel. Here was a horse with real speed, and in the 2000 Guineas he streaked away from the rest of the field to win by eight lengths, still a record. However, the extra half-mile of the Derby found out his lack of stamina, and he was beaten by a 40–1 shot, Pearl Diver. 1947 was still a memorable year. He beat his own record of wins in a season, and his final total of 269 is one of those that looks likely to stand for ever.

That year, Fred Darling retired, and Richards

'You just have to look at Gordon's numbers to realise that he belongs at the top. 4,870 winners and champion jockey 26 times, just think about it. He rode for 33 years and he once said that he was lucky in two respects: 1) He never had to diet to stay at 8 stones and was able to eat what he liked, so he was always at full strength. 2) He nearly always had good horses to ride – no matter how talented you are, you can't do it without the horse! I'm told his style was not one that you like to teach young jockeys, but I'm a great believer that form should follow function.'

IAN RUSH

**IAN JAMES RUSH
FOOTBALL – FORWARD
BORN: ST ASAPH, 20 OCTOBER 1961**

The greatest goalgetter of his generation, Ian Rush was forward supreme during Liverpool's great years in the mid-1980s. He was the spearhead of probably the best British club team of all, and a legend to the fans on the Kop.

Rush joined lowly Chester City from school as an apprentice, and forced his way into their first team as a teenager. He caused havoc among Fourth Division defences, and attracted the eye of Geoff Twentyman, a scout for the Anfield giant. Such was his praise for the youngster that Bob Paisley was persuaded to part with £300,000 for Rush towards the end of the 1979–80, considerable money for a lower division player in those days. After only thirty-four games at Chester, Rush was moving on to greater things.

Rush was a reserve that first season, watching from the bench as Liverpool lifted the European Cup with a single goal win against Real Madrid. He had a short run in the first team at the end of that season, and looked unimpressive. Paisley kept faith with him, though, and after starting the 1981–82 season in the reserves, he was brought back in October and told to be more selfish in front of goal. Suddenly he and Dalglish formed one of the most devastating partnerships in Liverpool's history. His electric pace took him away from defences and brought him seventeen goals, as a late-season run of eleven successive wins brought the title to Anfield.

he trophies and goals kept coming. The championship was Liverpool's in 1983, and again in 1984, as Rush banged in thirty-two goals. Liverpool had won a hat-trick of titles and, with a replay win over Everton, managed a fourth straight League Cup title, an unprecedented run of success. In 1984, in Rome, Liverpool won the

most important prize of all. They faced Roma in the European Cup final, in their rival's home stadium. It was a tense, exciting match, with Rush finding himself shackled by the Italian defence. It ended in a 1–1 draw, and Rush was one of the scorers as Liverpool took their fourth European title on penalties.

The next season, of course, was disastrous. No trophies, and then the terrible events at Heysel Stadium left Liverpool's reputation in tatters. Under player-manager Kenny Dalglish, the team were left to come to terms with what had happened. Rush found it especially difficult. In December, his seemingly endless goal supply dried up, and without the supply from their Welsh spearhead, Liverpool looked sluggish. As many who wrote them off found, Liverpool were at the best under pressure. Rush's nose for goals re-ignited with a vital goal at Watford in the Cup quarter-final: he got two in the semi-final and, as their rivals faded, and Liverpool headed for the championship as well. When they met Everton at Wembley in the Cup final, it was to secure the elusive Double.

The game was a personal triumph for Rush. After Lineker had given Everton an early lead, it was the Welshman whose pace carried him away

Ian Rush's Career (to the end of 1994–95)

Football League appearances	483
Goals	238
Italian League appearances	29
Goals	7
International appearances	71
Goals	28
European Cup	1984
Football League Championship	1982, 1983, 1984, 1986, 1990
FA Cup	1986, 1989, 1992
League Cup	1982, 1983, 1984, 1994
Footballer of the Year	1984
PFA Footballer of the Year	1984
PFA Young Footballer of the Year	1983

Facts about Ian Rush

- Rush scored five times in a 6–0 win over Luton in 1983. Opposition manager Davis Pleat called him, 'Painful to watch, but beautiful.'

- Rush was never on the losing side in a Liverpool match in which he scored, until the 1987 League Cup final where he scored, but Arsenal came back to win 2–1.

- Juventus bought Rush for £3,200,000 in 1987. At the time, it was a record for a British player.

Still going strong in 1995 as the Liverpool revival gathers momentum.

- With two goals in the 1986 FA Cup final, two in the 1989 game and one in 1992, Rush is one of only three players to have scored in three FA Cup finals, and, with five goals, has scored more in the season's showpiece than any other player. His 41 cup goals (to the end of 1994–95) equal Denis Law's record.

- When Rush appeared as Liverpool substitute during a game against Charlton in 1988, an opposition fan was heard to say, 'It's like Bradman coming in to bat with 500 on the board.'

- He received an MBE in the 1996 New Year's honours list.

- Rush scored his 42nd FA Cup goal in a 7-0 win over Rochdale in the 1996 3rd Round. It made him the FA Cup's leading scorer this century.

from the Everton defence to round Mimms for the equaliser. Rush set up Johnston to put Liverpool in the lead and finally he ran on to a chip by Whelan to crash the ball joyfully into the far corner of the net. Liverpool's Double was secure.

Rush was now the target of foreign interest, and in 1987 he was signed by Juventus. The move to Italy was a disaster. He missed his beloved Liverpool, taking every opportunity to return to see family and friends and after a miserable season the Kop's hero returned.

Had Rush not been a Welshman, his talents would probably have been seen more at international level. He is the principality's top scorer at international level, but has never appeared in the finals of a major competition. We can only be glad that his glorious club career gave him the chance to be as widely admired as someone of his talents deserves.

'"Rushie" has played an era when avoiding defeat has been the most important thing in the game. So, with packed defences and tight marking, his totals seem much less impressive than those of Dixie Dean, but they were just as effective. The game is so different now with only one or two forwards, who are also expected to be the first line of defence.'

TESSA SANDERSON

THERESA IONE SANDERSON
ATHLETICS – JAVELIN THROWER
BORN: ST ELIZABETH, JAMAICA, 14 MARCH 1956

Smiles during the event, tears on the winners podium. Sanderson's reversal of fortune in 1984.

Facts about
Tessa Sanderson

- Sanderson first threw the javelin at the age of 12 and was so bad at it, she told friends it was 'a silly sport for a girl'. She devoted herself to the discipline two years later when she challenged a classmate to a javelin contest and won.

- At her first Olympics in 1976, she weighed only nine stone. Seeing her waiting to enter the arena with the other throwers, Karin Smith of America tapped her on the shoulder and pointed to another entrance. 'Sprinters that way,' she said.

- Like a number of sports people, Sanderson has also done winter seasons in pantomime.

- Sanderson worked initially as a copy typist to make ends meet.

- She was awarded an MBE in 1985.

Tessa Sanderson was born in Jamaica, spent her early years being raised by her grandmother while her parents were in England looking for work. She joined them in the Midlands as a nine year-old and, although the transition to her new environment was not entirely a pleasant one, she settled down and started to display considerable athletic potential.

She joined Wolverhampton & Bilston, one of Britain's premier athletic clubs, and initially showed promise in the pentathlon, before finally deciding to concentrate on the javelin. By 1972 she had won her first title, the English Schools intermediates. In 1975, she won the British javelin title, and improved the British record three times. Obviously, here was a athlete of potential, and her tenth place at the Montreal Olympics the next year was a valuable learning experience.

The experience showed in 1977, when she improved her personal best by ten metres to 67.20 metres, moving into second place on the all-time list. She followed that with an easy win in the 1978 Commonwealth Games and, that same year, silver in the European Championships. Unfortunately, none of this promise was translated into a medal in Moscow. She gave one of the most disappointing performances of her career, and failed to qualify for the final. 'I was frightened to death of the competition', she said later.

The next year she decided to broaden her horizons, and she took up the heptathlon. She was not unsuccessful, twice beating the UK and Commonwealth records, but she decided that she did not have the all-round ability and did not continue in the event. The next year, she suffered from injury, and was forced to miss both the European and Commonwealth Championships.

By now, she had a rival in the British team, Fatima Whitbread, who had finished runner-up in the 1983 World Championship. Although Sanderson's best throw in 1983, 73.58 metres in a meeting in Edinburgh, was better than Whitbread's by over four metres, she would have her work cut out to stay as Britain's number one, let alone win the Olympics.

In Los Angeles, the women's javelin competition was not immune to the effects of the boycott. Sanderson took advantage, and a huge throw of 69.56 metres was not only good enough for gold, it set a new Olympic record as well. Her arch-rival

Tessa Sanderson's Career

Olympic Games

1976 (Montreal)	9th
1980 (Moscow)	did not qualify
1984 (Los Angeles)	1st
1988 (Seoul)	did not qualify
1992 (Barcelona)	did not qualify

World Championships

1983 (Helsinki)	4th
1987 (Rome)	4th

European Championships

1974	13th
1978	2nd

Whitbread could only claim the bronze. However, that seemed to be Sanderson's limit, and Whitbread started to overtake her. Sanderson lost on the next seven times the pair met in competition. She came good when it mattered, though, winning the 1986 Commonwealth Games title. She overtook Whitbread with her fifth throw of just short of 70 metres, and triumphantly danced around her distraught rival as she lay on the track.

That was her last major championship, though. Injuries meant that she had to be selected to go to the Seoul Olympics, rather than qualify in her own right, and once in Korea she sustained a nasty heel injury which prevented her qualifying for the final. She then left athletics to become a presenter with Sky Sports. However, she could not stay away and in 1991, she returned to the javelin and won the European Cup. The next year she was selected for the Barcelona Olympics and, at the age of thirty-six, became the first British athlete to go to five Games. Tessa Sanderson, a quintuple Olympian, was one of Britain's sporting greats.

'It has been a pleasure to have known Tessa since 1976, when we both went to the Montreal Olympics. She has a real hyper personality; she is always buzzing. Her strength is the fact that she has so much faith in her ability – she is even contemplating a return to competition, in 1996, in Atlanta, to raise money for charity.'

PETER SHILTON

PETER LESLIE SHILTON
FOOTBALL – GOALKEEPER
BORN: LEICESTER, 18 SEPTEMBER 1949

Peter Shilton is England's most capped player and his international career stretched for 20 years and 125 appearances. He became a byword for excellence and dedication to his craft.

He started his career as a junior with Leicester City, his hometown club. He was such a good prospect that Leicester felt able to transfer their World Cup winning goalkeeper, Gordon Banks, to Stoke to let young Shilton flourish. He was still a teenager when he made his first Wembley appearance, as a losing FA Cup finalist. In November 1970, he made his first England appearance in a 3-1 win over East Germany, and this while playing in the Second Division, Leicester having been relegated in 1969.

When Banks was forced to retire after injuries sustained in a car crash, Shilton was an automatic replacement. Some still harboured doubts about his ability, though, and when England played Poland in a vital World Cup qualifier in 1973, Shilton allowed Domarski's shot to slip under his body, and England were eliminated. It was a mistake that haunted him for many years.

Shilton moved to Stoke in 1974 for the then

Facts about Peter Shilton

- Up to the end of the 1994–95 season, Shilton had played 996 Football League matches, a record, and 1379 senior matches, another record.

- Shilton did not win a League Cup medal with Nottingham Forest in 1978. He was cup-tied, and understudy Chris Woods took his place in the cup run.

- Shilton's aura in goal was quite intimidating. Larry Lloyd, who defended in front of him at Nottingham Forest said, 'I've seen forwards get past me with all the confidence of a Pele or Johan Cruyff and then, faced by "Shilts", will suddenly lose their nerve.'

Shilton clearing from Macari in 1973 against Scotland at Wembley. England's Emlyn Hughes looks on.

England against Holland in the European Championships in 1988, a 100 cap milestone for Shilton.

- He was voted Professional and Footballers' Association Player of the Year in 1978 and won the PFA's Merit Award in 1990.

retained the trophy, overcoming strong favourites Hamburg by the only goal. Almost as an afterthought, they won the League Cup twice as well. Shilton provided them with the solid base from which these title challenges could be launched. Forest in their prime were virtually impossible to beat. Between November 1977 and December 1978, they went a record 42 League matches without defeat, and, in little more than three years, Forest went from the English Second Division to the World Club Championship in Tokyo.

The club allowed Shilton to move on in 1982, to Southampton for £300,000. It was an inspired move for the keeper. Southampton were playing marvellous football under Lawrie McMenemy and finished second, their highest position, in 1984.

Shilton was now established as England's number one. He kept goal in three World Cup finals tournaments. In Spain, he only conceded one goal in five matches, as England were eliminated in the second round without losing a game. In Mexico in 1986, he was the victim of Maradona's 'Hand of God' goal, as well as the Argentinian's rather better second effort.

He announced that he would retire from international football after the 1990 Finals in Italy. Shilton was in good form on the way to the semi-finals, but in the penalty shoot-out in the semi-final against Germany, he was beaten four times out of four, and England were eliminated. His 125th, and last, England appearance was in the third place play-off against Italy. They lost 2-1, and Shilton made a rare mistake for the Italian's opening goal, but it was still a memorable occasion. At the time, it was believed that Shilton held the world record for international appearances, but it later transpired that his total was already lower than that of Majed Abdullah of Saudi Arabia.

Shilton moved to Derby in 1987, and then, in 1992, became player-manager at Plymouth Argyle. Unfortunately, after promising beginnings, his managerial career ended in acrimony with revelations about Shilton's financial affairs.

enormous sum of £325,000. However, he failed to keep them in the top division and, when they were relegated in 1977, he moved to Nottingham Forest. Forest had just scraped promotion but, under the management of Brian Clough, they took the First Division by storm. They won the title by seven points from Liverpool, and then turned their attentions to the continent. The East Midlands club won the 1979 European Cup without losing a game, beating Sweden's Malmo in the final, and then

Peter Shilton's Career (to the end of the 1994–95 season)

Football League appearances	996
Goals	1
International appearances	125
European Cup	1979, 1980
Football League Championship	1978
League Cup	1979

'Peter is determined to make it to 1000 appearances in the league and, in 1996, I'm sure he will achieve it, but at 47, he hasn't got much time left.'

JACKIE STEWART

**JOHN YOUNG STEWART
MOTOR-RACING DRIVER
BORN: DUMBARTON, 11 JUNE 1939**

Jackie Stewart stopped racing in 1973, and just kept on going. After a career which brought him three Drivers' World Championships and a place among the sport's all-time greats, he simply applied all his considerable talents and energies to being even more successful after his sporting career than he was during it.

As far as his sporting record is concerned, along with fellow Scot, Jim Clark, he is regarded by the motor sports cogniscenti as out on his own among British drivers, and among the best four or five drivers of all time anywhere in the world. As a personality, as a publicist and as a leader in his sport he is unique.

Stewart wasn't from a poor background – his family had a garage and car dealership – but he did have his problems. He had a hard time at school and was miserable. What was then dismissed as Stewart's 'stupidity' turned out to be what is now known as dyslexia. But he had inner strength and

In his third championship year in 1973 at the British Grand Prix

**Facts about
Jackie Stewart**

- After the frightening experience of being trapped for twenty-five minutes at Spa, he always carried a spanner taped into the cockpit to help get the steering wheel off.

- Stewart's campaign for improved safety was long overdue. Between 1966 and 1973, fifty-seven drivers were killed in Grand Prix and sports car racing around the world.

- Of the many charity events he runs and supports, one of them is devoted to raising money for team mechanics injured in their work. Stewart always seems able to attract the high-born and leading celebrities to his charity functions. Guests often include friends like Sean Connery, The Princess Royal, Jack Nicklaus and Gene Hackman.

- His racing helmet was distinctive. It always had a band of the Stewart tartan around it.

The keen eyes of a great shot, a great Scot and a great driver.

was determined to overcome whatever obstacles he faced and he found refuge in sport. It was soccer at first and then shooting. If he couldn't see words he could certainly see targets. He became British Trap Shooting Champion in 1959, and was devastated to miss selection for the 1960 Olympic team.

His father's business, and the fact that his brother, Jimmy, had driven competitively, inevitably led him to gravitate towards cars. He, and others, soon discovered that he had a rare talent.

From the moment the young 'JYS' had his first race, his rise to the top was inexorable, shrewdly plotted and rapid. He drove Formula Three for Ken Tyrrell, in 1964, after a famous trial which has become part of racing folklore. Brue McLaren, Cooper's works Formula One driver at the time, set the standard for Stewart to follow. He matched it every time and then beat it without batting an eyelid. Tyrrell signed the precocious young Scot on the spot. He took the world of Formula Three by storm, and then Formula Two.

His first year in Formula One was 1965. The road to glory for the Stewart tartan continued straight and true. He scored a point in his opening race, was third at Monaco, second at Spa

Francorchamps and second at Clermont Ferrand. Then, to put the gloss on an outstanding debut, he won the Italian Grand Prix at Monza. In his first season in Formula One, he had scored thirty-three points and came third in the Drivers' Championship.

Stewart won the first race, in 1966, at Monaco and nearly won the Indianapolis 500 at his first and only attempt, but his engine failed when he was leading by a lap. Then, the wheels came off the Stewart bandwagon, almost fatally. The incident, and Stewart's reaction to it, was a watershed in motor-racing history.

During the first lap of the Belgian Grand Prix, Stewart came off in heavy rain, hit a telegraph pole and demolished a hut. He landed upside down, trapped in his car with fuel pouring all over him. Graham Hill and Bob Bondurant struggled for twenty-five minutes to get him out, in the face of the constant threat of fire. Neither an ambulance nor professional rescuers arrived. The only tools available were borrowed from a spectator. Eventually, Stewart had a bumpy ride to hospital in the back of a van, even though it was feared he had injured his spine. Thankfully, his injuries, although

Jackie Stewart's Career

World Drivers' Championship
Winner: 1969, 1971, 1973
Runner-up: 1969

World Championship Grands Prix wins: (27)
1965	Italian	(BRM)
1966	Monaco	(BRM)
1968	German, Dutch, United States	(Matra)
1969	French, British, Dutch, Italian, South African, Spanish	(Matra)
1970	Spanish	(Matra)
1971	Canadian, French, German, British, Monaco, Spanish	(Tyrrell-Ford)
1972	Argentinian, Canadian, French, United States	(Tyrrell-Ford)
1973	Belgian, German, Dutch, Monaco, South African	(Tyrrell-Ford)

Summary: 99 Grands Prix, 17 Poles, 15 Fastest Laps, 27 Wins, 359 Points

serious, were not life-threatening, but the incident led Stewart to use all his organisational and persuasive skills to mount a campaign radically to improve driver safety.

He single-handedly took on the establishment and eventually got his own way. 'The cocky little bugger', of whom it was often asked, 'Who does he think he is?', showed them exactly who he was.

It took Stewart two years to get back to winning races. His safety campaign can't have helped his concentration, but more importantly, the BRM's H16 engine in 1967 was seriously uncompetitive.

But in 1968 he drove a Matra for Ken Tyrrell and began a superb partnership, reminiscent of his Formulas Two and Three days. He won twice and came second in the Championship. It was the year of his famous victory at the Nurburgring when he won, in the rain and the fog, by over four minutes and left everyone gawping in amazement. 1969 saw the introduction of the Matra MS80, a beauty of a car, and with it Stewart won six races and his first World Championship.

Two more Championships followed in 1971 and 1973 as the little Scot established a fantastic record of success.

Stewart's great reign came to an end in sad circumstances before the final act of the 1973 season. His team-mate, Fran_ois Cevert, was killed in an horrific crash in practice for the United States

Grand Prix at Watkins Glen. Stewart was assured of winning the Drivers' Championship and had already decided to retire, but his colleague's death was an ironic and bitter blow at the end of an outstanding career, during which he had done more than anybody else to improve driver safety.

Jackie Stewart moved with all the nimbleness and deftness he had brought to racing into the chicanes, bends and curves of business after he retired. He was usually on pole, usually ahead into the first corner, and usually first to take the chequered flag in the world of advertising, promotions and management, just as he was on the track.

His business interests flourished and he became an even more prominent member of the glitterati after his retirement than before it. Not bad for a 'cocky little bugger' who was 'stupid' at school.

Early in 1996, Stewart announced his intention to return to Formula One racing with Ford.

'You can tell, just from being in his company for a few minutes, that Jackie Stewart is a meticulous and driven man. Like most of the people in the list, he wishes there were twenty-six hours in a day. For him the competition is not the racing, it's life itself. Racing introduced him to the spot light, and now he's proving that 15 minutes of fame can be turned into a life time.'

- One of the most chastening things he ever heard came from his son Paul who came home from school one day and asked, 'When is Daddy going to get killed?'

- He once said, 'Motor-racing accidents don't hurt, they happen too quickly. They only hurt afterwards, if you're lucky enough to survive them.'

- Stewart once described a feeling of heightened awareness, often mentioned by athletes in the midst of a peak performance, when being overwhelmed by the smell of freshly cut grass in the middle of a race. It had come from the impact of the tyres of a car that had spun off in front of him. This, despite the smells of the car, the speed he was travelling and all the paraphernalia of visor, helmet and clothing surrounding him.

- He is notoriously punctual, fastidiously tidy and obsessive about the smallest details.

- Stewart was awarded the OBE in 1972.

- He was BBC Sports Personality of the Year for 1973.

JOHN SURTEES

JOHN SURTEES
MOTOR-CYCLIST, MOTOR-RACING DRIVER
BORN: WESTERHAM, 11 FEBRUARY, 1934

Facts about John Surtees

- Surtees was known to be an incurable and often infuriating perfectionist about the performance of his cars and bikes.

- In order to race on four-wheels he needed an FIA (the French International Automobile Association) licence and the RAC required him to compete in a club race. He raced at Goodwood in a Tyrrell Formula Junior Cooper and came second. His licence was granted immediately.

- He made his Formula Two debut two weeks later and came second to Innes Ireland at Oulton Park.

- After his accident in Canada, the local doctor at the hospital described Surtees as, 'A stiff-upper-lip Englishman who is determined to make a rapid recovery.'

John Surtees has a unique place in motorsport, a fact that sometimes disguises his achievements rather than illustrates them. Most sports-buffs know that he is the only man to have won a World Championship on both two wheels and four, but very few people know the full record of achievement of a man who has a claim to greatness in one sport, and at least the accolade of one of the best of his era in another.

Like contemporaries, Hailwood and Stewart, Surtees was born into an environment heavy with the pungent smell of engines. His father was a South London motorcycle dealer who raced sidecars at grass track meetings; so the man with the unique two-wheel, four-wheel record started racing on three wheels, in his father's sidecar!

Surtees started racing in earnest by dispensing with the third wheel and finishing second to the great Geoff Duke in 1951 at Thruxton, on a Vincent bike he had tuned himself. He made his Isle of Man debut in 1955, but his career didn't take off until he signed with MV Agusta in 1956. In that year he won his first Senior TT and, after two Grands Prix victories in Holland and Belgium, won his first 500cc World Championship.

1957 was a fallow year, but still produced a runner's-up place in the TT and third place in the 500cc Championship. But then came three amazing years in 1958, 1959 and 1960 – he won everything there was to win. In 1958, he won the Senior and Junior TT, the 350cc Championship and the 500cc Championship. He repeated the double double again, in 1959, and in those two years he won all twenty-five of the races he entered. In the following year he repeated the 350/500cc double and won the Senior TT to become the first man to win it three times in a row.

John Surtees's Career

World Championships

1956	500cc	(MV)
1958	350cc, 500cc	(MV)
1959	350cc, 500cc	(MV)
1960	350cc, 500cc	(MV)

Total Victories (38)

250cc	1
350cc	15
500cc	22

Isle of Man TTs

1956	Senior	(MV)
1958	Senior and Junior	(MV)
1959	Senior and Junior	(MV)
1960	Senior	(MV)

Total Victories (6)

Senior	4
Junior	2

World Drivers' Championship

Winner	**1964**
Runner-up	**1966**

Total Victories (5)

1963	German	(Ferrari)
1964	German, Italian	(Ferrari)
1966	Belgian	(Ferrari),
	Mexican	(Cooper)
1967	Italian	(Honda)

Summary: 111 Grands Prix, 180 points, 6 wins

It was at the end of this unprecedented era of success on two wheels that he first doubled his wheel-base and moved into Formula One, and became the only man to do it with any real competitive edge.

In only his second race he finished second to Jack Brabham, at Silverstone, in the British Grand Prix, driving for Colin Chapman in a Lotus. The following year he gave up motor-cycles completely to concentrate on Formula One, but drove for the private team, Yeoman Credit, in a Cooper. It wasn't a good choice because Ferrari dominated the

A return to glory for Ferrari in 1964 and for Surtees and the World Drivers' Championship.

season. The following year he drove a Lola and had a little more success in finishing fourth in the Championship.

It wasn't until 1963, and his first drive for Ferrari, that Surtees' fortunes began to improve. He had his first Grand Prix win at the Nurburgring and, in 1964, with another win at the Nurburgring and one at Monza, he won the Drivers' World Championship. The following season was not a happy one. He had a bad accident in October, in Canada, in practice for a CanAm race, and, although he recovered in time for the season, he got involved in the Machiavellian politics of Ferrari and walked out on them at Le Mans and drove for Cooper. He won the final race of the season in Mexico to add to a brilliant win for Ferrari at Spa, earlier in the year, and was runner-up in the Championship.

After one more win in the Championship, in a great race against Jack Brabham in 1967, driving a Honda, Surtees' driving career gradually came to an end. Honda were not quite ready for the demands of Formula One and in 1968 he had an appalling year with BRM (British Racing Motors) which led him to retire and decide to build his own cars.

His team was never really successful, despite a monumental effort on his part to put it right, and the team was wound up in 1978. He finally retired from motor-racing and began a successful investment business, content in the knowledge that he had become the only man to succeed in the two senior classes of motorsport.

'John is an all-time great in the motor cycle world, just look at his record in world championships. He has as many world championships as Mansell in Formula One, but because he is the quiet, introspective type, he never got the headlines he deserved.'

- The Italian motorsport public gave Surtees his nick-name, 'Il Grande John'.

- His year at BRM was so distressing for him he could hardly bring himself to talk about it except to say: 'Without a doubt, my worst year in racing. I'd rather not discuss it. I was just paying penance. It was hell. At the end of the year my health, physical and mental, was at a very low level. I had come to the end of the road and seriously considered getting out of motor-racing.'

- Surtees's transition from bikes to cars was remarkable. In June 1960 he dominated TT week on the Isle of Man, and the following month drove a Lotus to second place in the British Grand Prix.

- His parting-of-the-ways at Ferrari was the result of a running battle with the aptly named team manager, Eugenio Dragoni.

- Surtees was awarded the MBE in 1961.

- He also raced successfully in North America and won the first CanAm Challenge in 1966

DALEY THOMPSON

FRANCIS MORGAN THOMPSON
ATHLETICS – DECATHLETE
BORN: NOTTING HILL, 30 JULY 1958

TOP 20

Facts about Daley Thompson

- He only competed in thirty-one decathlons in his entire career. He won nineteen of them and came second three times. From June 1977 to September 1987, he competed in just twenty decathlons, during which time he won all his major titles – he won sixteen events, came second twice and did not complete twice. Strangely, although he completed four decathlons in Wales and one in Scotland, he never completed one on English soil in his entire career and never lost to a fellow Brit.

- His ten personal bests would add up to a staggering 9289 pts.

- Only he and American Bob Matthias have won the Olympic title twice.

- Bruce Jenner, the Olympic Champion in

Note: *'Daley promised that we were free to write this without interference or pressure from him – except to say that he would beat us senseless if we said anything he didn't like!' Stewart Binns and Tom Lewis*

Honestly though folks, to say Daley Thompson is a unique athlete would be mild compared to the plaudits he has received over the years. Throughout the 1980s he was more or less unbeatable in a discipine which is specifically designed to find the best all-round athlete in the world. He faced at least three opponents who, at any other time, would probably have been world or Olympic champions themselves, and he brought front-page headlines and a charistmatic personality to an event that, up to then, and probably since, was no more than a sideshow for track and field purists.

He has been bracketed with Jim Thorpe, the great native American hero of the 1912 Olympics

and only a couple of others, such as fellow Americans, Bob Matthias and Bruce Jenner, as the greatest all-round athlete of all time. And there is compelling hard evidence, especially if one takes an objective non-American view, that he would be at the head of such an illustrious list.

What is certain is that Thompson was an unusual decathlete. Few of his predecessors, except perhaps Thorpe, Matthias and Jenner, had much impact outside the narrow confines of their sport and, perhaps uniquely, Thompson brought what is always the hidden dimension of sport – the ability to win – more directly to bear than anyone else did, in a sport where physical prowess is so obviously the key to success.

Thompson's own description of his background and upbringing is one of 'happiness in childhood, lots of help and support and a few lucky breaks'.

Daley Thompson's Career

World Records
1980	Gotzis	8648 points
1982	Gotzis	8730 points
1982	Athens	8774 points
1984	Los Angeles	8847 points

Olympic Games
1976	18th
1980	Gold
1984	Gold
1988	4th

Commonwealth Games
1978	Gold
1982	Gold
1986	Gold

World Championships
1983	Gold
1987	9th

European Championships
1978	Silver
1982	Gold
1986	Gold

European Junior Championships
1977	Gold

AAA Championships
1976	Winner

AAA Junior Championships
1975	Winner

The eyes of the tiger, going for gold in Los Angeles.

But his circumstances were not all that auspicious and could easily have led to an entirely different direction in his life.

He was brought up in Notting Hill in London, the son of a Nigerian father and a Scottish mother. His parents separated when he was seven and his father subsequently met a violent death when Daley was thirteen. Daley's hyperactivity, both mental and physical, were starkly apparent from an early age. He was sent to a boarding school in Haywards Heath, which specialised in combining a liberal educational philosophy with a well-organised and disciplined routine. The young man thrived on the experience.

His sporting talent became obvious very early on. He was one of those kids who could do anything, but his particular passion was running. Staff at the school talked fondly of their memories of him, running everywhere. His older brother Frank remembered visiting him on school sports days, 'He would just run and run and run. He won everything. He was so much better than everybody else, he won by miles.'

Thompson won the Sussex Schools 200 metre title in 1974 at the age of sixteen and in June the following year, while still only sixteen, won his first decathlon event, the Welsh Open at Cwmbran. From that moment his rise to the top was phenomenal. He won the AAA (Amateur Athletic Association) Junior title and came second for the British Senior team in an international against France before going off to Montreal for the 1976 Olympics, still aged only seventeen.

Montreal was a revelation for him. It was the games of Comaneci, Juantorena and Viren, while in the decathlon he watched in awe as Bruce Jenner achieved seven personal bests to defeat the 1972 Olympic Champion, Nikolai Avilov and the German, Guido Kratschmer. Thompson finished eighteenth, but he knew where his destiny would be – it was his eighteenth birthday.

The juggernaut of success began to gain momentum in 1978. He won his first major Championship in Edmonton with a gold medal at

1976 when Thompson made his debut at seventeen, picked him out and said, 'There's the next Olympic Champion.' Jenner also said that, throughout the entire two days of competition, Thompson never stopped asking questions.

- When Thompson looked back at the vital third throw in the discus event at Los Angeles, he remarked, 'It was like I went over to the cliff and looked over the edge.'

- Seb Coe, a good friend of Thompson's who knows a thing or two about the will to win, said of Thompson's commitment, 'He's an athletic stalinist. He doesn't just want to win, he wants to totally destroy the opposition; annihilate them.'

- Another famous example of Thompson's approach to winning comes from the often repeated answer when asked why he bothered to train on Christmas Day: 'Because I know Jurgen Hingsen doesn't.'

- The late Ron Pickering, a friend and mentor to Thompson, once said: 'It's a blessing that Daley had the talent to become a great

the Commonwealth Games. Three weeks later, against a much stronger field and tired from Edmonton, he came second in the European Championships in Prague, to Aleksander Grebenyuk of the Soviet Union. Thompson was still only twenty and for anyone else it was an amazing achievement, but he was devastated by defeat, saying that it was the only time in his life when he lost, knowing that he ought have won. He vowed it would never happen again. It never did.

1980 was a special year. He broke the world record at the world's leading decathlon event in Gotzis, Austria, scoring 8648 points, and later won his first Olympic gold medal in Moscow. The double year of 1980 became a triple in 1982. He repeated his victory and world record in Gotzis, this time scoring 8730 points, and followed it with his first European Championships gold medal in Athens and yet another world record at 8774 points, and then won his second Commonwealth title in Brisbane. It was a phenomenal year and in two of the events, Gotzis in May and the Europeans in September, he faced his most famous adversory, the German giant, Jurgen Hingsen. At six feet seven inches and 220 pounds, he was made in heaven for the decathlon. Hingsen would become the perfect competitor to push Daley onwards.

Thompson's next objective was the inaugral World Championships in Helsinki in August 1983. Hingsen was again the threat and what's more, another German had emerged, Sigi Wentz, to add to the huge presence of Hingsen and Guido Kratschmer. Thompson's preparation had been plagued by injury and Hingsen had set a new world record. But again, it was Thompson's two days. His competitiveness was supreme and again, was the telling factor. Mel Watman of Athletics Weekly wrote: 'His sheer competitiveness and coolness under pressure is without parallel.'

He now had the lot: Commonwealth, European, World and Olympic champion; he had set three world records; and he was still only twenty-five.

One of the great images from the memorable decathlon in Los Angeles.

The Los Angeles Olympics will always be remembered as Daley Thompson's finest hour – at least in terms of public perception. Hingsen had yet again taken away the world record and the television cameras had the perfect duel in the sun between the gladiators in the LA Coliseum. The scenario was perfect: the German adonis, hewn in classical marble, serious, unsmiling and grimly teutonic; against the British buccaneer, powerful and muscular, forever happy and jovial and irresistably unconventional.

The battle was a classic. It came down to two crucial moments. In the discus, the seventh event on the second day, Hingsen threw a massive 166 feet nine inches. Thompson stared defeat in the face. On his final throw he improved from 124 feet on his first throw and 135 feet on his second, to 152 feet, to save the day. He then had to consolidate his position in the pole vault; he achieved it with a clearance of sixteen feet and _ inch and celebrated with a memorable back-flip on the landing cushion. He'd done it again, Hingsen was vanquished and Thompson had his second gold medal and another world record.

1985 was a year of rest and relaxation. There was talk of a career in the movies, it was said the Dallas Cowboys wanted him as a running-back. But, in truth, he was rapidly withdrawing from an extrovert existence. His personality had not won him too many friends in the press. He didn't suffer fools and he regarded many of the press as just that. In turn, they often reported him as being rude and arrogant. He had whistled through the national anthem at his Los Angeles medal ceremony and then when he wore tee-shirts which had messages on them about the American TV coverage of the Games and a reference to the world's second-best athlete being gay, the press had a field day.

Mercifully for Thompson, 1986 was another double decathlon year and in July he won his third consecutive Commonwealth gold and a month later his second European gold in Stuttgart. It was then eight years since he had lost a decathlon (his silver medal in the Europeans in 1978) and he had a tally which will probably never be beaten: four World records, three Commonwealth, two Olympic, two European and one World Championship.

But then ten years of phenomenal training regimes and high-pressure competition began to take their toll. Injury hampered his performance in the second World Championships in Rome and he finished ninth behind the new Champion, Torsten Voss of East Germany. Similarly, at the Seoul Olympics, in 1988, he carried injuries throughout the competition but only missed a bronze medal by twenty-two points. However, on both occasions he won many friends for the way he behaved when not winning. Dutch competitor, Rob de Wit, was quoted in the Sun talking about Seoul, 'Since he lost in the World Championships in Rome, many of us looked at him with different eyes. But having watched him go through all that pain today and still refuse to give up, I realise we were wrong – he's still a god. There can't be anyone in your country who isn't proud he represents the British people.'

Injury also prevented Thompson from competing in 1990 in either the Commonwealth Games in New Zealand or the European Championships in Yugoslavia, but he made one last attempt to win this third Olympic gold medal in Barcelona in 1992. It was an enticing prospect, especially when the new American star, Dan O'Brien 'blew it' in the US Trials. However, a dislocated collar-bone ruined his final preparation and on the eve of the Games he had to accept the inevitable and he retired from competition. He was thirty-four years old.

Daley Thompson has enjoyed life since retirement from competition. He is involved in numerous promotional activities and has appeared in several television series and programmes as well as BBC sports commentary work. He also dabbled with a career in motorsport for a while, before pursuing his current obsession of becoming a professional footballer.

'I think 8 years undefeated says much about the way I performed at the top level. I am also proud of being the only man to win the Olympic; World; European; and Commonwealth titles, and to have broken the world record more times than anyone else. Above all that, after having mostly a bad press, the British public always had a soft sport for me and still do.'

---

athlete, because otherwise I'm sure he would have become an urban guerrilla.'

- Tom McNab, one of Britain's leading coaches and sports gurus, is reported to have remarked about the young Thompson, 'That boy is a bum.' Daley never let him forget it.

- When not competing in decathlons, he was a regular competitor for his club, the Essex Beagles.

- It took Thompson so long to provide a urine sample after his Moscow victory that by the time he got back to the athletes' village for a team celebration, everyone had gone to bed.

- Daley's registered Christian names are Francis Morgan. 'Daley' derives from 'Ayodele' a Nigerian name given to him by his father.

- Other titles he has won include a Commonwealth silver and European bronze in 1986 with the British sprint relay team and an AAA long jump title in 1977 and a UK one in 1979.

- He was awarded the MBE in 1982.

JAYNE TORVILL AND CHRISTOPHER DEAN

**JAYNE TORVILL
BORN: NOTTINGHAM, 7 OCTOBER 1957
CHRISTOPHER COLIN DEAN
BORN: NOTTINGHAM, 27 JULY 1958
ICE SKATERS**

Facts about Torvill and Dean

- Christopher Dean gave up a career as a policeman to become an ice dancer.

- Dean later married Isabelle Duchesnay, the world's second-ranked ice dancer, though the marriage did not last.

- Since retirement, Torvill and Dean have won four professional ice dance titles.

Perfection is not the easiest condition to achieve officially, especially in as subjective a sport as ice skating. The rows of sixes that followed most Torvill and Dean performances in 1983 and 1984 have never been seen before or since, and may possibly never occur again.

Both started skating at Nottingham Ice Stadium at the age of ten. Torvill was taken by her school, which had a programme in which pupils were taken to the rink, while Dean's stepmother thought Christopher needed an outside interest that would keep him out of mischief. In his case, skating did not appear to be the ideal solution. The first time he was left on his own at the rink he skated into a barrier and broke a leg. However, both showed enough promise and dedication to progress.

Initially, they were both paired with different partners. Torvill teamed up as a pairs' skater, a very

different discipline, with Michael Hutchinson. They won both a British junior and senior pairs' title, the latter when Torvill was only fourteen. However, a few weeks later, they finished last at the European Championships in Gothenburg, and the partnership ended.

Dean started as a competitive ice dancer, and was teamed with Sandra Elsdon. It was initially Elsdon who was the dominant partner, and her presence helped them to win the British junior title in 1974. Then the couple started quarrelling, and it was clear they would be going their separate ways.

Torvill and Dean teamed up as ice dancers in 1975. They did not seem to be physically well-matched, and Torvill as a pairs' skater was technically rather inferior, but they showed so much promise that the National Skating Association entered them in two tournaments abroad before they had skated competitively in Britain.. They won one of those events, in St Gervais, France, and finished second in the other behind a Russian couple who placed fifth in the next World Championships. The judges liked their routines, but they were criticised in some quarters. Some of their moves, particularly those that had accompanied Torvill from her pairs' skating, were not considered wholly in the spirit of ice dancing.

It didn't matter to the couple, though. In 1977, they placed third in the British Senior Championship, and they were selected for the European and World Championship teams. In the

Torvill and Dean's Career

Olympic Games

1980	(Lake Placid)	5th
1984	(Sarajevo)	1st
1994	(Lillehammer)	3rd

European Championships
1981, 1982, 1984, 1994

World Championships
1981, 1982, 1983, 1984

former, in Strasbourg, they finished a highly creditable ninth. The next year, they won the British title. By this time they were being coached by Betty Calloway. At the time, she was also coaching the Hungarian pair Regoeczy and Sallay, who moved to Nottingham to be with her. The presence of Calloway and the Hungarians, who went on to win the World Championship in 1980, gave Torvill and Dean's skating a tremendous impetus. Not only did they have a coach who would drive them hard and ensure they improved, they also had a world-class couple against which to measure themselves. And they were definitely improving. In 1979, they were eighth in the World Championship in Vienna, and at the 1980 Europeans they came fourth. They were definite medal contenders at Lake Placid.

However, the 1980 Olympics proved a disappointment. Torvill came down with the flu, they found the accommodation below standard

The perfect pose. In preparation for Sarajevo in January 1984.

(the Olympic village was later turned into a prison) and the amount of practice time they were allotted was less than they were used to. They finished fifth. Then in the World Championships in Dortmund, a mistake by Torvill cost them a bronze. 1980 was a year to forget.

With the next Olympics four years away, they now had to make a commitment to skate full time if they were to improve. They were in demand for exhibitions but, as they weren't professionals, they were able to claim no more than expenses. They needed a sponsor to be able to pay their training expenses, and eventually, shortly before the European Championships in 1981, they received a grant of £7000 from Nottingham City Council, renewable after six months. Buoyed up by the news, they went to Dortmund, and won their first major title. They followed that with the World Championship in Hartford, Connecticut. They had arrived.

For the 1982 season, Dean devised a routine using the music of Mack and Mabel, a Broadway musical that had closed after just nine performances. It was an instant success. In the British Championship, they got two sixes for the technical category and no less than seven for artistic impression. It was now no longer a question of whether they would win the European and World titles, it was a question of how many sixes they would get. The answer, in the Europeans, was three for their short programme, 'Summertime Blues', and eleven for 'Mack and Mabel'. For artistic impression, eight out of nine judges rewarded it with a six, a new record. Eleven more sixes for their short and free programmes at the World Championships confirmed their status far ahead of the field.

The next year, Torvill and Dean tried to push back the boundaries yet further. They selected a routine with music from Barnum for their free programme. The idea behind the routine was to express the joy of the circus and, because certain restrictions on lifts in amateur dancing had been removed, they were now free to perform more

Opposite: An emotional farewell and a bronze medal in Lillehammer in 1994.

daring movements than previously. It had its drawbacks, though. During practice, Dean slipped during a lift and Torvill fell heavily, injuring her shoulder. They had to withdraw from the European Championships as a result. However, by the time the Worlds were staged in Helsinki, Torvill had recovered sufficiently to participate and once again they walked away with the title. For the first time, they received a complete row of sixes, nine out of nine, for artistic impression. It was the first time such a scoreboard had ever been seen.

1984 was Olympic year, and now the couple had the chance to make up for the disappointment of Lake Placid. This time, their free dance programme was to the music of Ravel's Bolero. Once again, it broke new ground starting with the pair commencing the routine kneeling on the ice and once again it was a triumph. They repeated their complete row of sixes, and were awarded twelve in all in the competition. A month later, they took Ottawa by storm in the World Championships and, with a further six, scored even better than they had in the Olympics.

With nothing left to aim for, they turned professional, and toured the world giving ice shows. That, usually, is the end of an Olympic skater's career, but the 1994 Games in Lillehammer allowed back the professionals, and Torvill and Dean returned to try to emulate their earlier success. Sadly, though, there was no fairytale ending. They were very controversially given a bronze medal, some of the judges questioning the legality of one of their moves. After that, they retired from competition for good.

'Jayne and Christopher's dominance over their peers was absolute from 1981-84, but it's their impact that has pushed them way up this list. Ice dancing isn't something many of us know much about or would want our kids to take part in, but Torvill and Dean had us all watching it. This ability to get people to watch you, when otherwise they would have no interest, is what 'impact' is all about. Not many have had more impact. Style is another mark where they have excelled, because technique and image are everything in this kind of sport.'

FRED TRUEMAN

FREDERICK SEWARDS TRUEMAN
CRICKET – BOWLER
BORN: STAINTON, 6 FEBRUARY 1931

Fred Trueman's Career

Test Wickets	307
Average	21.57
Tests	67
First-class Wickets	2304
Average	18.29
County Championships	
1949 (shared), 1959, 1960, 1962, 1963, 1966, 1967, 1968	
Gillette Cup	1965

For 'Fiery Fred', the alternative to cricket would have been life as a coal miner. His father worked at Maltby Main, but the young Trueman's prowess at village cricket was such that he was very soon spotted by Yorkshire. He made his debut for them aged eighteen in 1949, a tearaway fast bowler with a long, curving run-up and a pronounced final back-foot drag on delivery.

He was capped by Yorkshire in 1951 and, in the absence of any other truly fast bowlers, was selected to play against India the next summer. It was a dramatic debut. In four Tests, he took twenty-nine wickets, and the Indian batsmen were thoroughly shaken up by him. In the second innings at Headingley, the Indians collapsed to 0–4, with Trueman taking three of those wickets in eight balls.

Not all was smooth progression, though. Trueman's bluff manner earned him a reputation for indiscipline and on the tour of the West Indies in 1953–54 he frequently fell foul of authority. Saddled with the label of being a difficult tourist, he was left out of the tours to Australia in 1954–55 and South Africa in 1956–57.

However, by 1957 he was developing a powerful reputation in domestic cricket. For ten straight seasons he took over 100 wickets, and in 1960 took 175 at an average of 13.98. As such, he became an automatic selection for England at home. In addition to his speed, Trueman developed prodigious away swing, and it was this that claimed a lot of his wickets. He developed great consistency and between 1959 and 1963 took twenty wickets or more in every series, except New Zealand in 1962–63, but then his fourteen wickets came in only two Tests.

In the 1963 series against the West Indies, Trueman was especially magnificent in a losing cause. He took thirty-four wickets, still a record for an English bowler against the West Indians, at an average of 17.47. Twice, he took ten wickets in a match, and in England's solitary win of the series, at Edgbaston, he took 5–58 in the first innings, and 7–44 in the second as the men from the Caribbean succumbed for ninety-one.

In 1964, he became the first bowler to reach 300 Test wickets. The milestone came against the Australians at the Oval. When the Australians batted, Trueman still had three wickets to take. The first two, Redpath and McKenzie, fell to the last two balls before lunch, which left the crowd with forty minutes to wait to see if Trueman could not only reach the landmark, but also get a hat-trick into the bargain. Sadly, the much anticipated delivery went just wide of the off stump, and Trueman had to wait a while before he induced Neil Hawke to edge an outswinger to Cowdrey at slip. He said afterwards that whoever broke his record would be 'bloody tired'.

Trueman pushed his total to 307 against New Zealand the following summer, before being dropped against the South Africans, many feel

'Fred Trueman had it all as a fast bowler. He was strong, aggressive and had a good action. Even when he lost some of the heat, his skill and control meant that he continued to take wickets. A good tail-end batsman and very good fielder, means that he was almost as good as he remembers he was!'

Facts about Fred Trueman

- At birth, he weighed a colossal fourteen pounds, one ounce.

- In Trueman's own words, he was 'the finest bloody fast bowler ever to draw breath'.

- Given the chance, he was a powerful hitter with the bat, and scored three first-class centuries.

- His late father treasured Trueman's Yorkshire cap, and was buried with it. He gave his mother his first England cap.

- He took four hat-tricks in his career, three of them against Nottinghamshire.

- He was England's leading wicket-taker in 1960 with 175 wickets.

Fiery Fred in 1953. Already awesome on the field and no less formidable off it.

prematurely. Others may now have left Trueman's achievement far behind, but the Yorkshireman only appeared in sixty-seven Tests. It was a phenomenal achievement.

Trueman finally retired from Yorkshire in 1968, after his twentieth first-class season. Yorkshire were County Champions for the eighth time in that period during his final season. They have never been champions since. After retirement, Trueman became involved in Yorkshire cricket's labyrinthine politics, but he is best known for his appearances as a commentator on both radio and television, and is as much treasured now as he was during his playing days.

RANDOLPH TURPIN

RANDOLPH TURPIN
BOXING – MIDDLEWEIGHT
BORN: LEAMINGTON SPA, 7 JUNE 1928
DIED: LEAMINGTON SPA, 17 MAY 1966

Facts about Randolph Turpin

- His brother, Dick, was British Champion before him and a hugely respected fighter. He also won the Empire title. He was eight years younger than Randolph and lost most of his best years to the Second World War, where he fought from El Alamein to Berlin, and to the pre-war colour bar, operated by the British Boxing Board of Control, which prevented black fighters from challenging the British titles. The colour bar wasn't dropped until after the war.

- Robinson's defeat at the hands of Turpin was his first loss in ninety-one fights.

Randolph Turpin's Career

World Middleweight Champion: 1951

British and Empire Middleweight Champion:
1948, 1950

European Middleweight Champion:
1950

British and Commonwealth Light Heavyweight Champion:
1952, 1955

British Light Heavyweight Champion:
1956, 1957

Fights: 75
67 Wins (45 inside the distance)
8 Defeats

Randolph Turpin was a rare talent. Perhaps, with Jimmy Wilde, the greatest pound-for-pound boxer Britain has ever produced. Certainly no one, Wilde included, had a night of glory quite like the one on 10 July 1951 when Turpin beat the legendary Sugar Ray Robinson, at Earls Court, to win the World Middleweight title.

It is a reflection of Turpin's status within the boxing fraternity, that he is one of the few British boxers to be included when American aficionados discuss the all-time greats. Sadly, like so many of those greats, Turpin's story is as much about tragedy as triumph. One of Britain's greatest ever athletes became one of its saddest; so much so that he took his own life, surrounded by debts and desperation.

Turpin had an upbringing not untypical in his chosen profession – it was hard. He was hardened by it, as were his brothers who also became boxers, but Randolph was the toughest. He was the perfect fighting machine for winning a world boxing title, but not particularly well designed for handling the life that went with it.

His father, from British Guiana, was a merchant sailor and died when Turpin was a child. His English mother, Beatrice, became partially blind and had to raise five children on a twenty-seven shillings-a-week services pension (£1.35 in today's money). Randolph was also the only black kid in his class. Being raised poor in the 1950s can't have been easy for any child; for the Turpin kids it must have been a nightmare.

Not surprisingly, Turpin fought his way out. He started boxing at the age of twelve and took up body-building, the effects of which were to give him one of the most famous physiques in boxing. He went into the navy and had an outstanding career as an amateur. He became ABA Welterweight Champion in 1945, aged seventeen, and then, a year later, became ABA Middleweight Champion. He first came to public prominence when the British amateurs beat the Americans, at Wembley, and Turpin knocked out Harold Anspach after ninety seconds.

Turpin turned professional in 1946, but it was his older brother, Dick, who became British Champion first. In doing so, in 1948, he became the first black British Champion. When Dick lost the title to Albert Finch, it became a matter of family honour. Randolph duly won it back and restored family pride in October 1950, when he stopped Finch in five rounds. At the beginning of 1951 he added the European title by flattening Luc Van Dam of Holland in forty-eight seconds.

Then came one of the most famous nights in boxing history. Jack Solomons, Turpin's promoter, was noted for being able to get things done and managed to get Ray Robinson to London to defend his Middleweight World title. For Robinson it was just a normal pay day, part of a European tour to knock down opponents and pick up cheques. To everyone's amazement, especially Robinson's, Turpin

Turpin's dramatic victory over the great Sugar Ray Robinson at Earls Court in July 1951.

- It is said that Randolph wasn't allowed to fight for the British title until Dick had a chance to win it – on strict orders from their mother.

- Turpin's total earnings from the second Robinson fight were thought to be over $200,000.

- His, not often used, fighter's name was 'The Leamington Licker'.

- The bookies' odds at the beginning of the first Robinson fight were 33–1 against Turpin winning on points. Even so, there were few takers.

- The Duke of Fife, who became President of the ABA, said that he had been with King George VI at a private party at Buckingham Palace during the first Robinson–Turpin fight. Apparently, silence had to prevail while the King listened to the commentary, and at the end he threw his hands up and exclaimed, 'He's won it! He's won it!'

won; and in style. He outpunched the great man and was on top for most of the fight.

After fifteen gruelling rounds Turpin had become the first Black Briton to make it on the international sporting stage.

Unfortunately, his reign lasted only sixty-four days. The return took place at the Polo Grounds in New York. American boxing fans had been stunned by Robinson's defeat in London. The crowd was over 60,000 and the receipts totalled more than three-quarters of a million dollars.

If the first fight went into boxing's Hall of Fame, the second was even better. For nine rounds the contest was even. Turpin was composed and controlled; the American audience began to realise that London hadn't been a fluke. Robinson came out of a clinch with blood streaming from a bad cut. It looked like Turpin would retain his title. But then, in one of the most famous sequences in boxing history, one that was seen as a mark of Robinson's greatness, the American launched a ferocious attack on Turpin, knowing that his cut was bad enough to end the fight. Turpin went down from a hook, but managed to beat the count – just. But Robinson tore into him again and Turpin got caught on the ropes and took relentless punishment. The referee had little option but to stop the fight. Ironically, it was only eight seconds from the end of the round.

Turpin had more years of success after his epic encounters with Robinson, but those two nights had been special.

In June 1952, Turpin beat Don Cockell to win the British and Commonwealth LightHeavyweight titles and then, in 1963, successfully defended his European Middleweight title against Charles Humez of France.

But domestic problems were beginning to loom large in Turpin's life and his career began to falter. An attempt to win back the World Middleweight title against American, Carl 'Bobo' Olsen, ended in a shock defeat amidst lurid stories and criminal charges of rape brought by a New York girl which were eventually settled out of court.

Turpin carried on fighting until retiring for the last time, in 1962, aged thirty-four. He had won some huge purses, but the money had gone. He made some unwise business moves and, by 1966, was in desperate straits. He shot himself a month before his thirty-eighth birthday.

'Turpin's story is really sad, he really did need looking after. In one respect, it shows the glory of sport, in that when allowed, anybody from any background can make it to the top. I never knew there was a colour bar on boxers fighting for the British title.'

ALLAN WELLS

ALLAN WIPPER WELLS
ATHLETICS – SPRINTER
BORN: EDINBURGH, 3 MAY 1952

The success of Allan Wells is a testament to hard work and also, let it be said, to good fortune. The Olympic 100 metres champion in 1980, many feel that he would not have been in the medal hunt had those games not been boycotted.

Wells started his career as a triple jumper, winning the Scottish title in 1970. He was also a promising long jumper, with a leap of 7.32 metres in 1972 his best. However, he was influenced by the performance of Jamaica's Don Quarrie at that year's Commonwealth Games, he decided that he would concentrate his efforts on sprinting.

He was relatively unsuccessful, only standing out from the crowd because he refused to use starting blocks, but under the influence of coach Wilson Young he developed a powerful physique through a punishing training routine. In 1978, he suddenly sprung to prominence by first equalling and then breaking the twenty-year-old British 100 metres record with a mark of 10.15 seconds. In August that year, in the Commonwealth Games in Edmonton, he surpassed himself, winning the 200 metres with a wind-assisted time of 20.12 seconds and taking silver in the 100 metres. He won a second gold in the sprint relay.

In 1979, Wells became a sprinter of definite world class. He twice improved the British 200

metres record, and then beat Italy's Pietro Mennea at the European Cup final in Turin. Despite a relatively successful year, he was not considered among the favourites for the Moscow Games until the boycott over the Soviet invasion of Afghanistan. With the Americans suddenly out of the picture, Wells was second favourite for the 100 metres behind Cuban Silvio Leonard. The race was desperately close. Both athletes went over the line in a time of 10.25 seconds, and initially it was believed the Cuban had won. It only became apparent when the race was replayed on the stadium scoreboard that Wells had crossed the line first. At the age of twenty-eight, Wells was at the time the oldest winner of the 100 metres title.

A few days later, there was an equally thrilling race for the 200 metres crown. Wells, in lane seven, looked to have had the race won when suddenly the world record holder, Mennea, appeared on his outside with a late burst. The time, the Scotsman had to settle for silver. His time of 20.21 seconds was a UK record, but that was his only satisfaction. He participated in a third UK record in Moscow, in the sprint relay, but this time it was only good enough for fourth place.

The next season, Wells continued his excellent form, winning the IAAF 'Golden Sprints' title, and taking victory in the World Cup and the European Cup. However, when the next season started, he was approaching his thirtieth birthday, and his abilities seemed to be on the wane. However, he had one final medal-winning performance left. In Brisbane, he took the Commonwealth Games 100 metres title, and then raced to a dead-heat with Mike McFarlane in the 200 metres. The judges took a long time before

Allan Wells's Career

Olympic Games

1980	(Moscow)	100 metres	1st
		200 metres	2nd
		4 x 100 metres	4th
1984	(Los Angeles)	100 metres	did not qualify
		4 x 100 metre	

deciding the two athletes could not be separated. For Wells, the second gold meant that he had retained his title from four years earlier.

Wells made the British team for the 1984 Olympics, but this time, at the age of thirty-two an with excellent American sprinters like Carl Lewis, he was outgunned. He was eliminated in the 100 metres semi-final. He was also one of the sprint relay team, which did reach the final, but got no further.

Wells may have owed his Olympic medals to the absence of others, but he still had to beat excellent runners like Leonard. His times remained British records for a number of years, before the rise of a new generation of sprinters in the late 1980s.

'There are those who say that Wells was lucky to win his gold in Moscow – I am not among then. True, the US athletes weren't there, but Wells beat the best of them, Floyd and Co., in Berlin straight after the Games. This must have been much harder for him than them (to try to scale a second peak in only a few days, quite incredible). This is one of the reasons for his success, mental strength, another was the quality and quantity of his training. It is said that Linford Christie is mentally tough but at least he is the first or second fastest in the field when he races, Wells never had that advantage so, to my mind, he is in a different class when it comes to getting it right on the day.'

Facts about Allan Wells

- Wells enrolled in a Charles Atlas bodybuilding course in order to build up his size.

- His father was a blacksmith, and his mother sewed nets for fishermen.

- Wells was the first British sprinter to experiment with the use of cycling shorts.

- Wells once said, 'the feeling of running fast is unforgettable, the exhilaration you feel running around a bend, it's like you're in charge, you're a Ferrari'.

- Linford Christie finally beat him in the 1986 European Championships, but graciously called him 'the Godfather of British sprinting'.

The world's fastest human. 100 metres gold in Moscow 1980.

FATIMA WHITBREAD

FATIMA WHITBREAD
ATHLETICS – JAVELIN THROWER
BORN: STOKE NEWINGTON, 3 MARCH 1961

Facts about Fatima Whitbread

- Her original surname was Vedad.

- Her incredible form in 1986 and 1987 led to a slightly unflattering self-assessment. 'People think of me as the Incredible Hulk.'

For many years, Fatima Whitbread was in the shadow of her rival Tessa Sanderson. In the late 1980s, though, she came through as a champion in her own right and for 1986 and 1987 was ranked the world number one.

She had a difficult childhood. Born: to Cypriot parents in London she was in and out of numerous children's homes before being adopted by Margaret Whitbread, an ex-international and UK javelin coach. Perhaps it was not so surprising that she eventually took up the sport. She showed good progress, sixth at the 1978 Commonwealth Games, and then European Junior champion in 1979, a year in which she broke the UK junior record three times. She was selected to go to the Moscow Olympics, more as a learning experience, but she failed to qualify for the final.

Whitbread showed steady improvement over the next two seasons, but she was still only given an outside chance of a medal when in the World Championships in Helsinki, though. Her first throw of the competition was one of her very best, 69.14 metres, and the Finns, who regard the javelin as their own event, were suitably generous in their praise. They fully expected their own heroine, Tiina Lillak to win. But round after round went by, and Whitbread still held the lead, although she had felt a twinge in her arm, and had not been able to throw any further. With the very last throw of the competition, Lillak flung the javelin beyond 70 metres, and the stadium erupted. Whitbread went over to her adoptive mother and burst into tears.

For the next few seasons, she still found herself unable to win any of the big events. She did win the European Cup shortly after Helsinki, but could only take a bronze medal behind Sanderson at the 1984 Olympics. Although she then proceeded to beat Sanderson in their next seven encounters, she lost the 1986 Commonwealth Games to her English rival after leading most of the way.

A few weeks later, she was in Stuttgart for the European Championships. In early morning qualifying, she let loose her first throw. It went way beyond the qualifying distance, and then kept going, finally landing 77.44 metres beyond the runway. It was a new world record. The final the next day was no formality. She had wrenched her arm slightly on the world record throw, and rain was falling. Her biggest rival, Petra Felke of East Germany, was in the lead for the first four rounds, before Whitbread unleashed a throw of 72.68 metres. In the final round, she did even better, 76.32 metres, and the gold was hers. She was the best javelin thrower in Europe, and had finally come out of Sanderson's shadow.

The next year, she won sixteen out of

Fatima Whitbread's Career

Olympic Games
1980	(Moscow)	did not qualify
1984	(Los Angeles)	3rd
1988	(Seoul)	2nd

World Championships
1983	(Helsinki)	2nd
1987	(Rome)	1st

European Championships
1982	8th
1986	1st

World Records
1986	77.44 metres in Stuttgart

seventeen javelin competitions, losing only on one occasion to Sanderson. Among her wins was the World Championship in Rome, making up for the disappointment of four years before. She had been nursing a damaged shoulder, but her fifth round throw of 76.64 metres was the third longest of all time, and there was nothing Petra Felke, who was now the world record holder, could do in reply.

1988 was Olympic year, but it started badly with an operation for an abscess on her back and a bout of glandular fever. She shone when it mattered in Seoul, although Felke was by now the world number one. Whitbread, after struggling to qualify, went on to pick up a silver medal. It was her last major prize. More injuries haunted her through the next couple of seasons, and she had a shoulder operation at the start of 1989. She was a popular champion, and took the pressures of success in her stride with great charm.

Not quite far enough. Silver in Seoul for Whitbread.

'Whitbread, along with Sanderson, finally put British field events on the map. In the years she was on top she was able to beat the best the Eastern block had to offer.'

JIMMY WILDE

JAMES WILDE
BOXING – FLYWEIGHT
BORN: TYLORSTOWN, 15 MAY 1892
DIED: CARDIFF, 10 MARCH 1969

Facts about Jimmy Wilde

- After starting work at twelve, he nearly lost his right leg in a mining accident.

- When he began professional boxing in 1911 he weighed only six stone six pounds.

- He had 140 full professional fights and lost just four. Numbers: 88, 117, 139 and 140.

- Wilde rose to the rank of Company Sergeant Major while in the army.

- Pete Herman was offered the huge sum of £8000 for the infamous fight in 1921 in London.

Jimmy Wilde was one of the most remarkable British athletes of all time. He never weighed more than seven stone ten pounds and stood only five feet two inches tall; not much bigger than a modern-day, pre-pubescent female gymnast. He had spindly legs, matchstick arms and a completely unorthodox boxing style which left his freakishly long arms dangling by his side.

Yet, before his first professional fight in 1911, it is estimated that he fought in more than 700 fairground boxing booth bouts to try to earn money to supplement his meagre miner's wages. He became the most feared boxer of his day. In 130 professional fights he lost only four times, either to much bigger men or at the end of his career.

His great strengths seemed to come from nowhere. He had a punch like a mule's kick with both hands, and a particularly devastating left-hook. He ducked and weaved incessantly, as he came in from his unorthodox stance, and attacked relentlessly. He would throw a barrage of punches and then retreat as rapidly as he came in. His hand speed was phenomenal.

Wilde was given several nicknames, all of them evocative of his awesome record, but the three most famous ones were: 'The Mighty Atom', 'The Tylorstown Terror' and 'The Ghost with a Hammer in his Hands'. He is regarded as the first world champion in the Flyweight division and probably the greatest of all time.

Wilde did much of his boxing during the First World War while serving in the army. He won the European title against Eugene Husson in 1914, but suffered a setback against Tancy Lee for the British and European title in 1915. He was ill with 'flu and had a massive swelling on his face, but fought on to the seventeenth round until his corner threw in the towel. After that setback, he was unstoppable.

Tancy Lee had lost the title to Joe Symonds after the Wilde fight and Symonds also claimed the

Jimmy Wilde's Career

Total professional fights: (140) 126 wins, 77 knock-outs, 4 defeats

World Flyweight Title fights

Year	Month	Opponent	Result	Method	Rounds
1916	(Feb)	Joe Symonds	Won	retired	12 rounds
1916	(Apr)	Johnny Rosner	Won	retired	11 rounds
1916	(June)	Tancy Lee	Won	stopped	11 rounds
1916	(July)	Johnny Hughes	Won	knock-out	10 rounds
1916	(Dec)	Young Zulu Kid	Won	knock-out	11 rounds
1917	(Mar)	George Clark	Won	retired	4 rounds
1924	(May)	Pancho Villa	Lost	knock-out	7 rounds

Elected Boxing Hall of Fame: 1959

The amazingly slight and deceptively frail physique of the Tylorstown Terror.

In 1919, Wilde went to America and returned undefeated, despite fighting much bigger men. However, it was a much bigger man who marked the beginning of the end for Wilde. The fight was for the World Bantamweight title against the American Peter Herman. As the contest grew near, Wilde learned that Herman had inexplicably lost his title to Joe Lynch. Wilde smelled a rat (in fact, Herman immediately won a return against Lynch after the Wilde fight) and wanted to pull out. He was eventually persuaded to fight by none other than the Prince of Wales. More skulduggery ensued at the weigh-in.

~Wilde weighed in at seven stone one pound, Herman was eight stone six pounds. Ludicrously, Herman was then allowed to go away and bulk up for the fight. Wilde fought courageously for seventeen rounds until the referee, Jack Smith, stopped the fight, saying to Wilde, 'I'm sorry. I have to pick you up because you don't know how to lie down.' Wilde retired, disillusioned by the whole sorry episode.

Wilde reluctantly made a comeback in 1923, when the American promoter Tex Rickard made him a huge offer to defend his World Flyweight title against the Filipino boxer, Pancho Villa. This time, a controversial refereeing decision interferred. Wilde appeared to drop his guard at the bell at the end of round two, and was knocked out by a late blow. He claimed not to remember much after that but struggled on for five more rounds until he fell down in the seventh. It took him weeks to recover and he retired at the age of thirty-two.

He became a manager and a promoter in his own right, and wrote a newspaper column for many years.

Jimmy Wilde's name may be less familiar at the end of the century than it was at the beginning, but his record speaks for itself. Certainly, the wise men of boxing history have no doubts about his status as one of the sport's all time greats.

'I didn't know much about Wilde until I started reading for this book but it seems to me, that this flyweight was indeed a big man in the world of boxing. During Wilde's reign, championship fights lasted 20 rounds or more.'

- When Wilde fought Joe Conn during the First World War, the army would not let him fight for money. So his wife was given a bag of diamonds worth £3000.

- Towards the end of life, when in ill-health and by then a broken man, he was beaten up by some teenagers on a lonely railway station. The culprits were never caught, and Wilde never really recovered. He died aged seventy-six in 1969.

world title. So, when a now fully fit Wilde beat Symonds on St Valentine's day 1916 he became the first Flyweight World Champion. He then reigned supreme for the next five years. He beat dozens of British Flyweight challengers, took on and beat Bantamweights, and even beat Joe Conn, one of the outstanding Featherweights of the day, in a war-time charity contest. During this time he also defended his world title five times.

The only blot on the Wilde copy-book at this time was a three-round defeat in an inter-services tournament, at the Albert Hall, which nearly caused a riot. His opponent, Memphis Pal Moore, was a Bantamweight, and the decision was a very controversial one. Seven months later Wilde reversed the decision.

DAVID WILKIE

DAVID ANDREW WILKIE
SWIMMING – BREASTSTROKE
BORN: COLOMBO, SRI LANKA, 8 MARCH 1954

Facts about David Wilkie

- Wilkie's attitude to training in the early 1970s was legendary. His coach called him 'The most unfit athlete at the 1972 Olympics', and he still won a bronzemedal.

- Wilkie lost the 100 metres breaststroke in 1974 in Vienna when he heard a horn in the crowd immediately after diving in. He thought it registered a false start, and stopped.

- Wilkie wore a cap and goggles for the 1974 NCAA (Northern Counties Athletic Association) Championships. He was the first swimmer to do so, and he was dubbed the 'Capped Crusader'.

David Wilkie's Career

Championship wins

Olympic Games
1976 (Montreal)	200 metres breaststroke

World Championships
1973	200 metres breaststroke
1975	100 metres breaststroke
	200 metres breaststroke

European Championships
1974	200 metres breaststroke
	200 metres individual medley

Commonwealth Games
1974	200 metres breaststroke
	200 metres individual medley

Wilkie was the most successful British swimmer since the heyday of Henry Taylor before the First World War. He was born in Sri Lanka of Scottish parents, and learnt to swim there. When he returned to Scotland in 1965 to attend school he was a keen swimmer, but had no serious competitive aspirations. However, he joined the Warrender Baths Swimming Club in Edinburgh, and met Frank Thomas, who saw the boy's potential.

Wilkie was clearly an exceptional talent and, without a terribly demanding training schedule, he won a bronze medal in the 100 metres breaststroke in the 1970 Commonwealth Games, and then took a silver over 200 metres in the 1972 Olympics. in January 1973, he went to the University of Miami on a marine biology course, and now he had the time and, after his medal-winning performances, the self-belief required to become the world's best breaststroke swimmer. At the World Championships later that year, he won the 200 metres, breaking the world record on the way. From that point on, his career was one of continued success.

Against the advice of his coach, he went to the Commonwealth Games in 1974, and he won both the 200 metres breaststroke and 200 metres individual medley. He followed that by winning the same events in the European Championships, setting a new world best in the medley. He still wasn't fully satisfied. Tiredness from travelling all the way to New Zealand meant that he only claimed a silver in the 100 metres breaststroke, and a poor start cost him the same race in the Europeans.

However, he went to Cali, Colombia, for the 1975 World Championships full of confidence. It wasn't the ideal venue. Wilkie and the rest of the team hated the accommodation, and most of the team suffered stomach upsets shortly before the races began. The Scotsman overcame the conditions in style, winning both individual golds in the breaststroke, and getting a bronze in the individual medley. The only factor preventing him setting new world records was a strong crosswind at the outdoor pool.

Wilkie started the 1976 season perfectly, with three wins in the US Championships, at both breaststroke events and the medley. He was the first Briton ever to win an American title, which put him in the perfect frame of mind for Montreal.

The American men had been dominant in the pool, and their mere presence at events had been enough to scare the opposition. Now the Americans were scared of Wilkie.

Wilkie trained hard for the Games, but so did the leading Americans, and the Scotsman's status as favourite was by no means a foregone conclusion. The 100 metres was the first event, and one that had given Wilkie trouble in the past: once again he was caught. John Hencken, the top American, touched first, and Wilkie had to settle for silver.

He gained ample revenge in the 200 metres. Wilkie started fast and was ahead at the first turn. He then let Hencken draw level by 100 metres and found that he had plenty in reserve. Over the last 100 metres, Wilkie simply pulled away. By the finish, he was two seconds ahead of Hencken, and

had beaten the world record by more than three seconds. It was an astounding performance.

Wilkie turned professional after the Games but in 1988 felt that his times were still so good at age thirty-four that he asked for renewal of his amateur status for one more try at gold. Perhaps fortunately he didn't go to Seoul so the memory of Wilkie in 1976 with the opposition trailing in his wake was left untarnished.

'David was one of the top sportsmen on our team when we travelled to Montreal. Also, his time spent going to school in America meant that like most Americans he was out-going and media-friendly and with only a few medals being won by Brits he was in huge demand.'

On his way to a world record and Olympic gold in Montreal in 1976.

JPR WILLIAMS

JOHN PETER RHYS WILLIAMS
RUGBY UNION – FULL-BACK
BORN: CARDIFF, 2 MARCH 1949

Facts about JPR Williams

- He was a very commanding figure on the rugby field with long flowing hair, mutton-chop whiskers and socks down to his ankles.

- His tackling was legendary. The most famous example was the audacious body-check to knock French winger, Jean-Luc Gourdon, into touch at Arms Park in 1978, to prevent a certain try in the corner in the Wales–France match.

- His speciality as a surgeon is sports injuries.

- One of his brothers, Chris, won three rugby blues at Cambridge.

- Williams was awarded the MBE in 1977.

- His nickname was 'Japes'.

JPR Williams was part of that unique cluster of talent that was Welsh rugby in the seventies. The same group of Welshman formed the heart of the two great 'prides' of Lions who were British rugby's finest ever ambassadors, in New Zealand in 1971 and in South Africa in 1974.

No one who knows and loves the game will ever forget the men of Harlech who dominated rugby in the northern hemisphere in the 1970s: Mervyn Davies, Barry John, Phil Bennett, Gareth Edwards, JJ Williams, John Davies, The Pontypool front-row. 'JPR' was the last line of defence of these great teams and often one of its most lethal attackers. He was universally respected for his unwavering courage under pressure and his ferocious tackling.

Like fellow Welsh hero Gareth Edwards, Williams was a product of Millfield School in Somerset, the private school which has produced so much sporting talent. He was also similar to Edwards in that he was a gifted all-rounder. He was an outstanding tennis player and won the Junior Wimbledon title in 1966 at the age of seventeen. Within two years, he was good enough at rugby to go on tour with the Welsh second XV to Argentina, having graduated from the Welsh School team. He was immediately recognised as having huge potential.

His tennis talent confirmed a sharp eye and good hands, but he was also quick, and big enough to play as a centre. In fact, he made one international appearance as a flanker on the 1978 Welsh tour of Australia, to become one of the few players to play at international level both as a forward and as a back.

These gifts, combined with his courage and aggression, made him into a very rare commodity,

JPR Williams' Career

Captain of Wales 1978–79

International appearances: 55
6 tries, 2 conversions,
3 penalty goals, 36 points

British Lions appearances
1971	New Zealand	(4 caps)
1974	South Africa	(4 caps)

good enough to keep Bob Hillier, the England full-back, out of the Lions team in New Zealand in 1971 and Andy Irvine, the Scotland full-back, among the reserves in 1974 in South Africa.

Williams quickly established himself in the Welsh team, and in 1969 won the Five Nations Championship and the Triple Crown in his first season, as well as going on tour to New Zealand with them.

An amazing catalogue of successes then followed. He won eight International Championships, six Triple Crowns and two Grand Slams from 1969 to 1979 and was captain in 1978 and 1979. This era also covered his two illustrious tours with the Lions in 1971 and 1974. He was the full-back and bullwark for both tours and played in all four tests on each tour, lending invaluable vocal support to the leadership of his captains, John Davies in New Zealand, and Willie John McBride in South Africa. In all, he made fifteen appearances on each tour. He was also a frequent tourist for Wales. After the tours to Argentina in 1968 and Australia and Fiji in 1969, he also went to Canada in 1973, the Far East in

- Williams's bravery led to a fair share of mishaps, including several sets of stitches. The most notorious incident occurred when he was playing for Brigend against New Zealand in 1978. He was caught at the foot of a rolling maul and was viciously stamped on by Kiwi forward John Ashworth. Williams' cheek was actually punctured in the incident. It was one of rugby's most unsavoury incidents, captured vividly on camera.

- As well as winning Junior Wimbledon, Williams also won the Welsh Junior tennis title, as did his three brothers.

- Williams was the first full-back to make full use of the Australian 'dispensation' law which prevented kicking to touch on the full outside the twenty-two yard line. His speed and strength made him an ideal vehicle for carrying the ball upfield.

1975 and Australia in 1978.

Williams retired in 1979 to concentrate on his career as an orthopaedic surgeon. However, such was his popularity, he was persuaded to return for Wales' centenary season and played against New Zealand in 1980, before making his final appearance against Scotland at Murrayfield in 1981.

'Isn't it amazing how often, when you get an all-time great, you find the level of everyone else around them lifted. JPR was another spoke in the wheel of Welsh rugby. Resolute defence; brilliant counter attacking and brave as you like; are what made him an all time great.'

BILLY WRIGHT

WILLIAM AMBROSE WRIGHT
FOOTBALL – DEFENDER
BORN: IRONBRIDGE, 6 FEBRUARY 1924
DIED: LONDON, 3 SEPTEMBER 1994

Billy Wright's Career	
League Championship	1953–54
	1957–58
	1958–59
FA Cup	1949
International appearances (90 as captain)	105

Facts about Billy Wright

- Wright's long run of England appearances included seventy consecutive games between October 1951 and October 1959.

- He was voted Footballer of the Year in 1952.

- Wright was awarded the OBE in 1959.

- One of the stands at the new Molyneaux Ground is named in honour of him.

- There is also a large portrait of him at Molyneaux which is not to everyone's taste. His only comment about the likeness was, 'we must have lost 7–0!'

- Initially, he was rejected by Major Buckley at Wolves because he was too small.

- As a boy, he once scored a hat-trick for Cradley Heath and was given three bars of chocolate as a reward.

It is forty years since Billy Wright's commanding presence in football made him a major British celebrity and a schoolboy hero. He was the supreme professional, had a flawless image and led his club and country with great dignity and authority.

Wright was the leader of an England team that included legendary figures like Matthews, Finney, Mannion and Lawton, and was the lynchpin of Stan Cullis' magnificent era at Wolves, when the 'black and old gold' dominated English football. With Bobby Moore, he is one of the few defenders to be regarded as being in the front rank of English football's greatest players.

He was not an instinctively talented footballer, but much more a leader of men. His gifts had more to do with his vision, his timing and his ability to motivate by example. After starting his career as a forward, he graduated to the centre of defence and was able to hold his ground and win challenges in the air, despite being a relatively small man.

For many years Billy Wright was English football. His marriage in 1959 to Joy Beverley, one of the Beverley sisters, was front-page news. The clean-cut blonde-haired 'Mr Perfect', captain of England, had married one of Britain's best-loved popular entertainers. What's more, he'd done exactly what the hit song had warned him not to: 'Lord help the mister, who comes between me and my sisters ...'

In an era when international teams played far fewer games than they do now, his record at international level was amazing. After making his debut against Portugal in 1947, he played in all but three of England's next 107 games. His total number of caps, 105, was a record, as was his ninety caps as captain.

Wright started his schoolboy football career as a centre-forward and once scored ten goals in a game. He was attracted to Wolves by an advertisement for young players in the local newspaper. Despite the daunting presence of Major Frank Buckley, Wright joined the Molyneaux groundstaff for the princely sum of £2 per week. He became a professional during the war, but in 1942 broke an ankle, in what was thought to be a career-threatening injury. However, he recovered and joined the army as a physical training instructor for the duration of the war.

Football began again after the war on a huge wave of popularity which seemed to carry Wright along with it. He quickly became a force in the resurgent Wolves team and took over the captaincy from Stan Cullis, in 1947. In 1949, Wolves won the FA Cup, 3–1, against Leicester. There were also three League Championships as Wolves became the dominant team of the 1950s. The Championships came in 1953–54, 1957–58, and 1958–59, but there were also two runners-up places and three third places between 1952 and 1959.

Wright made a timely and wise retirement in the summer of 1959, at the age of thirty-five. He had played his last game for England in the same year and had just led Wolves to their third Championship in six years, and decided to retire at the pinnacle of his career.

He continued to be a leading figure in the game and became manager of the England youth and Under-23 teams. In 1962, he became manager of Arsenal, a team he had supported as a schoolboy, but lasted only four years at Highbury. It was said he was too nice a guy to be a successful football manager.

However, many people close to Arsenal felt that much of his work in developing a youth policy paid off years later under the tutelage of Bertie Mac.

Wright was much more successful in the world of television and became a leading executive with ATV. He remained happily married to Joy and saw Wolves begin to plot the journey back to the glory days with a new Molyneaux and new ambitions in the 1990s.

Billy Wright died in 1994 and will always be remembered as one of football's all-time greats.

'Billy Wright and Bobby Moore were very alike when you consider, the image, the authority and the way each led by example, but in the end his legend is built on those 105 caps.'

- He discovered he had been made England captain by a 'clippie' on a Wolverhampton bus who showed him the 'stop press' column in the newspaper.

- His proudest day in an England shirt was the 10–0 defeat of Portugal in Lisbon. The England forward line that memorable day was: Matthews, Mortenson, Lawton, Mannion and Finney.

- Although he suffered the disappointment of the famous defeat at the hands of Puskas and the Mighty Magyars at Wembley in 1953, he was full of admiration for the way they played and took the defeat with great sportsmanship. He said he was 'supremely grateful' just to have played against the great Hungarians.

The England players carry Wright off the field to mark his 100th cap, as England beat Scotland in 1959.

SCORES FOR THE TOP ONE HUNDRED

The scores for the athletes are listed from 100 to 20, according to the five criteria outlined in the introduction.

The top 20 athletes, which will be the subject of the Channel 4 series, "The Greatest", are left blank to allow you to use the book in conjunction with the series and to allow you the opportunity to make your own scoring decisions.

The scoring for the athletes listed from 100 – 20 is entirely the product of the opinions of the authors, as is the choice of the athletes to be included in the top 20. However, the authors worked closely with TWI, the producers of the Channel 4 series, to reach a consensus on the top 100, on the scoring for the group between 100 and 20 and in the choice of the top 20.

The top 20 are not listed according to any hierachy. They are simply entered alphabetically. Please use the spaces provided to fill in your own scores and rankings if you wish to.

Criteria Score:	1 Achievement (out of 20)	2 Dominance (out of 20)	3 Style (out of 20)	4 Fortitude (out of 20)	5 Impact (out of 20)	Total (out of 100)	Rank (100th to 1st)
Ann Jones	10	9	9	8	9	45	100th
Martin Offiah	9	8	9	9	11	46	98th =
Harold Larwood	10	9	10	9	8	46	98th =
Richard Meade	10	8	10	11	8	47	96th =
John Curry	11	8	9	9	10	47	96th =
Fatima Whitbread	12	11	7	10	8	48	90th =
Rodney Pattison	13	10	8	10	7	48	90th =
Ann Packer	13	9	9	9	8	48	90th =
Lennox Lewis	12	10	8	10	8	48	90th =
Graham Gooch	11	9	9	10	9	48	90th =
Billy Boston	10	11	9	9	9	48	90th =
Jonathan Edwards	12	9	9	9	10	49	87th =
Geoff Duke	10	11	9	9	10	49	87th =

Criteria	1 Achievement	2 Dominance	3 Style	4 Fortitude	5 Impact	Total	Rank
Score:	(out of 20)	(out of 20)	(out of 20)	(out of 20)	(out of 20)	(out of 100)	(100th to 1st)
Eric Ashton	10	11	10	9	9	49	87th =
Peter Shilton	11	11	9	10	9	50	83rd =
Billy McNeill	10	11	10	10	9	50	83rd =
Peter May	9	9	12	10	10	50	83rd =
Colin Jackson	11	10	12	8	9	50	83rd =
Billy Wright	10	10	11	10	10	51	77th =
Alan Minter	11	11	10	10	9	51	77th =
Steve Davis	11	10	10	11	9	51	77th =
Frank Bruno	9	8	9	10	15	51	77th =
Phil Bennett	10	10	12	10	9	51	77th =
Ken Barrington	12	10	9	12	8	51	77th =
Alan Wells	12	10	8	14	8	52	69th =
Ian Rush	11	11	11	10	9	52	69th =
Stirling Moss	9	10	11	11	11	52	69th =
Adrian Moorhouse	12	11	10	9	10	52	69th =
Tony Jacklin	9	11	11	11	10	52	69th =
Joe Davis	12	10	10	10	10	52	69th =
Laura Davies	10	12	10	11	9	52	69th =
Henry Cooper	8	7	10	11	16	52	69th =
Randolph Turpin	14	11	8	9	11	53	62nd =
Gary Lineker	10	11	12	10	10	53	62nd =
Stephen Hendry	12	11	11	10	9	53	62nd =
Mike Hailwood	12	12	10	10	9	53	62nd =

Criteria Score:	1 Achievement (out of 20)	2 Dominance (out of 20)	3 Style (out of 20)	4 Fortitude (out of 20)	5 Impact (out of 20)	Total (out of 100)	Rank (100th to 1st)
Colin Cowdrey	10	10	12	11	10	53	62nd =
Henry Cotton	10	11	11	11	10	53	62nd =
Harold Abrahams	12	10	9	11	11	53	62nd =
Pat Jennings	11	11	12	11	9	54	58th =
David Gower	10	10	13	9	12	54	58th =
Tom Finney	10	11	12	11	10	54	58th =
Roger Bannister	11	9	11	13	10	54	58th =
JPR Williams	11	10	11	12	11	55	52nd =
David Wilkie	12	11	10	10	12	55	52nd =
Billy Meredith	11	13	10	9	12	55	52nd =
Willie-John McBride	12	11	10	12	10	55	52nd =
Ellery Hanley	12	12	10	10	11	55	52nd =
John Conteh	12	10	10	10	13	55	52nd =
John Surtees	14	12	10	11	9	56	49th =
David Hemery	13	12	11	11	9	56	49th =
Jimmy Greaves	11	12	12	10	11	56	49th =
Tessa Sanderson	12	10	11	12	12	57	44th =
Barry McGuigan	12	10	12	11	12	57	44th =
Jim Laker	12	12	12	11	10	57	44th =
Lynn Davies	12	10	12	12	11	57	44th =
Gordon Banks	12	11	12	11	11	57	44th =
Alex Murphy	11	11	12	12	12	58	39th =

Criteria Score:	1 Achievement (out of 20)	2 Dominance (out of 20)	3 Style (out of 20)	4 Fortitude (out of 20)	5 Impact (out of 20)	Total (out of 100)	Rank (100th to 1st)
Nigel Mansell	12	11	11	14	10	58	39th =
Anita Lonsborough	12	12	12	11	11	58	39th =
Denis Law	12	12	12	11	11	58	39th =
Graham Hill	12	11	12	11	12	58	39th =
Mary Peters	12	11	12	11	13	59	37th =
Mike Gibson	10	13	13	12	11	59	37th =
Eric Liddell	13	11	11	13	12	60	33rd =
Kevin Keegan	12	12	12	12	12	60	33rd =
Sally Gunnell	13	12	12	13	10	60	33rd =
John Charles	12	11	12	12	13	60	33rd =
Cliff Morgan	12	12	13	12	12	61	30th =
Ken Buchanan	12	13	12	13	11	61	30th =
Geoff Boycott	12	12	11	13	13	61	30th =
Fred Trueman	13	12	12	12	13	62	27th =
Wally Hammond	13	13	13	12	11	62	27th =
Steve Cram	14	13	12	12	11	62	27th =
Stanley Matthews	10	12	14	13	14	63	25th =
Dixie Dean	13	12	13	12	13	63	25th =
Gareth Edwards	13	13	14	12	12	64	23rd =
Jack Hobbs	13	14	13	12	12	64	23rd =
Gordon Richards	14	14	12	13	12	65	22nd
Jim Clark	14	14	14	12	12	66	21st

THE TOP 20 IN ALPHABETICAL ORDER

	Criteria	1 Achievement	2 Dominance	3 Style	4 Fortitude	5 Impact	Total	Rank
	Score:	(out of 20)	(out of 20)	(out of 20)	(out of 20)	(out of 20)	(out of 100)	(100th to 1st)
GEORGE BEST		___	___	___	___	___	___	___
IAN BOTHAM		___	___	___	___	___	___	___
BOBBY CHARLTON		___	___	___	___	___	___	___
LINFORD CHRISTIE		___	___	___	___	___	___	___
SEBASTIAN COE		___	___	___	___	___	___	___
DENIS COMPTON		___	___	___	___	___	___	___
KENNY DALGLISH		___	___	___	___	___	___	___
NICK FALDO		___	___	___	___	___	___	___
LEN HUTTON		___	___	___	___	___	___	___
BARRY JOHN		___	___	___	___	___	___	___
BOBBY MOORE		___	___	___	___	___	___	___
STEVE OVETT		___	___	___	___	___	___	___
FRED PERRY		___	___	___	___	___	___	___
LESTER PIGGOTT		___	___	___	___	___	___	___
MARY RAND		___	___	___	___	___	___	___
STEVE REDGRAVE		___	___	___	___	___	___	___
JACKIE STEWART		___	___	___	___	___	___	___
DALEY THOMPSON		___	___	___	___	___	___	___
TORVILL & DEAN		___	___	___	___	___	___	___
JIMMY WILDE		___	___	___	___	___	___	___

SPORTS ORDER FORM

☐	0 7522 1031 9	Championship '96	£3.99 pb
☐	0 7522 0229 4	Dermot Reeve's Winning Ways	£15.99 hb
☐	0 7522 1015 7	The Fastest Man on Two Wheels	£10.99 pb
☐	1 85283 466 8	John Wilson's Fishing Encyclopedia	£20.00 hb
☐	1 85283 956 2	Ryan Giggs Soccer Skills	£9.99 pb
☐	0 7522 1664 3	Venables' England	£15.99 hb

All these books are available at your local bookshop or can be ordered direct from the publisher. Just tick the titles you want and fill in the form below.

Prices and availability are subject to change without notice.

Boxtree Cash Sales, P.O. Box 11, Falmouth, Cornwall TR10 9EN

Please send a cheque or postal order for the value of the book and add the following for postage and packing:

U.K. including B.F.P.O. – £1.00 for one book plus 50p for the second book, and 30p for each additional book ordered up to a £3.00 maximum.

Overseas including Eire – £2.00 for the first book plus £1.00 for the second book, and 50p for each additional book ordered.

OR please debit this amount from my Access/Visa Card (delete as appropriate).

Card Number ☐☐☐☐☐☐☐☐☐☐☐☐☐☐☐☐

Amount £ ....

Expiry Date ....

Signed ....

Name ....

Address ....

ACKNOWLEDGEMENTS

To everyone at TWI for all their support and to Tish,
Lucy, Nancy, Gill and Tash for all their forebearance
and hard work.

Thanks to the following agencies: Allsport for pictures
on pp 8, 9, 10, 13, 24, 27, 29, 37, 38, 41, 45, 51, 52,
57, 59, 60, 71, 73, 77, 81, 83, 87, 92, 95, 97, 98, 101,
104, 105, 109, 110, 117, 121, 124, 127, 133, 134,
136, 137, 139, 151, 153, 155, 159, 161, 165, 177,
181, 189, 191, 193, 201, 203, 204, 206, 210, 212,
216, 217, 220, 221, 222, 225, 227, 228, 231, 232,
239, 241, and 245; Allsport/MSI for pictures on pp 16,
68, 143, 163, 178 and 186; Allsport/Hulton Deutsch
for pictures on pp 15, 19, 21, 23, 31, 32, 35, 39, 43,
47, 48, 55, 61, 63, 65, 67, 69, 76, 84, 89, 91, 100,
102, 108, 112, 115, 119, 122, 126, 128, 131, 141,
145, 147, 149, 156, 167, 169, 171, 173, 175, 183,
185, 188, 195, 199, 209, 214, 219, 235, 237, 247, and
249; and Kos pictures for picture on p. 197.